THE NEW FEMINIST MOVEMENT

THE NEW FEMINIST MOVEMENT

Maren Lockwood Carden

RUSSELL SAGE FOUNDATION   NEW YORK

PUBLICATIONS OF RUSSELL SAGE FOUNDATION

Russell Sage Foundation was established in 1907 by Mrs. Russell Sage for the improvement of social and living conditions in the United States. In carrying out its purpose the Foundation conducts research under the direction of members of the staff or in close collaboration with other institutions, and supports programs designed to develop and demonstrate productive working relations between social scientists and other professional groups. As an integral part of its operation, the Foundation from time to time publishes books or pamphlets resulting from these activities. Publications under the imprint of the Foundation does not necessarily imply agreement by the Foundation, its Trustees, or its staff with the interpretations or conclusions of the authors.

Poem by Ann Rosenberg on page 27 reprinted by permission. Copyright 1970 by *Women: A Journal of Liberation*, 3028 Greenmount Avenue, Baltimore, Maryland 21218.
Poem, "Bridal Suite" by Jody Aliesan on page 27 reprinted by permission. "Bridal Suite" was published in *Pandora*, II, No. 6 (December 28, 1971), p. 4; and in a volume of poetry entitled *To Set Free* (Seattle, Wash.: Second Moon, 1972), Copyright 1972 by Jody Aliesan.

Russell Sage Foundation
230 Park Avenue, New York, N.Y. 10017
© 1974 by Russell Sage Foundation. All rights reserved.
Library of Congress Catalog Card Number: 73-83889
Standard Book Number: 87154-196-3
Printed in the United States of America

To Guy

CONTENTS

FOREWORD

Several years ago I wrote that "there is not likely soon, or ever, to be a definitive study of the Women's Liberation Movement. The members would not cooperate with such a study; Movement Women do not want to be defined by outsiders."[1] I was wrong. Maren Lockwood Carden has made just such a study; she interviewed women representing a wide spectrum of feminist groups, including Women's Liberation groups, and met only three refusals. It was not always easy; but she succeeded.[2] And she has left us all in her debt.

The New Feminist Movement clarifies the kaleidoscopic nature of the feminist movement today. It is an ideal introduction to the movers and shakers who found Archimedes' point to stand upon. As he predicted, they could move the earth. Almost by accident I stumbled upon the Women's Liberation Movement some five—only five?—years ago. I was dumbfounded. Where had it been all my life? No one, male or female, among my professional colleagues could tell me anything about it.[3] I went around without a map trying to chase down clues.[4] It took a long time to trace the general outlines. Now Ms. Carden has mapped the terrain for all of us.

What remains almost incomprehensible is the enormous leverage a handful of women in a half-dozen cities were able to achieve. How was it possible for small bands of women to have such enormous impact, to change our thinking so radically in so short a period of time? They ignored standard male canons. They did not bow to male knowledge and experience. Yet less than a decade after their inception, with no foundation funds, no formal structure, no mass support, no consensus, no access to the media, and against strong opposition, they changed our minds (if not always our hearts) with respect to sex roles to an incredible extent. That these women achieved so much has to mean that they were doing something right; something that had to be done. In my opinion they were.

I agree with David B. Lynn who says that "if the Women's Liberation movement did not exist, society would have to invent one to help awaken the nation to the necessity of undertaking the new adaptations demanded of it."[5] The Lord, as we all know, moves in mysterious ways to perform His wonders. He seemingly has chosen mettlesome feminists to modernize our creaking societal structures, especially the sex-role structure.

II

The year 1972 was a time of tipping points. One of the most epochal had to do with the mother and worker roles of women.[6] For the first time since records have been kept, the proportion of mothers with school-age children (but with no pre-schoolers) who were in the labor force became greater than the proportion who were not. Admittedly the difference was not remarkable—50.2 percent versus 49.8 percent[7]—and no serious researcher would make much of it. (And admittedly the proportions may teeter for a while.[8]) But the mother of school-age children (with no pre-schoolers) who was not in the labor force was in the process of becoming "deviant" rather than "typical." These women are in the general age bracket, 35 to 54, and it is projected that by 1990, 56.3 percent of all women in this age bracket will be in the labor force. Ruth Hartley has reminded us that when any pattern becomes modal it tends also to become normative, even coercive.[10]

I believe the feminists have been as successful as they have been because they were—*malgré elles* in many cases perhaps—performing for our society the basic and urgent function Lynn was referring to above, forcing us to see what was actually happening rather than what outworn clichés and stereotypes misled us into thinking was happening. What do you *mean* women's place is in the home[11] when more than half of all women ages 20 to 55 are in the labor force, three-fifths of them married? What do you *mean* motherhood is the lifetime role of women when 54.3 percent of mothers with children under 18, living with their husbands, are in the labor force?[12] And even more women who are separated or divorced are in the labor force.[13] What do you *mean* women prefer the status quo when the mental health of married women is a disaster area?[14]

The feminists called our attention to the fact that a culture which drives those who try to follow its role prescriptions "mad" just has to be examined and exposed. The feminists have forced this examination on us, and not a moment too soon.

III

The two branches of the feminist movement have gone about their modernization task in somewhat different ways. The liberation-oriented women have turned to their own experiences for their data.[15] These experiences were part of the abrasive crunch that resulted when tradition crashed headlong into a newly emerging societal structure. These women were *there*. They were observing the crash first hand in their own lives. They were responding to the demands of the modern world, or trying to, shackled by anachronistic structures, beliefs, attitudes, and paradigms. The consciousness-raising groups, which Ms. Carden analyzes so well (pp. 33-37) dredged up material that no academic researcher ever could have remotely reached. Suddenly, under the bland questionnaire responses that surveys of women—in no-matter-what role situation—had uniformly reported, there was revealed the hidden anguish, anger, and resentment that had been festering in the minds of so many women darkly, hopelessly, for so long. No humane society could tolerate such a state of affairs. Airing the emotional malaise of women was essential no matter how hard it was to take. "You can't mean it!" "I never knew how you felt!" "Why didn't you tell me?" "It's just the doing of a bunch of outside agitators!" "You've got to be kidding!" . . . But it finally did get to us.

The rights-oriented feminists have followed more traditional styles. They have called our attention to the sexist bias in our scientific paradigms that has had dysfunctional consequences not only for women but also for our society as a whole.[16] And they have done the cold, hard-nosed, academically impeccable research that shows up in legal briefs, congressional hearings, court cases, formal resolutions, and even political campaigns (pp. 141-144). The anguish that is fed into their research in the form of the raw experiences of women comes out of the research process in the form of tables and charts in the best academic tradition. In whichever form, the movement has shaken loose, if not demolished, a structure that no longer fits a modern world.

IV

Ms. Carden helps us understand not only what makes the "women's libbers" tick but also the "anti-women's libbers." The tilt in the balance between labor-force participants and housewives has put the housewives on the defensive.[17] In the past they did not have to defend themselves; there were theologians and even scientists to take up the cudgels for them. Now they feel themselves denigrated. They are fighting a rear-guard action against inexorable forces. Ms. Carden's trenchant comments call our attention to the fact that even the women who are most hostile to the movement nevertheless state their case in almost precisely the same terms as do the feminists (p. 165). Some women in the process of rebutting the feminists find their own consciousness raised. Like the foe in Oliver Goldsmith's deserted village, they come to scoff and remain to pray. And some conclude that there has to be something to a movement that can survive the outrageous behavior of the more radical feminist women. They are the "I'm-not-a-women's-libber but . . ." group (p. 163). I am reminded of the second tale in Boccaccio's *Decameron*.[18]

In any event, Ms. Carden makes it all credible. She deserves deep appreciation from everyone who wants to understand what has been going on in our society for the last half decade and the remarkable women who have helped to make it happen. It goes without saying that this book will become required reading in all academic courses dealing with women. But I hope it reaches a far wider audience as well. The restructuring of a society is too big a job to leave to any elite.

So, here they are, the women whose power one should never underestimate.

JESSIE BERNARD

Washington, D. C.
August 1973

NOTES

1. Jessie Bernard, *Women and the Public Interest, An Essay on Policy and Protest* (Chicago: Aldine, 1971), p. 200.

2. Ms. Carden's description of her research techniques (pp. 173–179) is an intrinsic part of the book, illuminating as data.

3. Our collective ignorance, I might add parenthetically, is itself worthy of study.

4. I knocked, literally, but unsuccessfully, on Roxanne Dunbar's door, more successfully on Dana Densmore's. I attended classes in a free university, went to lectures, read everything I could get of that astonishing, brilliant quasi-underground literature circulating in network channels. More than most readers I believe I appreciate the skill, patience, and research talent that went into Ms. Carden's study as described in Appendix I.

5. David B. Lynn, "Determinants of Intellectual Growth," *School Review*, 80 (February 1972), p. 245.

6. The "tilt" in our thinking from a basically pronatalist to an antinatalist position triggered by concern for the environment is another example of a "tipping point." Motherhood was being viewed as "an occupation in decline" (Jeanne Binstock, "Motherhood: An Occupation in Decline," *The Futurist*, 7 [June 1972], pp. 99 102). The decline in the rate of first marriages was another such "tipping point" (Paul C. Glick and Arthur J. Norton, "Perspectives on the Recent Upturn in Divorce and Remarriage," paper presented at Population Association of America, April 1972). For other examples of "tipping points" see notes 11 and 17 which follow.

7. *The President's 1973 Manpower Report*, p. 168.

8. In only three years since 1948 (when it was 26 percent)—1960, 1963, and 1965—had the proportion of mothers with school-age children (no preschoolers) declined, always less than one percentage point (*Ibid.*).

9. *Ibid.*, p. 220. Not all of these women will be mothers, but most will be.

10. Ruth E. Hartley, "American Core Culture: Changes and Continuities," in Georgene H. Seward and Robert C. Williamson, eds., *Sex Roles in Changing Society* (New York: Random House, 1970), p. 129.

11. Another interesting "tipping point" was also reached in 1972. For the first time, fewer than half (46.7 percent) of entering male freshman—presumably an avant garde—did not subscribe to the women's-place-is-in-the-home ideology. In private two-year colleges, the proportion was still high (55.9 percent) but in the private four-year universities it was only 34.6 percent. Among women, only 25.6 percent accept this conservative position (Staff of the Office of Research of the American Council on Education, "The American Freshman: National Norms for Fall, 1972," *Research Reports*, 7, No. 5, 1972).

12. *The President's 1973 Manpower Report*, p. 168. Because the bearing of children is the one function that cannot be shared by both sexes, the ultimate feminist issue, even when others have been appropriately dealt with, will be how to institutionalize motherhood. As it is institutionalized in our socety today it is not good for either women or children. Yet there is no consensus on how to improve it. It is because of the critical importance for the redefinition of the role of mother now in process that my own thinking for the past year has been directed to an analysis of the problem. See my forthcoming book, *The Future of Motherhood, The Severence and Attrition of a Role*, to be published by Dial Press in 1974.

13. Women's Bureau, *1969 Handbook on Women Workers* (Washington, D. C.: U. S. Government Printing Office, 1969), pp. 47–48.

14. Jessie Bernard, *The Future of Marriage* (New York: World, 1972), Chapter 3; Walter R. Gove, "The Relationship between Sex Roles, Marital Status, and Mental Illness," *Social Forces*, 51 (September 1972), pp. 34–44.

15. In this way, wittingly or unwittingly, they have been following C. Wright Mills' advice: "Do not allow public issues as they are officially formulated, or troubles as they are privately felt, to determine the problems that you

take up for study. Above all, do not give up your moral and political autonomy by accepting in somebody else's terms the illiberal practicality of the bureaucratic ethos or the liberal practicality of the moral scatter. Know that many personal troubles cannot be solved merely as troubles, but must be understood in terms of public issues—and in terms of the problems of history-making. Know that the human meaning of public issues must be revealed by relating them to personal troubles—and to the problems of the individual life. Know that the problems of social science, when adequately formulated, must include both troubles and issues, both biography and history, and the range of their intricate relations. Within that range the life of the individual and the making of societies occur; and within that range the sociological imagination has its chance to make a difference in the quality of human life in our time." (C. Wright Mills, *The Sociological Imagination* (New York: Oxford University Press, 1959), p. 226.

16. In a recent book (*The Sociology of Community* [Glenview, Ill.: Scott-Foresman, 1973], passim), I made the point that the classic paradigms for community study have become so weighted down with "anomalies of fact" in the Kuhnian sense that they can no longer serve adequately as guides for either research or policy. The same can be said of other paradigms. For example, although women in the household contribute indispensable services to the economy, the gross national product has been conceptualized in such a way as to ignore it, resulting in dysfunctionalities not only to women but to the economy itself. As long ago as 1961, Gardner Ackley was noting that "failure to include the value of services rendered in the household by family members . . . not only understates the national product and income, and gives a false impression of the proportion of total output originating in business, but also biases seriously all measures of the long period trend in national product" (*Macroeconomic Theory* [New York: Macmillan, 1961], p. 56). Juanita Kreps has also commented on the errors introduced into economic thinking by its disregard of the work of women (*Sex in the Marketplace: American Women at Work* [Baltimore: Johns Hopkins University Press, 1971]. An award-winning book whose objective was "to present a systematic analysis of the American occupational structure, and thus of the major foundation of the stratification system in our society" omits two-fifths of that structure (Peter M. Blau and Otis Dudley Duncan, *The American Occupational Structure* [New York: Wiley, 1967], p. 1). See also Rae Carlson, "Understanding Women: Implications for Personality Theory and Research," *Journal of Social Issues*, 28, 1972, pp. 17–32). I consider the correction of dysfunctional paradigms to be a major contributiuon of feminists (Jessie Bernard, "My Four Revolutions, An Autobiographical History of the ASA," in Joan Huber, ed., *Changing Women in a Changing Society* [Chicago: University of Chicago Press, 1973], pp. 11–29).

17. In 1966, Alva Myrdal and Viola Klein noted that already women who were not employed were on the defensive. They "almost have to give an explanation for staying at home" (Alva Myrdal and Viola Klein, *Women's Two*

Roles [London: Routledge and Kegan Paul, 1968], p. xi). See also pages 163–165 of this book. The year 1972 was a "tipping point" in this context also. After a decade which had aimed at a redefinition of the "career woman" she ceased to be a deviant misfit and became an admirable human being (Ravenna Nelson, "The Changing Image of the Career Woman," *Journal of Social Issues*, 28, 1972, pp. 33–46).

18. In that story a devout Catholic in Paris has tried hard to convert his good friend Abraham to his faith. After repeated affirmation of his own faith, Abraham consented to run down to Rome to take a look. His friend's heart sank. No one who saw all that corruption would ever accept conversion. The Jew went, saw all the corruption (as only Boccaccio could describe it), and then, much to his friend's surprise, accepted conversion. Any faith that could survive all that corruption had to have something going for it (Giovanni Boccaccio, *The Decameron*, trans. Richard Aldington [New York: Laurel ed., 1962], pp. 55–58).

PREFACE

In any study of such a contemporary and controversial topic as feminism, it is important for the reader to know the author's viewpoint and possible biases. I should therefore say at the outset that I am, in general, sympathetic with the goals of the new feminist groups I describe. I shall not attempt to state my own views in detail: some of my ideas are distinctly "radical" while others are distinctly "conservative." In the account which follows I have tried to allow for the possibility that my own views might color my description and analysis; my aim throughout has been to produce an objective sociological study.

While I have worked on this book, the people who have helped the most are the 104 movement participants who gave freely of their time and attention during lengthy formal interviews and many other participants who answered questions and talked to me at meetings and conferences. While I cannot name my respondents, I can thank them.

Several movement members read earlier drafts of the manuscript. I received especially valuable comments from Roberta Benjamin, Jo Freeman, Wilma Scott Heide, Muriel Fox, Bernice Sandler, and Barrie Thorne. Professor Thorne also made useful comments on the sociological analysis.

While I was a Fellow at the Radcliffe Institute (1970–1972), Dean Alice K. Smith and other members of the Institute provided valuable support and encouragement. In addition, Institute Senior Scholar Janet Zollinger Giele made insightful and provocative comments on Chapter Eleven.

Marie Lindahl applied her administrative and intellectual abilities to being a first-rate research assistant. Ruth Hein's editorial comments made me see the necessity for complete reorganization of the manuscript I had sent her.

Special thanks go to Russell Sage Foundation which provided funds to cover research expenses and a year's leave (1970–1971) while I did the initial field work. Within the Foundation I received particular assistance from Eleanor Bernert Sheldon who helped me shape the project in its initial stages and from Vivien Stewart who made very useful comments on the manuscript's first draft.

Maren Lockwood Carden

New Haven, Connecticut
August 1973

INTRODUCTION

I n the late 1960s a new feminist movement burst upon the American public. Even those who were in tune with the newly emerging series of protest movements—civil rights, peace, the New Left, antipoverty—found the revival of feminism a startling event. Men and women with traditional views gasped. These must be sick, unbalanced women, or at best, just bored housewives. Everyone knew that American women were better off than women anywhere else in the world or at any time in history; they were spoiled and pampered. What did they have to fuss about? What were they after? What did they mean by "liberation" or "oppression"?

The press and other mass media had a field day making fun of the "women's libbers." The reactions they reported were often highly charged emotionally, negative, and frequently contradictory. These women were sexually promiscuous, sexually deprived, lesbians, or frigid. They hated men, "wanted to take over the world," or wanted to subordinate men to women. They were portrayed variously as rejecting both marriage and motherhood, as considering childbirth a barbarous experience, as rejecting the aid of obstetricians at childbirth, as unwilling to sacrifice any personal whim for the sake of their children. They were unhappily married or else divorced or single. Physically unattractive, they were compensating for their "failure" as women. Strident, hostile, hysterical, and maladjusted, they lacked human compassion and perspective.

Few observers had any clear idea about the new feminism, and even fewer knew anything about the groups to which the new feminists belonged.

By now the dust has cleared. "Women's lib" was not just a fad. It did not fade away. People began to realize that behind the bizarre elements played up by the media lay a serious reform movement. The new feminism is not about the elimination of differences between the sexes, nor even simply the achievement of equal opportunity: it concerns the individual's right to find out the kind of person he or she is and to strive to become that person.

It is time now to begin the scholarly task of looking at the new feminism in the social context within which it arose, to study the historical forces that have shaped it, to note who has been attracted to it, what these people have been attacking and what weapons they used, what they have been seeking and what tools they have used, what they have believed and what they have rejected. The present study is designed to supply answers to questions of this kind. They are not simple answers, for the phenomena themselves are not simple. The movement is complex, multifaceted, and not amenable to categorical treatment. This book does not force such treatment on the data.

The research reported here is limited in coverage. It focuses primarily upon the years between the mid-1960s and the first years of the 1970s and upon two major types of groups which have been active during that time—Women's Liberation and Women's Rights.[1] Both Women's Liberation and Women's Rights appeared during the mid-1960s; feminist objectives were their primary concern; they each possessed at least a minimum of organization as a way of coordinating their change-making efforts; and both were independent of any established institution.

Women's Liberation consists of numerous independent groups scattered throughout the country, each generally composed of from six to twelve young women. The groups' primary function, "consciousness raising," has involved intimate, personal discussion among the participants. Through this group process of sharing experiences and feelings the participants discuss the social forces that mold them in the traditional behavior patterns of the feminine role, and they evaluate other possible styles of life. Perhaps as many as 15,000 women belong to these very loosely coordinated Women's Liberation groups, which have flourished with astonishing vigor and, as will be seen in Chapters Five-Seven, have in some cases moved beyond the goal of consciousness raising into social action.

In contrast to the fragmentation of Women's Liberation, most Women's Rights groups are larger, more formally structured organizations. Like members of Women's Liberation, almost all members of the Women's

Rights groups see the issue of women's role definition as central to the new feminism. They have worked for reform of women's status by applying legal, social, and other pressures upon institutions ranging from the Bell Telephone Company to television networks to the major political parties.

The Women's Rights groups are both large enough and have sufficient national influence to identify the principle organizations. These are the National Organization for Women (NOW), the National Women's Political Caucus (NWPC), and the Women's Equity Action League (WEAL). These three groups are organized on a national level and are subdivided into state or other local chapters. Most of the remaining Women's Rights groups are officially national in scope but, in fact, draw most of their members from a single locality. Their total membership is probably between 2,000 and 3,000. The total membership of all the Women's Rights groups is about 75,000.

I chose to focus this research upon the Women's Liberation and Women's Rights groups in order to limit it to a manageable size. In so doing, I have excluded a large number of women, and men, who legitimately see themselves as playing a very important, active role in the new feminist movement. These people fall into three categories. First, there are the sympathizers—people who agree with the new feminist objectives but do not belong to any feminist organization. Second, there are members of the long-established traditional women's organizations which have always professed feminist objectives but which, prior to feminism's recent revival, had neglected these objectives or had been disregarded by the outside world. Such groups include the National Federation of Business and Professional Women's Clubs, the YWCA, the League of Women Voters, as well as such little-known groups as the American Medical Women's Association. Third, there are the newer women's interest groups formed since the appearance of Women's Liberation and Women's Rights organizations. They represent women's interests within the professional societies and trade unions, among federal government employees and in religious organizations, in radical student groups and among the white-collar staffs of business firms. Relevant groups here include the Stewardesses for Equal Rights, the Task Force on Women of the United Presbyterian Church in the U.S.A., and caucuses within professional societies ranging from the American Association of Law Schools to the Modern Language Association.

A great many highly committed and very active feminists are included in the category of "sympathizers." Although I have chosen to focus upon a different part of the movement, I wish to emphasize that these other feminists have played and are playing as important a role in social change as the Women's Liberation and Women's Rights groups.

I have limited this study not only in the groups studied but also in the questions posed. Two main questions guided the research. Why do women participate in Women's Liberation and Women's Rights groups? And, how do these groups operate? These issues (discussed in Parts Two, Three and Four) form the main body of the book. In addition, I give an account of the ideas to which the new feminists subscribe (Part One) and an overview of the origins and future of feminism in the United States (Part Five).

A prerequisite to an understanding of the membership and operation of the new feminist groups is an understanding of the ideological positions held by participants. Many serious discussions of the new feminism have been empty intellectual exercises because they are based upon inaccurate accounts of the movement derived from presentations in the mass media. Intent upon providing entertaining news, the media play up the sensationalism in the movement. One wonders, for example, how many people know the unsensational fact that Betty Friedan, once the driving force behind NOW, left the presidency in March 1970 on being elected to the far less exhausting job of Chair—One of NOW's National Advisory Committee; or that Germaine Greer has never participated in any of these new feminist organizations. Or, one wonders how many people know that only a tiny minority of participants hates men. The account of movement ideology given in Chapters One and Four is based primarily upon interviews with women throughout the movement—rank-and-file members, marginal members, leaders, media "stars" (who may or may not be movement leaders), and others.

Although I have described the new feminist ideology in some detail, I have avoided discussing its social, philosophical, or scientific merits. For example, I state in Chapter One that participants question the authority of psychologists who assert that woman's traditional role is her natural role, but I do not discuss which psychologists have taken this position nor have I evaluated the bases on which feminists or psychologists have reached their conclusions. Such important discussions belong in another type of book, and many people are writing such books.

While this research concentrates upon the membership and organization of United States' Women's Liberation and Women's Rights groups it is not a comprehensive survey of the topic. The new feminist movement is too complex to be adequately described in a single book. Nonetheless, it is important that the work of recording and analyzing its history be begun as soon as possible. Contemporary feminists, in contrast to nineteenth century feminists, rarely keep journals or write more than cursory letters upon which social scientists may draw in the future. Certainly, a mass of published, xeroxed, and mimeographed periodicals and other literature exists, but it is generally produced by a small minority of unrepresentative members, or it is limited to news items. For these reasons it is important that we record this particular piece of contemporary social history while its actors are available to re-tell their parts.

PART ONE
THE NEW FEMINISM

CHAPTER ONE

IDEAS AND ISSUES

Much of what the general public hears about the new feminism concerns the groups' many and varied efforts to introduce social change. Movement advocates have supported repeal or reform of abortion laws; they have opposed legal restrictions on the distribution of birth control devices; many have objected to the impersonality, male dominance, and sexism of modern medicine whether this is practiced by the obstetrician, psychiatrist, or internist. Child care is a crucial issue: members advocate, and often establish, many kinds of child-care facilities.

All forms of economic, job, and educational discrimination have been attacked by legal, legislative, and less direct social pressures. Feminists have sued companies which pay women less than men for the same work, they have worked for passage of the Equal Rights Amendment to the Constitution, demonstrated against and sued newspapers which list "Help Wanted" advertisements separately under "Male" and "Female" headings, encouraged secretaries and blue-collar women workers to form unions, joined women on welfare in protesting both the inadequate support payments and the rude treatment given them by local government authorities, and publicized the degrading treatment afforded women prisoners.

Modern marriage forms have been attacked. Many feminists have tried to eliminate inequities regarding the married woman's right to own and dispose of property, her rights and her husband's to custody over children in the event of a divorce, and the payment of child support by a former husband. Inside and outside of marriage feminists insist that women should not be treated as sex objects but as complete human beings for whom sex is only one part of their experience. They object to seeing women demeaned as Playboy Bunnies, or as the "come on" in an advertisement for liquor or cars. When women reject heterosexual relationships in favor of lesbian relationships, many feminists support that choice.

A majority argues that any woman who wishes should keep her maiden name when she marries, they protest requirements that women vote only under their married names, complain to credit card companies because they issue cards in the name of Mrs. John Jones instead of Mrs. Mary Jones or Mary Jones, and object when banks will not give mortgages to single women. They try to remove from schools and libraries books which show women only as brides, housewives, mothers, stewardesses, or secretaries. They write books of their own; they introduce courses on women in schools and colleges, and urge that more research be done in the area of women's studies.

These activities represent a scrutiny and criticism of and, often, an attack on all institutions—prisons, welfare systems, churches, the law, industry, local and federal governments, schools, colleges, unions, and the mass media. The resulting actions are varied but they have an underlying coherence based upon the feminists' analysis of women's position in society. One must understand this analysis, theory, or ideology before one can understand why feminist groups act as they do or why people espouse the cause.

THE NEW FEMINIST IDEOLOGY[1]

Many people view the contemporary feminist movement as a revival and continuation of nineteenth-century feminism. Certainly participants in both movements have worked for female equality; but the two movements differ significantly in the basic argument on which they have based their demands for equality—the nature of the biological differences between the sexes.

Most nineteenth-century American feminists saw far greater differences between the "male" and "female" nature than do their modern counterparts. They were firmly convinced that, as women, their biological inheritance included many distinctively "feminine" characteristics and that woman's natural instincts suited her primarily for homemaking and child care. However, they argued that these differences by no means justified the unfair treatment afforded them by society. It was, they felt, their human right to be freed from such crippling restraints as those which gave husbands rights over their wives' earnings and allowed women only minimal opportunities for education or denied them the vote. When women possessed this sort of freedom, they would be better able to contribute their special feminine qualities to the general improvement of the society outside of the home.

In contrast, today's feminists argue that far too much has been made of the biological differences between men and women. For them, different socialization processes account for a larger part of the observed differences in men's and women's behavior, while biology plays only a minor role. Thus their argument for equality is based upon the belief that the biologically derived differences between the sexes are relatively minor and that a vast inequitable system has been built upon the assumption that such differences are basic and major.

To a far greater degree than their nineteenth-century predecessors today's feminists examine and protest the degree to which social institutions (supported by cultural values and normative expectations) channel women into an unreasonably narrow role. They point out that women are expected to commit themselves primarily, if not exclusively, to being wives and mothers and that social expectations give them very little latitude even in the ways they can interpret their wifely and motherly responsibilities. The great majority of new feminists object not to marriage and motherhood, but to the excessive restraints these roles involve. They argue that in a truly equal society women would be in a position comparable to that of men who at the present time are able to combine occupational and other roles with those of husband and father.

The new feminists feel that consciously or unconsciously almost everyone cooperates in this "oppressive" socialization or "conditioning." Parents, teachers, toy manufacturers, and writers of children's books encourage girls to be "feminine." Girl babies are "pretty," boys are "sturdy." As they grow older girls are kept home near mother, who teaches them to be passive, disciplined, and obedient. Boys, on the other hand, are allowed greater freedom; they roam the neighborhood, climb "dangerous" trees, get soaked in rainstorms, and are scolded—but also admired—for their adventurous spirit. Even if parents encourage a girl to be adventurous, other adults discourage the idea. At a church group's discussion of the movement, one participant commented:

> When we were in graduate student housing, Susan [her daughter] would play "fire-engines" and race tricycles with the two little boys who lived in the next apartment. Then we moved to the suburbs. Here the girls and boys always play separately. It's uncanny. If Susan doesn't join the girls with their dolls, she has no one to play with.[2]

Toys manufactured for girls encourage them to "play house," to tend babies, to practice "helping men" as nurses, and to learn how to make themselves look "beautiful." Boys, on the other hand, can let their imaginations run riot playing with space missiles, trains, erector sets, or racing cars. As in games, so in stories; men "go places, struggle against nature, direct large enterprises, boss women, make money, and gain respect and fame." They "are elected to chair meetings and be officials. . . . Women are present . . . but they hardly say a word."[3] Little boys "do"; little girls "are."

As a girl progresses through school and college, parents and counselors discourage her from embarking on a career because, after all, they expect her to marry, and it is far more realistic to acquire a good general education and some secretarial training. With such experience she then can move in and out of the labor force (albeit at a low level) whenever her family situation so demands. Thus her advisers, with her best interests in mind, have contributed to the perpetuation of her stereotyped role.

Even the adult woman constantly is reminded of her secondary role. In mixed organizations—churches, recreational clubs, community improvement associations, political parties—she performs essentially the same service functions: she bakes cakes, contributes to bazaars, rings doorbells soliciting contributions, and serves refreshments. At work her typical job as secretary, waitress, nurse, or teacher, involves helping others (frequently men) and often involves working under men's supervision. Women workers can expect to remain in dead-end jobs in the telephone company or on the assembly line with no hope of advancement to positions like those held by their male supervisors.

Socialization has such a pernicious effect, say most feminists, that women are forced to suppress the greater part of their human potential. A member of NOW's board of directors said,

> I want to have a part in creating a new society. . . . I want women to have something to say in their own lives. . . . I have never reached my potential because of social conditions. I'm not going to get the rewards. I've been crippled. . . . I want to see the kind of system that facilitates the use of potential.

Movement members see the mass media as contributing continuously to this socialization process. Here they draw heavily upon Betty Friedan's analysis.[4] They say that the men running the mass media actually believe in the stereotyped female they portray. The woman who sees herself only in these terms and lacks the challenge of anything outside her immediate environment believes the soap operas and the advertisements that portray her as a scatterbrained, dependent, submissive, and passive creature with very little intelligence—"They're dumb but they're fun" go the words of a song coming from her radio. It is also argued that the media present as unhappy those women who show initiative, independence, and competitiveness because they have denied their essential "feminine" identity. Constantly told that she is different and special, the American woman comes to believe in her otherness, and that otherness is, quite simply, inferiority.

The one area in which women are seen as exercising a certain amount of initiative is in controlling their physical appearance. Indeed, it is argued that a woman's prestige often depends less on her personal qualities or performance than on her looks. The ideal American woman is supposed to be young, fresh, and beautiful. She dresses to please men rather than for comfort; she spends much time putting on makeup and arranging her hair; she uses deodorants, perfume, and vaginal sprays.[5] But not all women are beautiful, and all women grow old; here too, then, women are doomed to failure.

A woman is caught within all these social institutions and these institutionalized attitudes. She finds herself in a vicious cycle: by trying harder to attain the ideal, she becomes more passive and subordinate, more preoccupied with appearance and less with ideas. She becomes less and less sure of herself and more and more willing to believe that men are superior beings.

The mass media are not seen as the only supporters of the American woman's demeaning image. Feminists have pointed out that, over the past thirty or forty years, scholarly discussions regarding the nature of woman and the nature of society in general, have helped to sustain the above concept of the feminine role. Recently such scientists' assertions that women possess an inherent and profoundly different psychological makeup from that of men have met vigorous protests. Thus movement members reject Freud's theory of penis envy, Erikson's modification of Freud's argument that, for woman, anatomy is destiny, and Bruno Bettelheim's assertion that women "want first and foremost to be womanly companions of men and to be mothers."[6] They will no longer accept without question the psychologist's authority as justification for assuming the woman's traditional role.

Another development of this general argument that the American social structure has restrained or "oppressed" women lies in the way the work force is organized. It is hard for anyone, man or woman, to begin or retrain for a career at the age of thirty or more. Stimulating part-time work that could lead to other jobs is almost unobtainable. Very few companies have introduced flexible hours to accommodate the needs of mothers. Industry is simply not set up to meet women's requirements, even though in some cases the necessary changes would be relatively minor.

When feminists claim that women are oppressed, they are referring to such practical, social, and psychological restraints placed upon the woman who wants to step outside the traditional role. They realize that prejudice, discrimination, and "male chauvinists" (with their belief that men are naturally superior) contribute significantly to this oppression; but they also see the whole American social structure as neatly coordinated with and furthering that oppression.

Obviously, throughout their analysis, the new feminists are describing an overgeneralized role. They recognize that many women do not center their lives exclusively in the home and that many housewives have remained independent and assertive people; such women have been happy and have been admired. But the force of the feminists' argument lies in their objection that on the whole the traditional feminine role has remained an excessively confining standard against which all women's behavior is measured.

In searching for some resolution of these difficulties, the feminists have endorsed the traditional American faith in progress, and the belief that experiment will lead to a better way of life. Thus they argue that only when we have found out what the unfettered woman can do can we discover what, if any, characteristics are truly "womanly" as opposed to simply "human."

Many movement participants believe that if women achieve greater freedom in determining their life styles, a series of other changes must follow. Most important, the traditional male role will be modified as women move into the men's working world and as men assume new duties inside the home. Such changes may, it is thought, have beneficial effects upon both men and women: a man can assume responsibility for his children without feeling emasculated; a couple may even decide that both would be happier if the husband stayed home while the wife worked; and, most important, men can abandon the impossibly demanding ideals of "masculinity." Men need not constantly "prove" their superiority or defend their "fragile male egos." In particular, they will be free to adopt more so-called feminine traits while women can take on so-called masculine ones. The qualities most feminists would like to see both men and women adopt combine parts of our male and our female role stereotypes. All people should be warm and concerned for others' welfare, they should be sufficiently self-assured to reach out to others, they should be self-motivated, adventurous, competent and, above all, they should be free to realize their individual potential.[7]

In addition to reevaluating male/female relationships, the feminists have reevaluated women's attitudes and behavior toward each other and concluded that they have much to gain from establishing closer ties with their "sisters." The concept of sisterhood is of great importance in the movement. If women are to cease living their lives through men, male friends and husbands should not play an exclusive role in a woman's life. If women consider their whole sex inferior, they are unwilling to establish friendships with each other. Those who believe in sexual equality must also believe that it is worthwhile "really relating to" other women. This does not mean that feminists exclude friendships with men; it simply means that they extend their interests to include other women. Some of those women will become friends, many will be interesting acquaintances, all will be "sisters" with whom they identify and whom they support.

New feminism's emphasis upon sisterhood has contributed to some outsiders' perception of movement members as lesbians. In fact, the great majority of participants do not want their most intimate and emotional and/or explicitly sexual relationships to be with women, but they believe that lesbians should be free to express themselves as they wish and they support them in the spirit of sisterhood.

From its support of lesbians to its emphasis on sisterhood to its questioning of what are the biologically based sex differences, the new feminism presupposes social change. In order to better serve women's needs changes must be made in people's attitudes, in laws, institutions, and, ultimately, the whole social structure of American society. Perhaps the changes need only be minor, perhaps they need to be drastic. In any event, feminists feel that not only will such social reorganization benefit women but that ultimately it will genuinely improve all of society.

WOMEN'S LIBERATION AND WOMEN'S RIGHTS GROUPS

The basic ideas of the new feminism, which I have described in composite form, have been developed in a wide variety of ways by different groups and different people within both the Women's Liberation and the Women's Rights segments of the movement.

Prior to 1971, the Women's Liberation contribution to the overall movement was primarily through the development of feminist ideology and the creation of public awareness of the feminist position. The small consciousness-raising groups encouraged independent thinking and, as they proliferated, the spread of new feminist ideas. Those which were particularly anxious to promote certain ideological interpretations published position papers, newspapers, and magazines. (In fact, Women's Liberation has contributed by far the greater part of the movement magazines and newspapers as opposed to action-oriented newsletters.) Ideas were discussed, evaluated, and enlarged upon at conferences and at periodic meetings of loosely federated groups from a particular locality. At the same time these feminists' personal contacts and public actions contributed to the spread of their ideas and to the creation of new consciousness-raising groups. In those early years the actions were precisely the sort that would gain attention for their ideas: a noisy demonstration outside a Playboy Club, a confrontation with a movie theater manager who showed sexist films, and the take-over of a building for use as a Women's Center. Such protests, however, were second in importance to the promotion and development of a new feminist ideology.

The Women's Rights groups, on the other hand, characteristically, have paid far less attention to theory and far more attention to practice. The two oldest groups, the National Organization for Women (NOW) and the Women's Equity Action League (WEAL) (founded in 1966 and 1968 respectively) espoused an ideology that, from the point of view of the movement, we may call relatively conservative. While they (particularly NOW) and other Women's Rights groups have since adopted more radical ideas, all have retained their emphasis upon producing change at the cost of theory. NOW and WEAL, together with the National Women's Political Caucus (NWPC) founded in 1971, remain the largest and most important of the several dozen Women's Rights organizations.

Like the Women's Liberation groups, Women's Rights groups have been organized in ways consistent with their orientation toward theory and action. In keeping with their focus upon "change now," they are usually formally organized around statements of organizational purposes to which a national dues-paying membership subscribes. In practice, most of them operate very informally and flexibly, but the underlying structure facilitates their efforts to introduce change. Their goals and actions reflect their overall interpretation of feminist ideology. NOW has the most general objectives, extending from equal employment rights through divorce law reform, abortion law repeal, improving the image of women represented in the media, and consciousness raising; these objectives are pursued in many different ways, ranging from legal action to lobbying and demonstrations. The Women's Political Caucus has similar objectives but, as its name implies, seeks to achieve these through party politics. WEAL's objectives are narrower; they are limited to rectifying inequities in the areas of law, education, employment, and taxation. Most of its members are committed to achieving these changes through thoroughly "establishment," if not always orthodox, channels.

The commonly heard characterization of Women's Rights groups as "reformist" and Women's Liberation groups as "revolutionary" reflects the more dramatic differences of their early years. Since 1970, both types of groups have attracted members who are representative of a wider range of ideological positions and the contrasts between these two segments of the movement have been blurred.

PART TWO
THE NEW
FEMINIST

CHAPTER TWO

SOCIAL AND PERSONAL CHARACTERISTICS OF THE NEW FEMINIST

As outsiders and participants repeatedly state, the majority of Women's Liberation and Women's Rights groups' members are middle- and upper middle-class whites. Although relatively more of the less-prosperous and less-well-educated women have joined during the 1970s, they probably still compose fewer than 10 percent of the total membership.

SOCIAL CHARACTERISTICS

Almost 90 percent of the Women's Rights groups' members interviewed had at least a B.A. degree; a third held Ph.D.'s, M.D.'s, or law degrees. This sample probably is biased in favor of the more highly educated women; nonetheless, members of Women's Rights groups in general are likely to be preparing for, trying to gain entry into, or actually participating in some professional or semiprofessional career. At the end of 1970 the occupations listed for the first 21 of the 120-odd members of Pittsburgh NOW were: teacher, psychoanalyst, realtor, retired couple, freelance writer, doctor, secretary, social worker in an adoption agency, demographer, two nurses, teacher, telephone-company employee, Demo-

cratic Committeewoman, city planner, dog trainer, employee at the
YWCA, physician's wife, television station employee, labor organizer.
Leaders of that chapter reported that "most" of its members are employed. Officials in other chapters report that between 20 and 40 percent
of their members are "housewives." Incomes varied considerably; but
the household income for both single and married women was generally
over $10,000, and for nonworking married women often over $15,000.

The social class position of Women's Liberation members cannot be
measured adequately by income or occupation because only about one-
fourth have settled into a particular occupation. Many hold temporary
secretarial or service jobs which are traditionally low status. They were
usually undecided about their future plans, but the alternatives they speak
of are generally within the professions. They are distinctly unwilling to
look upon a dull, repetitive job as permanent. Another measure of social
status is the participants' style of life. They take inexpensive vacations,
but they go to such middle-class resorts as Martha's Vineyard. Their
low-rent apartments often are decorated with inexpensive but unusual
items rather than with the products of a large retail store's basement sale.
Their social behavior follows middle-class norms. For example, they
formally introduce strangers and serve even the simplest of meals with a
habitual attention to etiquette obviously learned from middle-class parents.

In addition to being middle class, the new feminists are cosmopolitan.
Whether they live in a large city or a small town in Wisconsin, they are
far less interested than their nonfeminist neighbors in local events and
more involved in national and international issues. Politically the Women's
Rights groups have attracted primarily independents or Democrats. Women's Liberation groups at first attracted women who leaned towards
socialism: later recruits' political preferences resembled those of the
Women's Rights group members. Institutionalized religion (in the sense
of attendance at religious services) rarely plays a significant part in the
lives of participants.

Although the women vary in age from their teens to their sixties,
most are in their twenties and thirties. The median age for Women's
Rights members is in the late twenties and early thirties and for Women's
Liberation members in the middle and late twenties.[1] Contrary to the
stereotype, most of these women are married. Participants in Women's
Rights groups report that about 80 percent of their members are married
with higher proportions among suburban groups and lower proportions
in central city groups. Five to ten percent have been married more than
once. Leaders are far more likely than nonleaders to be single or nonwork-
ing married women with a school-age family. These people have more time
to give to the movement than have married women who work or who

have young children.[2] About one-third of the married women have no children. This figure includes the women who have been married only a short time and do intend eventually to raise a family.

In contrast to the members of the Women's Rights groups, members of Women's Liberation are less likely to be married and more likely to be divorced. In my sample, biased in favor of unmarried leaders, about one-half are single, one-fourth married, and one-fourth divorced.[3] About half the married women have children. I have the strong but unsubstantiated impression that, among the more recently formed Liberation groups whose members are less radical and less urban, the proportions of people in each marital category more closely resemble those of Women's Rights groups.

PERSONAL CHARACTERISTICS

There has been a good deal of speculation about the kind of woman who joins the new feminist movements. At one extreme are those observers who suggest that the feminists are expressing a very reasonable protest against an unreasonable social situation in which they are caught. At the other extreme are the people who see the participants as man haters, lesbians, sexually frustrated, or psychologically disturbed.

Is There a Movement Personality?

Very few social scientists have attempted to analyze the personalities of members of any type of social movement, and none has successfully proved the existence of a characteristic "movement personality." Yet the belief that such a specific personality exists recurs not only in the popular press, but also in scientific literature.[4] The confusion on this point is due partly to the writers' inadequate specification of what they mean by "personality."

If by "personality" we mean basic psychological makeup—involving, for example, needs for security, strivings toward autonomy, or tendencies toward aggression—we must conclude that there is no evidence for the existence of a "movement personality." We know that there are patterned ways in which these needs, strivings, and tendencies are combined, but we also know that these patterns take many different forms. Furthermore, there is a wide range within which any one of these patterns can be expressed in *observable* behavior. Thus, it is very difficult to trace the many complex connections between basic personality and such behavior as showing an even temper, being talkative or an extrovert, selecting a spouse, choosing an occupation—or joining a social movement. Within any social movement, as within an occupation, these connections will vary greatly as one moves from person to person.

On the other hand, movement members, like "bureaucrats" or "Englishmen," do seem to share certain characteristics which often are considered to form a particular type of personality. If "personality" in this context is interpreted to mean relatively "superficial" attitudes, values, and beliefs, then common characteristics can be identified for people in particular occupations, cultures, or social movements. Thus, a particular Englishman may have highly developed aggressive tendencies and a strong desire for autonomy, which basic psychological traits he expresses in ways acceptable to other English people—for example, through an impenetrable social reserve and excessive social restraint. Any society, or group, channels its members' idiosyncratic basic impulses into such "acceptable" forms[5] which we usually think of as typical, stereotypical, or modal personalities.

Like members of cultures and societies, members of social movements share certain personality characteristics of the sort I have called "superficial." In this case they share the values, attitudes, and beliefs associated with a conscious conviction that the movement's ideology explains certain common problems. It is a serious oversimplification to suggest that there are simplistic causal relationships between movement membership, basic personality, and child-rearing practices. We would overlook the complexity of human personality if we said, for example, that rebellious student protesters have never outgrown the temper-tantrum stage because of their parents' permissive child-rearing practices.

Movement participation should be seen as performing two very different functions for any one member. First, it allows for the expression of a conscious commitment to an ideology which puts into perspective a series of common experiences. Second, it allows for the expression of other idiosyncratic personality needs, often unconscious, which might be satisfied less well, equally well, or better within some other group. Some of the needs which fit into this second category will also be shared with other movement members. For example, many members may desire social contact with others whereas only a few may be seeking power. Undoubtedly, needs which fit into this second category motivate feminists to join the movement. However, they would probably try to satisfy them in less controversial groups outside the movement if they did not also share a belief in the feminist ideology.

It is, of course, possible that within any one movement, some participants will be seriously disturbed neurotics and even psychologically disabled. But the same generalizations can be made about businessmen, physicians, nursery school teachers, or any other group in the general population. They all attract a wide range of personality types, representing a wide range of psychological adjustment.

In one respect the members of this new movement can with certainty be called "abnormal": they have rebelled. Thus, they no longer belong to the *statistically* "normal" population. However, this argument reveals nothing definitive about a movement member's mental health. A rebellious minority may be making a "healthy" reaction to an "unhealthy" society, or it may be making an "unhealthy" reaction to a "healthy" state of affairs.

Potential Recruits

The potential recruits to the new feminist movement are those women who feel most acutely the conflict between the social expectations associated with their traditional role and the generally accepted "American" values. Sociologists and others have described this dilemma.[6] They point out that the middle-class woman in particular has been taught the feminine virtues associated with her traditional role—concern for others, adaptability, dependence, unassertiveness, a capacity to express her feelings, gentleness, supportiveness, and nurturance. On the other hand, she has also learned the values of the larger American society which are sometimes applied to men only and sometimes applied to both men and women. To be consistent with these general societal values, a woman must be active, aggressive, individualistic, independent, unemotional, objective, competitive, and achievement oriented.[7]

The sets of traits associated with being "feminine" and those associated with being "American" are each internally consistent. But, when a woman tries to combine them, she finds them to be contradictory. In the course of her life, the middle-class American woman faces many such contradictions. For example, to achieve in college or in a career, she may need to put her own interests ahead of her personal relationships and her concern for others. Such achievement will certainly also require her to be individualistic and therefore to reject in part the traditionally feminine traits of dependence and unassertiveness. Similarly, she must select more or less consciously from among other traits associated with stereotypical masculine and feminine roles.

These conflicting choices are translated into practical terms when a girl has to decide on such questions as whether she should take secretarial or college preparatory courses in high school; whether she should follow an inclination to become an excellent tennis player; whether her primary concern should be social life, school work, or even sports; whether she ought to spend an afternoon visiting relatives with her mother or go off to a museum by herself; whether she should prepare for a career, and the sort of career for which she should prepare. In sum, should she develop the personal qualities and the behavioral experience that prepare her for the traditional feminine role of wife and mother; should she instead develop those that agree with the general societal values; or should she attempt to work out a compromise and develop for herself a role which combines with motherhood a greater involvement in the larger society?

Although we do not have comparative data on the experiences of nonjoiners, the interviews showed that those who do participate are, in fact, seriously bothered by the evident conflicts in values.[8] The conflict experienced by members of Women's Rights groups generally took one or more of three forms: frustration at being confined exclusively to the home in the role of housewife and mother; the practical difficulties associated with combining career with motherhood; and the overt or covert discrimination they had met in the working world from people who assume, consciously or unconsciously, that the traditional role is the only appropriate one. Typical comments came from a mother with two children aged four and six:

> When I was home full-time, the isolation was very hard. It is very difficult to make friends when you have young children. I . . . and others had . . . a kind of vague, chronic depression. A feeling that you can't do anything. One's memory for recent events becomes poor. You can't distinguish one day from the next. You are helpless and not able to function outside of the house.

Another mother, whose children were one and three years old, commented:

> There is nothing more creative than bringing up children; but not twenty-four or twelve hours per day. . . . My aim wouldn't be to get away for all the day but for half the day. This amount of frustration shouldn't be forced upon one. [With a college degree one is] vastly overeducated for the task of housewife. One hopes the present generation will have thought it through and will not drop everything to get married.

Those who had "thought it through" and had been trying to juggle career and family responsibilities still met with many problems. A European woman who was about to give birth to her first child said that one reason she got involved in NOW

> was the whole problem of having children in this country. My parents . . . do not see it as incompatible to have a career and children and husband. It seemed, in Europe, that it was not incompatible. When I got here a male friend said, "You have to make a choice between motherhood and career." That is the general feeling around here. . . .
> I just felt that among the women I knew here that there was a fantastic feeling of uneasiness, unhappiness about this. I have a couple of friends in Switzerland who don't seem to experience the conflict.

A married woman with a Ph.D. in science from a top-ranking university found herself unable to get a satisfactory academic job despite the fact that she was living in a large metropolitan area with many local colleges:

> After I got my Ph.D. in 1965, I was an instructor at [one of the middle-level universities in the area] and did the work of a teaching assistant. I was not even allowed to teach evening courses or in the summer school, while a male graduate student, without his Ph.D., taught summer courses. The . . . department chairman was antifeminist. I realized I could not teach except at the [lowest status] type of college—which is the type of place where qualified women are teaching in [this area].
>
> Between June 1968 and June 1969, I could not get a job at all . . . not even as a medical secretary—only typing.
>
> I have had two post-doc jobs in areas I'm not specially qualified in. I didn't want to continue doing post-doc work for someone else at $6,000 [a year].

Another (single) woman who had made her career in industry said that "discrimination in employment" was the primary reason she joined NOW:

> I was not aware of it for years because of my low expectations. Salary increases and advancement were never taken as seriously as with a man "because you married and got pregnant." I had a manager who got me as far as a position ready for a career jump. (There was never any question of my competence.) But then there was no place to go in that company. They wouldn't let me [make that jump]. There was the frustration of never getting through the glass wall.

Although members of Women's Liberation faced similar conflicts, they did not spell these out in such specific terms because, being at an earlier stage in their life cycles, they had less experience as housewives or as paid workers. Instead, they expressed ambivalence about their situation. Looking to the future, they were not sure they wanted a life composed exclusively of housewifery and motherhood and, looking to the present, they questioned the subordinate role women of their age traditionally assumed with males. A twenty-one-year-old undergraduate referred to her uncertain future:

> for the past year, I had had difficulty identifying myself as a real person. I felt myself to be an incipient schoolteacher, a wife-to-be, a potential mother. I was not sure what I was. Something seemed to be missing.

A recently married woman commented on her efforts to find fulfillment as a housewife: "I had thought that the homemaker role *ought* to be a source of satisfaction and [after I joined the movement] realized that it need not be. . . . I had used mystical explanations to explain what it meant to be a woman. The Ying and Yang, body-mind stuff." Another married woman who had a young child expressed her feelings of inferi- ority: "I was hung up about not going back to school. . . . My small group of bright, politically active, sensitive women all had similar prob- lems—feelings of inadequacy about their work in the house, and else- where."

Many such women had assumed that, after college, they need not make a life of their own but could live their lives through boyfriends and, later, husbands. They agreed with the young woman who said: "I had always been taken in by the myth that all you have to do is find a man and you'll be happy." If they were "to find a man" they must not be too self-assertive:

> I had always been told that men wouldn't like me because I was too aggressive. I thought I had gotten over that. I had, to a large extent, but . . . in my senior year, when lots of women were getting married, I worried about not being married and about there being no position in this society for a single woman. Until I left [college] . . . I accepted the myth that women are submissive, not speaking at SDS meetings, sit- ting in the dorms waiting to be asked out.

Former members of the New Left commonly objected to the way the movement men treated them as inferior. For example, "One of the main reasons I got into [Women's Liberation] . . . was because the [New Left] movement is male supremacist. . . . You can see the inequality under your nose." Respondents' ambivalence to the conflicting social pressures were summarized by a twenty-five-year-old woman who was working as a secretary. Before joining the movement she had had a

> desperate feeling of "got to get a man but don't want to be tied." . . . I felt I had a mind inferior to that of men. . . . The men in the [New Left] movement always made you feel irrelevant. . . . I was just a passive fol- lower.

Members of both Women's Liberation and Women's Rights often share one further experience. Some female or male role model has directly or indirectly encouraged them to "be an individual" or to "make some- thing of themselves." These same role models, to whatever social class they belong, have usually set an example by doing more with their lives than have other people in their immediate family or community. It is, then, the relative ambition of such role models, not the absolute social position they have reached, which inspires the nascent feminist.[9]

Emotional Involvement in Feminist Issues

The high emotional level found in all the new feminist groups under- scores the view that the conflicts are of great concern to the women involved. Such emotion is demonstrated at large and small meetings of Women's Liberation groups, where participants are likely to express publicly their anger at women's oppression and to receive sympathetic responses from the other participants. During the 1968 Chicago conference workshops, for example, "woman after woman started crying." At home, talking together in their consciousness-raising groups, women "got very angry. We were very raw." For some groups, "There was a stage when none of us could watch TV. It made us so angry."

The Liberation movement literature contains many highly personal and emotional biographical accounts, often of traumatic experiences—for example, abortion:

> A pain started from deep within the core of life and rose up in my gut like a roar of lava leaving the earth. . . . Sweat ran into my eyes. . . .
>
> God damn you! God damn you to hell! You are hurting me. Stop! Stop! . . . The pain came again, and I grunted and cursed and fought it. . . . The masked figure worked swiftly. Each time I cursed, he laughed. . . . For each curse, another strike, and another agonizing twist that rose from the depth of my body.[10]

There are many accounts of painful love affairs, unhappy marriages, the problems of an "aging" forty-year-old woman, the demeaning nature of secretarial work, women's hatred at the catcalls and whistles they hear from men, and the plight of welfare women. The poetry, which appears just as often, reflects a similar depth of feeling.

> They all want to come and drink from my well,
> Drown in my pussy in liquid passion,
> Scan my topography,
> Search all the crevices,
> And ultimately bury their bone, the dogs.[11]

And:

> After the wedding he watched basketball
> On the motel TV, hunched in underwear
> At the foot of the bed. She sat at the head,
> Against the wall, fingering rosebud buttons
> On the obvious white chiffon nightgown
> Her mother gave her for the occasion.
> It wasn't that he hadn't told her about the game.
> It wasn't that she expected any joy.
> Years later, before she asked for the divorce
> They used to laugh and tell their friends about it,
> How reasonable it was, unsentimental,
> Convenient, realistic, and urbane.
> She never forgave him; he never apologized.[12]

Similar strong feelings are evident throughout the Women's Rights groups—although there they are more tightly harnessed. A member of a relatively conservative NOW chapter comments that "people's emotions are running wild," and as an observer at a meeting where there was an exchange between the general membership and representatives of the communications industry I could see these emotions expressed. The women, even accomplished public speakers, could not prevent their voices from shaking as they asked polite but pointed questions about discriminatory practices. Evasive answers from the panel were met with icy silence broken occasionally by an exasperated sigh. Even WEAL, which of all the groups places greatest emphasis on "correct" demeanor, found that some of its members' polite exteriors shattered when, at its 1971 annual meeting, California Assemblyman Charles Warren opposed equal quotas for women in professional schools as long as the majority of heads of households were men. "Hands flew in the air as angry women responded" with explanations of how that view was unfair to women. "Visibly shaken as hands continued to wave . . . [Warren] exclaimed that the women were extremely rude."[13]

RELUCTANT RECRUITS

Members of Women's Liberation and Women's Rights organizations are sensitive about how few lower middle-class, lower-class, and black women have joined their groups. They believe that such women are worse off than themselves: they are confined to a narrower role, live with more oppressive males, or experience greater economic restraints and discrimination than do white middle- and upper middle-class women. In an attempt to rectify these inequities the new feminists have, for example, worked to reform welfare regulations and to improve the working conditions and advancement opportunities of service, factory, and clerical workers. They have also tried, with little success, to recruit to the movement women who are not middle-class whites. For example, one Women's Liberation group tried to attract the predominantly lower middle-class college students of San Francisco City College by distributing 1,000 leaflets urging attendance at a meeting for women interested in learning about the movement. They received almost no response. Yet only a short time before from the slightly higher status students attending San Francisco State College they had attracted "quite a number of people" (probably about fifty) after distributing only 500 leaflets. Even movement members who have gone to live in lower-class neighborhoods and talked at length to the women there have sparked little enthusiasm for the new feminism.

Despite their obvious economic and social deprivation, it is reasonable that lower middle-class and working-class women should not be attracted by the new feminism and should therefore not even belong to the pool of potential recruits. The sociological literature substantiates the view that these women are more likely to feel satisfied in the traditional role.[14] Compared with women higher in the class scale, they receive far greater exposure to the values associated with that role. A girl's peer group, parents, and counselors rarely urge her to prepare herself for any job more skilled than that of a secretary or of a beautician. Unlikely to go to college, she is therefore unlikely to be exposed to the alternative viewpoints available there. In addition, the society immediately outside her home offers little opportunity for an individualistic achiever. Most of the young men in her own social class have only routine jobs, and nothing more challenging is available to her. Indeed, comparing herself with the men, she might reasonably feel that to be married with a house or apartment of her own, a group of women friends, and a sociable neighborhood in which to live, offers more opportunities for self-realization than would "going out to work."

Significantly, the few working-class women who are found in the movement, whether in Women's Liberation or Women's Rights, were usually attracted by the "equal rights" aspect of the ideology. In matters of pay, job security, working conditions, and fringe benefits, they have had *personal experience* of discrimination and can demand equality in such areas without feeling threatened in their feminine role. For them economic inequities, not role inequities, are paramount. It is for this reason that they often come into the women's movement via traditional union activities. Trade unionists, in addition, represent the small minority of employed working-class women who have both the time to give to a protest group and the conviction that organized action will effectively change their situation.

Efforts to recruit black women have met with even less success than efforts to recruit socially and economically deprived whites. In 1969 and 1970 a common complaint of movement members was that all blacks regarded feminism as a white middle-class movement unrelated to the concerns of blacks. At meetings and conferences rarely more than 1 or 2 percent of the women are black (unless these meetings have been planned as coalitions that include such black groups as the Welfare Rights Organization). Since 1971 more black women have come out in favor of new feminist ideas, an occasional black Women's Liberation group has been formed, and feminist ideas have penetrated black women's organizations. While public opinion polls show that black women are now more likely than whites to favor the efforts of "women's liberation groups,"[15] most black women remain concerned *primarily* with what to them are the more pressing issues of racial discrimination and economic privation.[16]

Other women who have not been attracted to the feminist movement in the proportions one might expect are middle-class high school and college students. While they have been more likely to join than have been black and working-class women, surprised movement members found them much less enthusiastic than expected. For example, a "Female Liberation" conference held at a large eastern urban university in February 1971 attracted only twenty-five or thirty women. At an eastern regional conference participants in a workshop on "campus organization" struggled with the question of dealing with student apathy toward the movement. While many universities throughout the country report the existence of some kind of Women's Liberation group, the total number of women involved is generally less than fifty—and even then the group often is supplemented by women from the outside community. Liberation groups on campuses with as many as 20,000 students regularly attract only twenty-five to fifty women to their meetings.[17] The few feminists who are active in high schools report even greater difficulty in drawing attention to women's issues.[18]

Several reasons could explain this apathy. First, high school and college students are often poorly informed about the objectives of Women's Liberation: like many people, they tend to see the "women's libbers" as "a bunch of man haters and bra burners." A second, and probably more important, reason is that, for women of their age, even the implied rejection of men is very threatening. Third, and perhaps most important, they will not feel the full impact of conflicting values until they experience or seriously anticipate what their lives will be like after graduation.

In conclusion: all American women grow up learning, on the one hand, such societal values as achievement and individualism and, on the other hand, the frequently contradictory demands of the traditional feminine role. Middle- and upper middle-class college graduates are likely to feel the ensuing conflicts most acutely; their expectations are highest and their relative deprivation is the greatest. It is from these women that, so far, the new feminist movement has drawn the majority of its members.

CHAPTER THREE

BECOMING A
NEW FEMINIST

Many women experience the role-related conflicts described in Chapter Two without becoming involved in the new feminist movement. The decision to join is one step in the process whereby people reconceptualize their thoughts in terms of the new feminist ideology: they reject the socially accepted view of the appropriate role for a woman and construct a new interpretation of much broader scope. Some people join the movement after they have reconceptualized their view of women's place in society; others do not change their perceptions until they participate; and still more find that, although they had changed their views before joining, they continue to change them afterward.

LEARNING ABOUT THE NEW FEMINISM

The founders of the earliest new feminist groups, NOW and Women's Liberation, were brought together, in the one case, by their work with the federally authorized state commissions on the status of women and, in the other case, by their work in the New Left movement. In 1966 NOW's charter members founded what they then called their "civil rights group for women" in response to their frustration at the commissions' excessively slow progress toward realizing women's equality.

Independently in 1967 and 1968 the first Women's Liberation groups were formed in five different cities by women who had become exasperated by the New Left males' refusal to treat seriously their complaints about being treated as inferiors.[1] The events preceding and accompanying the founding of Women's Liberation and NOW will be described in Chapters Five and Eight.

During the movement's crucial formative years, personal contacts were the most important means whereby the founders reached potential recruits. As one person put it, "Recruitment was only by the grapevine. There was no advertising. We had a hard enough time coping with the women who came. There were always too many as it was." All of the women interviewed who joined Women's Liberation, NOW, or WEAL before the end of 1969 heard of the movement through friends or acquaintances. Occasionally, the Women's Rights group members knew these friends through their work in other volunteer organizations such as political parties, or the National Federation of Business and Professional Women's Clubs; but well over half of those interviewed had heretofore not belonged to or only been nominally involved in any kind of volunteer group.[2]

Since the end of 1969, participation in both segments of the movement has increased rapidly.[3] There is evidence that this increase was partly stimulated by the increased publicity given the new feminists by the mass media. The then executive director of NOW described the media's sudden discovery of the new feminism. In August 1969, she "went crazy" trying to answer inquiries from periodicals, newspapers, radio stations, and TV stations. Evidence of this surge of interest is found in the listings of articles on feminism in the *Reader's Guide to Periodical Literature*. Between March 1966 and March 1967 the *Guide* reports fifteen articles on some aspect of feminism. The numbers increased gradually during the next two years, but the greatest change occurred later. Between March 1969 and March 1970 over 200 articles are listed; most of them appeared in the latter part of 1969 and in the beginning of 1970.

Although much of the media's coverage of the movement was critical, the publicity caused many women to look into the movement. The young suburban housewives who began to get involved in Women's Liberation during 1970 frequently report that they learned about the movement through the mass media; suspecting that the movement might be useful to them in their own endeavors, they decided to explore it.

Members of Women's Rights groups were especially likely to attribute their initial interest to something they had read in the popular press or had heard about on radio or television. Of those respondents who had joined after 1969 only about one-fourth had learned about the movement exclusively or primarily from other people. In contrast, about half were influenced by both personal contacts and the media; and, most interestingly, about one-fourth decided to look into the movement entirely on the basis of what they had learned from the mass media. A number of NOW chapters including those in New York City and Los Angeles noted a sudden influx of new members following the publicity associated with the protests of August 26, 1970. On that day demonstrations, marches, speeches, and personal "strikes" marked the fiftieth anniversary of the date women gained the vote.

In a sense, therefore, the movement has been created by the media, because without their publicity the ideas would not have spread so rapidly. But in another sense the mass media were only the means whereby an already established movement was suddenly brought to the attention of large numbers of people. Women's liberation is a topic that impinges on everyone's life. Its more bizarre forms made good press, and for better or for worse, the movement received a great deal of publicity. Perhaps the contemporary women's movement would have progressed as slowly as the nineteenth-century movement if modern society were not able to disseminate ideas so rapidly. Perhaps, also, it would have taken a different form if the media had not emphasized dramatic but often unrepresentative events and figures and if potential members as well as opponents had not learned about the movement through the media's often sensational presentations.

PARTICIPATION IN WOMEN'S LIBERATION

Women who are eventually to become committed to the feminist ideology as members of Women's Liberation do not accept that ideology as soon as they hear of it. They join a Liberation group because feminist ideas interest them and because the group offers the opportunity to talk about and perhaps resolve the role-related problems which worry them. In the course of participation, they achieve a changed perspective on these problems and on their identity as women.[4]

This process of reconceptualization, which is the essence of consciousness raising, occurs in many different ways and over varying periods of time, but it follows a single general pattern. A woman questions, rethinks, and revises her old conceptions of womanhood as this manifests itself in innumerable parts of her life. The process is best exemplified in those small discussion groups frequently called consciousness-raising groups, which have been central to the growth of the Women's Liberation part of the new feminist movement.

The idea of the consciousness-raising group probably derived from the New Left's discussions of Chinese Communists' group criticisms and from the young radicals' encouragement of open, democratic, and non-hypocritical expression of feelings. The groups are given many different names including "cells," "affinity groups," "rap groups," "collectives," "support groups," "small groups," or simply "my Women's Liberation group." They consist of from five to twelve women (experienced organizers suggest that eight is a good number) brought together through informal movement channels and, more recently, through the initiative of women who have no prior involvement in the feminist movement. No one leads the group sessions although, for the first few meetings, an experienced member of Women's Liberation may help guide discussions. The meetings, which generally take place once a week in one of the participants' homes, are informal. In the movement's early years they followed no specific guidelines but more recently participants have adopted suggestions about first, organizing and second, running the groups from the movement literature.[5]

In the course of the meetings, participants discuss openly and at length topics related to their position as women. A great deal of personal experience is shared and discussed with other group members. As meetings continue, each participant begins to think over a series of previously unconsidered questions. How, for example, should she dress? Are fashionable but uncomfortable clothes, carefully set hair, and elaborate makeup necessary? Is it her way of trying to attract men? Why should she go to such trouble to make herself essentially "unnatural"? Ought a wife to devote herself primarily to caring for her husband? Should she cook all his meals, care for his clothes, clean the house, type his term papers, type his thesis, and eventually type his book in return for a sentence in the Acknowledgments which includes the words "love" and "without whose help"? Do women have to sacrifice more than men for the sake of the companionship and intimacy of marriage? Ought a mother to be in sole charge of her children? What should be the father's responsibility? Should he play baseball with the oldest son on Saturday afternoon or should he get up to give his youngest child its bottle on alternate nights? Should women refrain from being assertive and aggressive? Why do they characteristically lack self-confidence? Ought almost all physicians, lawyers, and businessmen to be male, while almost all social workers, nurses, and elementary schoolteachers are female? Is there such a thing as the "essential feminine"? Do they like other women? Or do they consider all women inferior?

A great range of topics is introduced and many personal experiences are exchanged. Almost in tears, a young mother tells that her husband wants to take a job in another city and asks whether it is her duty to do what he wants when she hates the idea of being uprooted. This will be her second move. Will she have to move again and again, each time her husband gets an offer of promotion? Another may ask what she can reply to her husband when he claims that since, historically, women have always held a lower status than men they must be inferior; she has, she realizes, always gone along with that view herself. Yet another woman may express for the first time her resentment about waiting on her husband and may wonder aloud, for example, why he never gets up from the dining table to collect a forgotten item from the kitchen.

A single woman may describe her anguish in waiting for a man to call her to ask for a date. Another may explain how silly she feels sitting passively in a car while her escort gets out from the driver's side, locks his door, walks around the car, and finally opens the door for her. A very composed young woman may ask the group members whether they, like her, are infuriated when men stare or whistle at them in the street while they can do nothing to retaliate but must simply walk on, feigning dignified indifference.

Sex is another frequent topic. Women discuss whether their husbands or lovers really satisfy their sexual needs. (As one would expect from the changing sexual mores and the cosmopolitan orientation of the participants, very few are virgins, though promiscuity is uncommon.) Women suddenly begin to question whether it is really a failing on their part if they do not experience orgasms. A participant may be astonished to discover that she is not alone in having frequently "faked orgasm" because she felt that the man would consider her "inadequate" or because she did not want to hurt his male pride or because he had not succeeded in "turning her on" and she wanted to "get the thing over with" as soon as possible.

The group members will discuss all such problems at length. As a result, they often discover with surprise and relief what is, in fact, an article of faith in the movement—that they share very similar problems. Many feel they have no control over their lives. If they are single, they must keep all their options open—work, recreation, where to live—so that, on marrying, they can adjust to whatever it is their husband does. They confess to and discuss their ambivalence about such matters as competing with husbands or male friends, working when they have children, having children, and even being married.

Eventually, they begin to question the woman's role which until that time they have taken for granted; and they begin to change their behavior. They cease tiptoeing round the male ego yet treat men and women with equal consideration; they refuse to tolerate males' put-down comments (e.g. "Women never understand mechanical things."); they break up relationships in which the men see them primarily as sexual partners; they begin to share housekeeping responsibilities with their husbands and insist on having some time each week to themselves; they return to college, or change to a new job. Each group member is affected differently, but the overall consequence of the small group experience is that "You learn to give the world a very hard look." In many different ways members ask each other repeatedly what is so sacred about the woman's traditional role and what right "society" has to "force" women into that role. Why cannot a woman be as free as a man to pursue her own interests and ambitions?[6]

Once a group member has evaluated her own life experiences and has begun to ask general questions, she is in a position to be "converted" to the new feminist perspective. The conversion is a matter of a conscious shift of thought processes from acceptance of the status quo to seriously questioning it.[7] By the time the turning point comes for a woman she is usually not surprised, she has seen it coming. "Before, I knew I didn't like the Doris Day image and I didn't like a lot of TV. Now . . . it's rather like the new analysis of a sociology course. It has helped me focus my malaise." Another woman said:

> The movement has explained the ways I was brought up and the ways people treat me and society treats me because I'm a woman. It was not a religious conversion but like an understanding of the situation you are in. I had never bothered to itemize before the lots of little examples of the ways women are treated. I had an enormous increase in consciousness as a woman. I couldn't walk down the street, read advertisements, watch TV, without being incensed . . . at the way women are treated.

Many comment with surprise on their previous image of all women as inferior:

> You realize that here are all these interesting women. It is really amazing. . . . You begin to see women as real people. It is the most mind-blowing of things. You realize that before, women were not people, they were women.

Occasionally the conversion to the Women's Liberation perspective is a dramatic event. "Everything just jelled." Or:

> My ideas began to change, talking to Women's Liberation people. . . . They got accentuated when I joined a group. Then when [a friend] listed to me all the things about women's oppression, they suddenly sounded very real all at once. I mostly had never thought of how women are oppressed.

One woman, who experienced this sort of change after participating in the national Women's Liberation conference held near Chicago in November 1968, noted, "Far back then it was such a revelation. It hit with such emotional force. We didn't expect it."

For many the newly derived conviction that their problems are of social rather than personal origin leads to a great sense of relief and of enthusiasm for the cause. One woman reporting her reaction to a two-day "Female Liberation" conference held in Boston early in 1969 said, "The week after the conference was spent in euphoria. It was very mystical. . . . I felt my whole life had changed. It has."

Even after they had adopted a new perspective on the feminine role, many members expected to undergo further consciousness-raising. The expectation of continued consciousness-raising was characteristic particularly of the New Left oriented participants who joined in the movement's first years: "I have not yet . . . got to the point where I can accept karate, no family, no capitalism and the revolution."

Among the more recent newcomers to Women's Liberation groups are an increasing number of suburban housewives who, unlike the original participants, are settled in a specific way of life and frequently feel trapped. Their problems are as unformulated as those of the earlier participants, and they also need other people with whom to discuss them. Such a person has a larger investment in the status quo than has the younger unmarried woman working as a secretary. She does not expect to make any radical changes in her life; communal living does not interest her—she believes that "It is hard enough to relate to one person, let alone twelve people." Indeed when one listens to such a woman describe how difficult she found it to ask her husband to come home before their children go to bed so that he may spend half an hour with them, or how she has, for the first time, begun to ask him to share in the housework, one realizes that she will probably never accept the more radical manifestations of the Women's Liberation perspective.

Whether they accept the less radical or the more radical interpretation of the ideology, Women's Liberation participants become committed to that ideology in the same way. They exchange accounts of personal experiences, identify shared problems, and interpret these problems in terms of the movement's ideology. Having examined all aspects of their lives from this new perspective, they eventually reconceptualize their thinking and accept that perspective as the correct way to interpret women's experience.

PARTICIPATION IN WOMEN'S RIGHTS GROUPS

Just as the members of Women's Rights groups differed from members of Women's Liberation in the role-related conflicts which initially they identified, so also they differed in the process whereby they reconceptualized their view of the feminine role.

Even before they had heard of the new feminist movement, women who later became members of NOW and WEAL had questioned certain parts of the feminine role. One person told how for years she had objected to

> the unnatural position of women in society, the lack of opportunity, the detailed definition of a role that was not necessarily a hole into which you fitted. It was a subject I was sensitive to in being a [scientist] . . . and intellectually involved . . . to a level of excellence that women don't usually aspire to. I am working exclusively in a man's world . . . I had these feelings verbalized before I joined NOW.

When she first learned about NOW in January 1970 she "became violently upset that a feminist movement could exist without my knowing about it." She joined immediately. Another professional person spoke specifically about discrimination. She "already knew that women were discriminated against" when she became a member of NOW. "What I was hoping was to find a way to help other women who did not know how badly off they were because the more each of us attains, the easier it is for each of us to attain."

A lawyer became an active member of WEAL because of her previous experience of sex discrimination:

> I have been burned very badly as far as sex discrimination is concerned— and only very recently. I was totally unaware of it until . . . three or four years ago. For the first five years out of law school there was no discrimination, not until . . . [I reached the stage] where there was a possibility of bossing men.

Another woman said that her experience staying home with two infant children had made her aware that homemaking and child rearing could not "fill one's life satisfactorily." Many such house-bound women "decided to look into NOW," went to a meeting, and discovered that they "had found a group of women willing to say the things I had been thinking about for years," or "Looking around the meeting, I felt . . . these women are like me." Others who had older children joined because of their experiences when their children were smaller. One such woman, a part-time artist and part-time housewife, said:

> I really felt I should have been better prepared for the wife and mother role. When I was in college, I couldn't think beyond June '55 [graduation]. Girls should be prepared long before they get married. For example, a social worker [with children] who lives down the street does part-time work. She has her life under control. This is the way life should be worked out. . . . Having children can be confining, dull, very lonely. . . . When you were young you were supposed to think it was wonderful. I

always felt it was wrong but had no support at all for my view. You don't have time [to object] when you have children. I was fortunate in some ways. There was a group of five women . . . [with children on this] street. We had a lot of fun.

A minority of these first participants in NOW and WEAL did not accept the Women's Rights ideology until they had gone through an experience comparable to that of the consciousness-raising group. They had to talk with other feminists before reconceptualizing their situation in feminist terms. One such person became convinced after traveling to a civil rights demonstration in the company of several NOW members and spending the greater part of the trip discussing feminism. Another woman, a NOW national board member, was one of the few women whose reconceptualization of the woman's role was precipitated by reading movement literature. She began her feminist career in 1967 when she encountered some of the early Women's Liberation literature (in particular, the periodical *Voice of the Women's Liberation Movement*):

I read it and I was home. I said, "My God, here are women who are not just sitting around." . . . I looked over all the organizations and decided which was the best for me—which made the best use of my talents. I got the faith, like religion, with that first publication.

Most members of NOW and WEAL did not, at first, think about their problems in such overarching terms as does the average participant in Women's Liberation. They objected, for example, to sex discrimination but were not so bothered by the differential socialization of boys and girls or the demeaning image of women portrayed by the media. In the course of their movement work, however, many underwent a form of consciousness raising so that they eventually adopted a broader ideology. When asked if they had experienced further consciousness raising since joining, members usually replied, "Of course," and continued with such comments as:

It's bound to happen. The more you are in the movement, the more facts you learn. . . . I have become more aware of insulting advertisements [and that] . . . at a party with my husband's friends, nobody mixes. The men form a circle to talk about engineering and the women—it's really kind of pathetic.

Or, "The more you read, the more you learn. For example, in a tennis tournament, you see that the men's first prize is $12,000 and the women's first prize is $1,200." And, "I have become more and more radical since I joined. I see the politicians at the statehouse being so moralistic [about abortion laws]. 'The woman pays and the man does not.' It makes me angry."

Thus, for the typical, involved member of a Women's Rights group, acceptance of the new feminist ideology is progressive. Her first formulation of a nontraditional view of women is modest enough: she sees women as deserving of opportunities to work outside the home (should they want to do so). Later, she enlarges upon this view until, questioning the whole process of socialization, she concludes with the Liberation participant that, as presently constituted, American society deprives women of all but a few means of realizing their human potential.

ADDITIONAL INCENTIVES TO PARTICIPATION

Participants in both Women's Liberation and Women's Rights groups find that involvement leads to additional satisfactions besides those already described. Some of these are shared by many participants; others are peculiar to a few.

Women's Liberation

An ancillary function frequently served by the consciousness-raising groups is to help the members cope with a social environment which lacks a clear set of normative rules for behavior.

The politically radical women who composed the majority of the first small groups' members were particularly affected by the new informality introduced in heterosexual relationships. One woman described the sorts of minor problems that, multiplied, made social relationships difficult within the New Left in 1969.

> It was not easy to figure out what is the proper way to behave. . . .
> A lot of guys in the movement are having a lot of trouble. One paid for a girl's ice cream and after was embarrassed about what he had done. A lot of people are aware that a new attitude is developing. They are up tight because they are not sure what they are still allowed to do. Girls and men are up tight about it.

Sexual partnerships in particular created considerable tension for members of Women's Liberation. When they rejected the prohibitions on premarital sex in the days before the women's movement had started, these women discovered that "living-with-a-man" brought its own set of problems. The new arrangement often turned out to be essentially like that of traditional marriage. The women performed the "wife" role: they did the household chores, were supportive of their men, adapted to their needs, and subordinated their interests to those of the males. Through such experiences, younger women who were finishing college or who had recently graduated became disillusioned simultaneously with traditional marriage and with their new life styles. The experiment had not "worked," and their general sense of normlessness was increased.

Despite her demands for freedom, the woman herself sometimes automatically assumed the traditional role. One woman said that after establishing a close relationship with a man, she

> shifted from being 'a girl people went out with' to being 'a housewife.' "What am I?" I asked, "only twenty years old and a housewife." I was acting as if it was required of me, whereas basically . . . [the man was]not oppressive in any way. . . . I've found out I assumed he had attitudes he doesn't have.

Although their lifestyle was called "new" most such women's roles remained essentially unchanged.

Another common problem associated with the new sexual partnerships' lack of guiding norms was summarized by a former member of the New Left, "The alternative life style of the Left gave no stability for women." Each partner behaved in accordance with both the traditional and the modern expectations. Under the old rules sexual relationships were forbidden unless accompanied by deep personal involvement, generally accompanied by marriage. Under the new rules, sexual relationships could be based on a certain amount of mutual affection, with intense involvement being considered unnecessary and even undesirable. Nonetheless, both partners (but particularly the woman for whom the change was greatest) were likely to fall into the traditional pattern. When, under these circumstances, a man leaves his partner, she finds herself thinking of him in the "old-fashioned" possessive and dependent terms: she feels angry and hurt. Yet she also knows that she agreed not to become "involved." She is caught between her very reasonable desire to maintain the close relationship and her expressed conviction that two sensible people can enjoy a brief sexual relationship without serious involvement on the part of either person. Intellectually she has no one to blame but herself, but emotionally she can be deeply hurt. Naturally, women who have been in situations of this sort are likely to express these feelings and to want to work out a new and better way of "relating to men."

Such young women may face another problem in their attitudes toward the sexual experience itself. If they do not always find sex thoroughly enjoyable they feel guilty or inadequate at their "failure." They do not excuse themselves as they well might with the thought that they are trying to break down within a few months the values inculcated in them since they were children. Even women who enjoy sexual intercourse may feel inadequate if they fail to live up to the ideal of multiple orgasms implied by Masters' and Johnson's research.[8]

The preceding account is based on respondents' reports of their own experiences and the experiences of other women in their groups, and therefore includes an element of hear-say evidence. Although none of the women interviewed was asked to or gave detailed accounts of their sexual experiences, they were clearly much preoccupied with their relationships with men. This issue is also a frequent topic of discussion in the conscious-ness-raising groups, particularly among the younger unmarried women. They talk with others about their inability to reach orgasm, their lack of interest in sex with the man they happened to be going with, their boy-friends' dominant behavior, and the men's demands that they play a sub-servient role if they wish to maintain the relationship. Talking with others, expressing their hurt feelings, and discussing how they should behave helps these members of the fluid youth culture to create a certain normative structure for their lives.

Such experiences probably contribute to the "man-hating" attitudes and the near-Victorian picture of man as an animal which some movement rhetoric reveals. Speaking of her experience in a radical consciousness-raising group one somewhat older graduate student said that she had been "shocked at the absolutely callous way people talked about sex . . . 'the man poking it around.' . . . 'old hot hands' [professors] trying to 'make them' when they were their graduate advisers." Sex—and men—had often disappointed these women badly. Sexual liberation, paradoxically, left these women more exploited by men than before, as they found them-selves in a position with all the disadvantages and none of the advantages of the traditional wife's role.

The less radical women, including the young housewives who began joining Women's Liberation groups in the 1970s, are bothered by a dif-ferent sort of normlessness. Since the feminist movement had voiced for them problems which they had previously avoided or considered the consequence of poor personal adjustment, they were seriously questioning whether marriage could give them a reasonable proportion of the satis-faction they need in life. Some of them realized for the first time that "the romantic interpretation of marriage is a myth." As one woman put it, "By sharing the idea that romance is a myth, people feel less unhappy at not getting it—though some expectations are very difficult to purge." Having reached this conclusion, she joins other Women's Liberation participants in wondering whether she wants to spend her life as a housewife and what alternatives, if any, are open to her.

Many of the problems brought up in the consciousness-raising groups are familiar to the older woman participant. She, however, did not have to cope with them within a few short years. The older single or divorced woman may have had to decide under what circumstances to have intercourse with a man, but she did not have to make this decision at the age of eighteen or twenty. The older married woman has realized gradually that pure romance is a myth and, with the explicit or implicit support of her friends, has learned to adjust to the fact. Compared with older participants, the younger women have been introduced abruptly to a large number of complex role-related problems. One woman in her late thirties expressed this idea with the comment, "What surprises me is the number of young women [in my group] who are involved facing issues which, at their age, I had not thought about. I was just running around and enjoying life."

Another recurrent theme in the movement is the participant's search for community within a large, impersonal society. Although very few women suggested this as a reason why they were attracted to Women's Liberation, many mentioned it as an advantage of participation.[9] Almost all referred to the personal satisfaction they derived from knowing very well a small group of women. For example, one young woman attending a large state university was among a small group of students working for the Women's Liberation movement. "You can talk to [those students]. You have people to say 'Hi' to on campus. The university is impersonal. The dorms are for freshmen and sophomores and everyone else lives off campus." Another student who had always lived in small towns before starting graduate work commented on how very difficult she found the transition to big-city life. Her consciousness-raising group encouraged her to expand her abilities. She learned to meet people, to engage in easy conversation, to give public speeches, to follow a map, to drive all over the city, and to organize and publicize meetings.

The sense of belonging experienced by this respondent and many others was, in part, the result of the movement's emphasis upon sisterhood. Once members tried establishing real friendships with other women, they enjoyed the interesting company and the relaxed, noncompetitive atmosphere of all-female groups.

Women's Rights

The same themes of normlessness and lack of community, so clear in Women's Liberation, are repeated in subdued tones in the Women's Rights groups.

Members of these organizations often face a personal normlessness or hiatus situation associated with their particular choice of life style. For example, a woman whose children have all started school wonders what she will be doing for the remainder of her life. Like the man in his middle forties, she asks herself whether she wishes to continue in her present pattern or whether she should change while she has a chance. Another may have earned an advanced degree while raising her young children and, all ready to go out into the working world, finds that no one will employ her. Some of the older single women have found that, because of discrimination, their careers are leading nowhere. A few others are facing the probability or actuality of divorce. For the participant in the Women's Rights groups this sort of personal hiatus—epitomized by the question, "What is to become of me?"—is the parallel to the normlessness that afflicts many participants in Women's Liberation.

Having joined a Women's Rights group, the more active women in particular discovered an unexpected satisfaction in a new sense of community. This satisfaction can be quite abstract: "By belonging to NOW, you give yourself some sense of identity." Often, it is more concrete: "To me it is a great relief to be with other women where I don't have to excuse [myself with comments like] 'Yes, I'm working and my children are not juvenile delinquents.' I am not constantly being judged." And: "It was not a reason for my joining, but the social support was very definitely a factor in strengthening my feelings."

Frequently participants not only benefit from their fellow members' support; they also actively enjoy these associations. "The people are marvelous. . . . [There is] the stimulation of a lot of extremely bright and dynamic women. I have never met so many outstanding individuals collected in one place." Or, "It's lots of fun. For example, for the first time in my life I've met a genuine raving neurotic and have been in a TV studio. . . . I didn't go into it expecting to like the people. As it happened, I did." "You see fascinating women perform in national executive roles, and you can participate in the same activity." For these women, therefore, working with like-minded, interesting women on stimulating projects is a happy but unexpected consequence of their involvement in the movement.

A final reward commonly appreciated by the more active members of both the Women's Rights and Women's Liberation groups is a sense of achievement that comes with being involved in an action-oriented group.

Idiosyncratic Reasons for Participation

Every movement member has her individual set of reasons for participation. While some of these are likely to be shared by a number of other members, others are found infrequently. For example, some of the first members of Women's Liberation seem to have been in search of a new movement of their own which would replace the disintegrating SDS and draft resistance movements. As one person said, "[I find it] more amusing and less threatening to have Women's Liberation to belong to than to be organizing a women's caucus within SDS." Some young single women, under pressure from their friends and families to marry, find a partial escape in the Women's Liberation or Women's Rights groups where they find a critique of that pressure. Others have unhappy family lives and find contributions to the feminist cause distracting as well as satisfying. Some chapter presidents and other active members of Women's Rights groups have a great desire for achievement and accomplishment which they channel simultaneously in their own interests and in the interests of all women. A few find participation a way to at least temporarily avoid facing and making important life decisions. For some, demonstrations are exciting: "I discovered it was fun to picket." Others find that, despite many such experiences, they still tremble as they stand in a picket line or demand to speak at a meeting they have interrupted.

Such idiosyncratic gratifications—and penalties—of participation vary greatly from person to person. With them are included the gratifications of the neurotic or even psychopathic people with excessive needs to have a place in the limelight, or to have power. We even find the occasional person whose grasp on reality is so slight that she believes her small contribution to the movement will be seen by future generations as gigantic. Or we see another filled with such deep hostility that, one by one, she destroys each of the groups she builds up around her.

However, we should notice very carefully that such examples do not constitute evidence that psychological disturbance is characteristic of the women's movement. They merely illustrate that new feminist groups, like the Lions Club or the American Medical Association, attract a wide range of personality types.

A final point of crucial importance to this study must be made. However well adjusted, or maladjusted, the different types of members are, all share a common concern with the restraints of their social role. It is this common concern, not the members' various degrees of psychological adjustment, which is the impelling motive behind the new women's movement. Had these women not agreed upon this *common* concern, they would have sought more or less consciously for other available avenues to express their *varied* conscious and unconscious motivations.

CONSEQUENCES OF COGNITIVE RESTRUCTURING

Women who participate in the new feminist groups find it difficult to live within the traditionally defined feminine role. As a consequence of their joint reevaluation of their lives, they consciously change their perspective on their roles and on what it is to be a woman. While all participants experience such a cognitive restructuring, the amount of restructuring varies. For some it involves only a few aspects of their role. For those less settled in life and those who have been in the movement the longest, it encompasses the greater part of that role. We know less about nonmembers. Outside sympathizers undergo similar experiences especially now that the feminist ideology is more commonly discussed. People who do not sympathize with the ideology, however, are unable to understand, let alone agree with, the way the feminist thinks. They ask in genuine puzzlement, "What is it these Women's Liberationists want?"

For example, outsiders cannot communicate effectively with a young, divorced movement member. When they ask her, "What are you going to do? How are things going?" they expect her to answer that she has taken a job with reasonable prospects, that she hopes to remarry, and maybe, that she is already dating seriously. For her part, the feminist is wondering whether she ever again wants to establish a "permanent" relationship with a man, let alone marry in the traditional sense, and whether, if she does enter into such a permanent relationship, she might not prefer to live in some form of communal situation rather than a house in the suburbs. As one feminist writes, "It's useless to try to answer these questions, since they are asked from a frame of reference which we have rejected, and explanations are only misunderstood."[10]

This conviction that their uncommon, and unpopular, views are "right" has often caused outsiders to call the new feminists "arrogant." Any people who express firmly held convictions can easily be so misinterpreted. Having become convinced that their views are correct, many movement members are no longer interested in objective discussions about the merits of their ideas. They want either to preach or to get involved in social action. At best, such an attitude annoys the unconvinced outsider; at worst—as when it happens to be combined with some idiosyncratic, personal quality, such as hostility or impersonality—it becomes offensive.

The consequences of the feminists' reevaluation of woman's position in society puzzles outsiders in yet another way: they cannot distinguish between their own and the feminist's view of "equality." Many men and women who sympathize with feminist demands for equal pay and equal opportunity in the job market are unable to see why feminists go on to attack the traditional role of women. They continue to wonder, "What do these women want?" In this chapter we have discussed the process of consciousness raising, similar to "conversion processes" in other social movements, by which the movement participants proceed from instances of "objective" oppression to the conclusion first, that objective oppression cannot be remedied without substantial changes in role and life style in the larger society; and second, that the traditional feminine role is bad in itself. This conceptual move distinguishes the committed movement participant from the sympathetic but puzzled outsider.

CHAPTER FOUR
THE RADICAL FEMINIST

Because of their unorthodox views, the new feminists have often been called "radical." Radicalism is an elusive concept. Behavior and ideas that the outsider calls radical, the movement member may call ordinary or even conservative. Neither people outside the movement nor movement members agree among themselves about what aspects of the new feminism are radical. Furthermore, they change their minds over time: something that is considered radical at one date may, in a few months or a few years, be generally accepted. In the following discussion I avoid the question of whether certain behavior or beliefs are appropriately called "radical" and simply describe those that *have* been called "radical" either by outsiders or by movement members.

The behavior and beliefs described here as radical may strike outsiders as "weird" or "abnormal." Some say it is abnormal for a woman to wear no makeup or to sign herself "Mary Jones" rather than "Mrs. John Jones." Others find such behavior perfectly reasonable but grow concerned when they hear feminists supporting the rights of lesbians or threatening men with physical force. For their part, the more radical feminists believe that their conservative sisters remain abnormally oppressed when, for example, they do not demand that their husbands share equally in the child-rearing responsibilities.

Rather than engage in a fruitless, value-laden discussion of the relation between, on the one hand, abnormal and normal and, on the other hand, radical and conservative, I shall outline some of the ideas and actions that outsiders or movement members at one time or another have classified as radical and shall describe the social and intellectual contexts from which they arose.

RADICAL IDEOLOGY

In their search for an adequate social analysis of women's position in society, some feminists have developed radical variations of the basic feminist ideology. Those who previously have adopted the New Left's Marxist orientation have generally grafted their feminism to their earlier ideas and emphasized the feminist aspects of socialist analysis: they see women's oppression as a direct consequence of class oppression. The only strict Marxist interpretation of women's position, however, is made by feminists who also belong to the Socialist Workers' Party/Young Socialist Alliance. A few other women, particularly those who subscribe to the views of Roxanne Dunbar, draw their inspiration from both Marxism and analyses of the blacks' position in American society. Not only, they argue, does America have a class system in the traditional Marxist sense, but the classes are themselves cross-cut by castes. "Castes" by this definition, include blacks as opposed to whites and women as opposed to men. At the present time the dominant castes oppress their subordinates in the same way as do the dominant social classes. No meaningful change in American society can be achieved unless both caste and class distinctions are attacked simultaneously.[1]

Another small group of theorists call themselves "anti-imperialist" women. They combine feminism with an objection to "capitalist oppression" of underdeveloped countries and argue that women from such countries cannot be free until their homelands are first freed from "capitalist domination."[2]

Politically radical women who have tried to integrate their feminism into a complete social analysis have most frequently worked within the general framework of democratic socialism. They speak of creating a "democratic socialist society with full equality for women . . . [where] people are the government rather than are represented in the government." Or they say:

> I just want people to see that capitalism is bad and that a society where you sink or swim on your own merit is bad. . . . Russia has failed as a good society. . . . It is really undemocratic. The fear of *1984* is valid. I see America taking responsibility. . . . Women active in all areas of life. . . . We need to get everybody together to show that the system is not viable.

Some such women hold a utopian view of the future society as a place "where everyone works for everyone's welfare and where everyone has all his needs filled."

When they considered the means whereby they would achieve their objectives, these socialist-oriented feminists generally held to a position they had learned from the New Left: satisfactory change could only be achieved through revolution. This was both imminent and inevitable. "I envision a mass-based revolution from below coming from people who are the most affected—students, and women, and workers. Hopefully, altogether they would make a majority. It doesn't necessarily have to be a violent revolution. I think probably it won't be." Such beliefs are often combined with disillusion with efforts at reform through the system. "I would never work for reform . . . [although] I think there is such a thing as radical reform. . . . You don't have to arm people to get a revolution. Maybe revolution will happen through continuous revolution."

Such ideas were heard most frequently before the end of 1970. By 1971 these feminist revolutionaries, like members of the New Left, had concluded that the revolution was not imminent and that significant social change for American society depended upon years of purposeful work. "Long-term action is required. . . . Most of us who have been in the movement for more than two years realized recently that we have to work for about ten or twenty years. You have to learn to live with that. It's scaring a lot of people."

Other feminists have been less interested in analysis of contemporary society and more interested in the historical origins of women's inferior status. For example, they suggest that when civilization supposedly moved from an economy based on collecting and hunting to an agricultural and pastoral economy, childbearing women were put in a dependent situation from which the dominant males have never allowed them to escape.[3]

One also finds feminists who, like certain members of the youth culture, take the "social conditioning" argument to its extreme. Women's socialization experiences are seen as the source of all their problems. One such interpretation was presented by a small east coast Women's Liberation group at a public meeting. A member asserted that, apart from the obvious primary and secondary sexual characteristics, no inherent differences exist between men and women. A "visit to the public library" had convinced these women that even women's musculature was inherently identical to men's, though its development was stunted because girls were not encouraged to engage in the same sort and the same amount of strenuous physical exercise as boys. Other radicals take the social conditioning argument to another extreme. Having decided that the "socially imposed" feminine role places excessive restraints upon women, they go on to argue that neither women nor men can be free unless they reject social roles in all their forms; the objective is a society that has no "roles" at all.

The most common way to extend the feminist ideology in a radical direction is to use the notion of oppression to explain all of a woman's problems: discrimination, not a tight job market, explains her failure to find employment; a bus driver's deprecation of women, not his habitually bad temper, explains his brusque behavior toward her; or, parents' double standards, not their judgment that females run greater risks than males, explain their objections to a daughter's hitch-hiking. Being constantly alert for, and constantly discovering evidences of antifeminism, movement members see oppression everywhere and begin to use it as the sole explanation of all the problems they encounter in life. All issues are assimilated to a single issue: antifeminism.

RADICAL ACTIONS

"Man Hating" and Physical Aggression

Whereas the radical developments of feminist ideology described above remain in the discussion stage, others have been translated into action. One such development that has caused much consternation both inside and outside the movement is the feminists' allegedly anti-male orientation. They were judged to be both rude and man-hating when, for example, they interrupted legislators' hearings on abortion laws with cries of "Hypocrites!" "Murderers!" Yet, from their viewpoint it was murder for the legislators to force women to risk death through incompetent illegal abortions and hypocricy for them to pass laws that effectively denied abortions to poor women, but not to the daughters of rich legislators. Such legislators, they would argue, deserve to be hated because they represent the male attitude that women must suffer the consequences of unwanted pregnancies, and because they were supporting the status quo for selfish political ends. A somewhat less radical position states that, indeed, "men collectively, are the enemy" but that, like women, individual men may be innocent victims of the social structure into which they are born.

Some women adopt a fiercely anti-male position in the period immediately following their adoption of the feminist perspective. "I was so sensitive then. It made me just furious to be 'looked over' by men. I remember one guy on the street saying something [obscene] to me. . . .

I remember the blind fury." Soon the violence of this reaction diminishes and it becomes a general intolerance of male dominance. Such intolerance seen in the context of the traditional feminine role can be called "man-hating": from the feminist perspective it is merely a justified dislike for men who oppose women's equality and freedom of choice. We should note also that the apparent anti-male stance is emphasized by movement members' unwillingness to discuss the advantages of marriage (or of child-rearing) for fear their opponents use this information to argue that women are, in fact, content in their secondary, subordinate role.

In the course of their movement experience, women have questioned more and more readily the assumptions that men should speak first, decide issues, or dictate how women should behave. They have such a low tolerance for dominating males that, attending a public meeting, they react to a man's pompous speech with cries of "Relevance?" and "Sit down!" When a man makes a pass at them in the street, they spit out some four-letter words and walk on. The movement has taught them that excessive modesty is debilitating: human dignity demands that they retaliate.

The use of obscene or scatological terms common in parts of the movement can, itself, symbolize the escape from men's dominance: a man cannot use such language to embarrass and insult a woman if she replies in the same vein. More commonly, however, this language which seems so shocking to the outsider is adopted simply because the feminist belongs to the larger radical subculture where it is a convenient, common, and group-identifying means of expression.

The use of other "man-hating" expressions like "male chauvinist pig" and "man as the oppressor" has disturbed many people. When first introduced, the terms were used by a few women to insult unsympathetic males. Within a short time, however, they became accepted as neutral concepts, used by all but the most conservative feminists as an efficient means of communication. "Male chauvinist" and "male chauvinist pig" (sometimes abbreviated to MCP) describe the man who, despite hearing feminist arguments, asserts that women are naturally suited only to their traditional role. Similarly, to speak of "man as the oppressor" became shorthand for saying that many fundamental social problems can be explained in terms of sexual inequities rather than inequities based on social class or some other variable. "Oppression" is used primarily in the context of harmful sex-based inequities. It may refer to serious physical and mental harm, or it may refer to minor inequities that are recognized as such by movement members.

In order to defend themselves from male oppression that takes the form of physical violence, some feminists have learned karate.[4] While

most such women are interested only in self-defense and healthful exercise, a few are prepared to initiate physical attacks. At a public meeting
(open to women only) sponsored by such a radical Women's Liberation
group, an uninvited male stood listening at the rear of the hall. A woman
interrupted the proceedings—"I want you to know there's a man in the
room." He was asked to leave. When he replied rather weakly that he
wanted to stay, he was "just interested," three of the organizers (at least
two of whom were learning *tae kwon do* or karate) walked silently down
the aisles toward him, clearly intending to remove him by force. Before
they reached the rear of the hall the man had left. The spectators' dismayed faces and worried comments showed that they did not approve of
threats of violence. Yet, the women concerned would argue that if
the tables are turned, men feel perfectly justified in forcibly removing
a man—or a woman—who intrudes upon their private meeting. They
would ask why the prerogative of exercising physical force should belong
solely to men.

Some of the strongest anti-male sentiments are voiced over the question of rape. It is said most women are vulnerable to the humiliation,
harm, and pain caused by rape. Although men are traditionally supposed
to protect women they, in fact, overtly or covertly side with the rapist.
The police, medical, and legal officials involved in a rape case say or assume that the woman invited assault, that she is trying to stir up trouble
for the accused man, that she has a "bad" reputation, or that she got what
she deserved. In response to such unsympathetic, even fantasy-shaped reactions, feminists often feel that all men cooperate to protect their traditional "right" to be sexually aggressive—even brutal. They say: "Men
fuck women over literally and figuratively."

A few women take anti-male views even further: they argue that
women cannot be free until they are entirely independent of men. In
New York City the twenty-odd members of The Feminists have attracted
much attention by advocating celibacy and allowing no more than one
third of their members to be married or living with men.[5] For them
sexual intercourse is men's expression of their power over women.

Such deliberately espoused celibacy represents also a radical interpretation of the feminist notion that women should be free to develop
their own personhood. A number of feminists argue that, while men have
control of the establishment—the medical profession, the educational
systems, the economy, and so forth—women can never be free. They have
therefore tried to create alternative, feminist, structures: these include
health clinics (that might even practice menstrual extraction and early
abortion[6]); self-education with classes on topics such as women's health,
women's history, women in literature, or auto-mechanics; and "buy

feminist" advertisements that aim at eventually establishing a feminist economic system that operates independently of society's established economic system.

Lesbianism

Since the movement's early years, members and outsiders alike have recognized that lesbianism is a logical alternative to a male partner's dominance. Yet, during the 1960s, few feminists were prepared to risk being called lesbians. As a consequence those who first supported the rights of lesbians were considered distinctly radical. An incident that took place in February 1970 illustrates the heterosexual feminists' fears. A group of about 100 women attended a meeting in Boston organized around a five-person panel of radical Women's Liberation participants. During the question period it became evident that about twenty gay women had come to the meeting in a body. One of these, indirectly identifying herself as a lesbian, asked why Women's Liberation was excluding gay women (who, with gay men, had begun to organize within the tolerant youth culture during the later 1960s). The speakers on the platform and the remainder of the audience were shocked. Several speakers responded feebly, but basically they hedged and turned the topic. The lesbian group grew angry. A spokesperson pointed out that the question had been disregarded. "It is a question about treating *all* women as equal." They had been involved with Women's Liberation ideas for two years "and this is the last appeal we are making to be treated equally and accepted as a real part of the movement." Neither the panel of speakers nor the audience was willing to pursue the matter, and the meeting ended.

Since 1970 most of the Women's Liberation and Women's Rights group members have changed their attitudes in favor of supporting their gay sisters. They were convinced in part by ideological arguments: lesbians ought to be accepted because the feminist movement sees all women as sisters; because lesbians, like all other women, should have control over their own bodies; and because it is only social conditioning that makes people disapprove of homosexuality. The more important reasons why lesbians were accepted were practical. Lesbian participation did not harm recruitment; and lesbians did not attempt to take over the movement for their own purposes.

Whereas in 1970 only radical feminists openly supported the rights of lesbians, within a couple of years most Women's Liberation and Women's Rights groups had discovered from experience that there was no real "lavender menace." They encouraged lesbians to join their groups and supported their demands for legal and social equality without encountering damaging repercussions. Within those few years the radical position as defined within the movement shifted drastically. It became one in which heterosexual women deliberately established lesbian sexual relationships. By this means, they argued, they became entirely independent of men. They "came to women from a political choice, experiencing men as an energy drain."[7] Such relationships it is argued represent the highest form of sisterhood. Consequently some women "feel that they are not real women unless they have had a lesbian experience." Occasionally, as in the following quotation, one sees women trying to resolve conflicts between a radical (or lesbian) interpretation of sisterhood and a fear of homosexuality:

> But can we be in love with each other in our collective without any physicality? . . . What I still don't know is what I want from a collective-women experience. Every time I experience moments when I see glimmers of what it's about I feel frightened because of the amount of love I feel, sort of an opening of all the protected areas of myself.[8]

Such deliberate courtship of homosexuality strikes many outsiders as pathological but the radical movement member would say that the outsider is imposing his or her definitions of health and sickness; the feminists are merely discovering for themselves what is the most satisfying life style to adopt.

(True lesbians are not always pleased with the newly adopted radical espousal of bisexual experience. They point out that these heterosexual women do not have to suffer the penalties of being lesbian. They have less need to fear public exposure and they do not suffer the strain of constantly pretending to be straight. Further, they sometimes hurt gay lovers by breaking a close relationship in order to return to the heterosexual world.)

Appearance and Demeanor

Many people, including movement members, believe that among new feminists the radicals are unattractive, badly dressed women who care nothing for their appearance. In fact, there is little evidence to support this view. The revival of feminism only correlates with the decline of the neat, well-groomed look of the 1950s and early 1960s. Today, the young woman wearing a T-shirt and old jeans is as likely to belong to the local choral society as to Women's Liberation.

As regards personal appearance, the radical position vis à vis the conservative outsider is for feminists to oppose dressing as "sex objects." Claiming that clothes should be functional as well as reasonably attractive, they reject the sort of tight, short-skirted outfits, high-heeled shoes, elaborate hair styles, and extensive use of cosmetics which attract men's attention at the cost of personal comfort and time. Shirts and jeans, pants suits, or simple dresses are their normal attire. I believe that bralessness is far more characteristic of young nonmovement women than of partici-pants.[9] Nor are movement women unattractive. A few outside observers corroborate my judgment that the movement has more than its share of inherently "beautiful" women.[10]

Within the movement, members who adopt what is thought of as the most radical position regarding personal appearance find their ra-tionale in an extension of the "sex object" argument. They avoid colorful clothes, cut their fashionably long hair, cease shaving their legs and underarms, and even smile less. Such behavior is often the culmination of a genuine moral struggle to cast off what are objectively unimportant but subjectively highly symbolic aspects of their old role.

Like dress, feminists' language can be seen as radical or conservative depending on one's perspective. The typical feminist of the late 1960s would have agreed with the typical outsider of the early 1970s that use of the title Ms. and retention of one's maiden or "birth" name on marriage were radical acts. By 1972 such usages were accepted but uncommon. Women in all parts of the movement were dropping titles entirely. They addressed envelopes, for example, to "Jane Smith" and began letters with "Dear Jane" or "Dear Sister." For them, a more radical position regarding surnames is a woman's refusal to use her father's name because it identifies her solely through her male ancestry. A few have invented new names— for example, Ann Fury, Dair Struggle, Ann Forfreedom, Kathy Sarachild, and Varda One.

A few years ago movement women astonished outsiders by objecting to words like "mankind," "manpower," and "chairman" because they im-plied that women were excluded from the category. Outside the movement one now occasionally encounters words like "chairperson," "chairone," or "chairwoman"; but other words and expressions like "womanpower," "womaning picket lines," and "herstory" (rather than "history") are used only by the moderately radical and radical feminists.

Many women are dissatisfied with the personal pronouns; in particular the pronoun "he" which can refer exclusively to a male or to someone of either sex. They believe that when "he" is used in contexts ranging from job descriptions to treatises on human society most people give it the "male only" interpretation. Consequently, almost all replace "he" with "he or she," "he/she," "she or he," and "she/he." They treat "him" and "her" similarly. A few women have suggested replacing existing personal pronouns with terms that are not sex linked. Proposals include replacing "his" and "her" possessives with a single pronoun such as "vis," "cos," "heris," "ter," or "their"; replacing the "he" and "she" nominatives with a single nominative such as "ve," "co," "she," "tey," or "they"; and replacing the "him" and "her" accusatives with a single accusative such as "ver," "co," "herm," "tem," or "them."[11] Very occasionally these terms are actually used in the movement literature, but I know of no cases where Women's Liberation or Women's Rights group members use them in conversation.[12]

From language to ideology, from lesbianism to physical prowess, feminists hold a variety of attitudes and behave in a variety of ways. The "radical feminist" is a mythical creature. Some people think of her as *any* feminist; others think of her as having ideas that are more radical than those of her colleagues; some think that she belongs only to certain Women's Liberation groups; others that she is found within both Women's Liberation and Women's Rights groups; some cannot agree whether she or some other feminist is the "more radical"; and others find that, while she was radical at one time, she keeps becoming outdated. One definite statement can be made about her: she has persuaded others, inside and outside of the movement, to adopt new ideas and attitudes that in her absence they would never have considered.

PART THREE

THE NEW FEMINIST GROUPS: WOMEN'S LIBERATION

CHAPTER FIVE

THE EMERGENCE AND GROWTH OF WOMEN'S LIBERATION

Women's Liberation and Women's Rights group members sometimes disagree over which of these two segments of the new feminist movement was founded first. In fact, the National Organization for Women (NOW) was founded in 1966 and the first generally recognized Women's Liberation groups were founded in 1967. In each case, several years of preliminary discussion and exploration preceded the actual formation of the groups.

WOMEN'S LIBERATION, CIVIL RIGHTS, AND THE NEW LEFT

Although the principal impetus for Women's Liberation came from within the New Left, its ideas were voiced first by women within the civil rights movement. As early as 1964, Ruby Doris Robinson, one of the Student Non-violent Coordinating Committee's (SNCC) black founders, presented to a SNCC conference a paper in which she protested the inferior status accorded to women within the organization.[1] Her remarks were received with the same ridicule with which young male radicals, for the next five years, would greet similar remarks. Stokeley

Carmichael voiced the prevailing male view in responding with a comment that later became notorious within the women's movement, "The only position for women in SNCC is prone."[2] Women, however, at all levels in the civil rights organizations, were beginning to discuss views similar to Robinson's. An example, described later by one of my respondents, was an incident that took place in the spring of 1966 within Chicago's Southern Christian Leadership Conference (SCLC) where a small group composed mostly of black and white women and black men was working on the open housing campaign. Because the group was isolated from the Chicago community, black and white women competed with each other for the attention of black males. Responding to the high tensions developing among the small group of about fifteen women, one white woman brought the others together to listen to extracts from Betty Friedan's *The Feminine Mystique* and to discuss their situation. The women talked about such problems as how, in competing for the men's attention, they grew antagonistic to each other; how they did all the uninteresting jobs—such as typing, making posters, canvassing, and arranging meetings—while the men confined their activities to strategy decisions, consultation with the more important community leaders, and speaking at the meetings which the women arranged. "We talked about how we did the shit work, and how we were competing over who was sleeping with whom." Although the discussion did nothing to change these women's relative status, it helped them to realize that the real cause of their complaints was not their relations with each other but their relations with the male members of the group.

Such Women's Liberation ideas originated within all the radical movements of the 1960s but particularly within civil rights, Students for a Democratic Society (SDS), and the antiwar movement. By the end of 1966 they had been crowded out of the civil rights movement by the concept of black power but had taken hold within the other two groups. Although most nascent feminists at first discussed their complaints in private, a few were willing to state them in public. Feminists had already spoken publicly at the December 1965 SDS national convention.[3] Despite the ridicule with which their remarks were then received, they returned the following year with the demand that the convention members accept a plank supporting women's liberation. The women who made this proposal were "pelted with tomatoes and thrown out of the convention."[4] A year later, in 1967, at the New Left "National Conference for New Politics," the issue was treated more gingerly though still unsympathetically. When the feminist women presented a "civil rights plank for women" political maneuvering, as well as ridicule, was used to replace it with a traditional plank concerning "women for peace."[5] During the next year most of the New Left men disregarded the women's movement growing within their ranks—but many of the women did not. Gradually they began to take sides on the issue. Some identified themselves as primarily feminists; others as primarily members of the New Left.

Eventually the New Left women split on the feminist issue. Two incidents in particular illustrate the growing schism. The first occurred in January 1968 at an anti-Vietnam war protest that took the form of a march on Washington organized by the Jeannette Rankin Brigade, a coalition of conservative women's peace groups such as the Women's Strike for Peace.

While the main demonstration was being held, some 500 New Left feminists left the other 4,500 women to hold an "alternative action" that would express their disillusion with women's contribution to the conservative and radical segments of the antiwar movement. At Arlington National Cemetery, they symbolically buried "traditional womanhood." Kathie Amatniek's[6] "Funeral Oration" stated clearly the relation between the new women's movement and women in the peace movement. "It would seem [to some of our sisters] that our number one task is to devote our energies directly to ending this slaughter [in Vietnam] or else solve . . . problems at home. . . . We cannot hope to move toward a better world or even a truly democratic society at home until we begin to solve our own problems [as women which render us] . . . powerless and ineffective over war, peace and our own lives."[7] When they evaluated the responses to the burial of traditional womanhood, the feminists realized that women outside of the New Left were unresponsive to their ideas. As a result of this and other similar experiences, during the remainder of 1968 and 1969 they rarely tried to proselytize outside New Left circles.

The second incident which marked the emergence of an independent Women's Liberation movement occurred a year later in January 1969 at the counterinaugural demonstration organized in Washington, D. C., by "Mobilization for Peace," another coalition of peace groups this time dominated by the radical left. Throughout the previous year New Left women had started to define themselves either as "politicos" (those who wished feminism to remain a part of the New Left) or as "feminists" (those who favored an independent women's movement). Women representing each of these viewpoints were to speak at the counterinaugural. The first speaker, Marilyn Salzman-Webb, a politico from Washington, D. C., gave what she and the opposing schismatic feminists believed to be a mildly feminist, strongly pro-Left speech. She referred to New Left people working "toward our revolution" through "a new pattern" and asked "all women to join this struggle and march with us today."[8] A number of factors combined to assure her speech a poor reception, thoroughly arousing the indignation of the more fervent feminists who were present. First hand reports show that before and during Webb's speech the audience had objected to the crowd of women milling around the stage. Some of these women, WITCHes[9] from New York City, were planning to perform guerrilla theater. Another group from New York were planning to mount the stage and publicly destroy their voter-registration cards to illustrate how useless the vote had been to the feminist cause. When Webb spoke, the audience had difficulty hearing her, partly because of the inadequate public address system and partly because Webb had a high voice and was not skilled at speaking into a microphone.[10] Given these confusing conditions, it is little wonder that there is general disagreement on the exact cause of the incident which followed. It is clear however that the men in the audience believed that the women were deflecting attention from what they felt was the real issue—opposition to the Vietnam war. They reacted by booing Marilyn Salzman-Webb and shouting such remarks as "Take her off the stage and fuck her." Many women were deeply shocked; others were infuriated. These last included the women who were already considering breaking with the New Left. One of them, Shulamith Firestone, the second woman scheduled to speak, "went right up, grabbed the mike," and told the radical men that it "was the end."

For a minority of New Left women, this day did indeed mark the end. They abandoned the "male-dominated" movement for the caucus-like Women's Liberation groups which, during the preceding two years, they had founded within the New Left in some half-dozen cities. Others followed later.

The schism with the New Left was never complete, however; soon the male radicals were taking the representatives of the newly independent Women's Liberation movement seriously and making its ideas part of their philosophy. For example, in the same month as the counter-inaugural, Chicago's SDS organized a sit-in at the university to protest the administration's refusal to reappoint to the faculty the political radical, Marlene Dixon. During the preceding two years, a few dozen women had been trying to promote Women's Liberation at Chicago.[11] The previous summer they had held a class on women's liberation at the Free University's Center for Radical Research. Subsequently several women's groups formed and reformed. One of them, the Women's Radical Action Project (WRAP) argued that antifeminism was one of the reasons underlying the university's failure to reappoint Marlene Dixon. At the sit-in WRAP demanded and received the men's consent to a number of feminist demands, the best-known of which was the insistence that WRAP hold a special press conference to which only women reporters were admitted.

Another 1969 sit-in (this time at Columbia University), also demonstrated the radical male students' growing awareness of the women's issue. When Columbia students were occupying Fayerweather Hall in protest over the university's expansion at the local community's expense, a "male leader asked for girls to volunteer for cooking duty." Many of the men present knew that the women considered cooking just as much a man's job as a woman's, and they joined in the laughter which greeted the request.[12]

At the same time as the male members of the New Left were beginning to take Women's Liberation seriously, the mass media, focusing upon the new movement's "newsworthy" elements, held it up to ridicule. In attempting to get publicity for public protests the feminists unintentionally contributed to the media's unsympathetic image. The best-known of the early demonstrations took place in September 1968 at the Miss America Pageant. The women who organized this action wanted to show how the pageant symbolized male—and female—Americans' preoccupation with a woman's physical appearance and their neglect of such features as character or personal attainment. In futile attempts to attain an impossible cultural ideal, women spent hours dressing their hair and making up their faces and suffered considerable discomfort from the clothes they wore. Symbolically, the feminists dropped into a trash can some of those uncomfortable clothes, including girdles, high-heeled shoes—and bras. Their actions were misunderstood. Many observers believed that the feminists wanted to behave like men and wanted other women to join them. Others believed that they despised and hated men. The media, seeing a good news story, highlighted their "unfeminine" "bra-burning" activities. In fact, no bras were burned, but the label "bra-burners" has stuck.

After the Miss America protest, the New York City WITCHes put a "hex" on Wall Street by means of a guerrilla theater presentation, feminists in San Francisco and New York disrupted bridal fairs, and others demonstrated outside of Playboy Clubs. These and other actions brought the new movement considerable publicity but little serious consideration. "Women's lib" (a term rarely heard in the movement) made good copy only if it was treated as a joke. This treatment encouraged many movement members to continue their work privately and, for the present, to avoid contact with the mass media.

THE GROWTH OF WOMEN'S LIBERATION GROUPS

Even before 1968 and 1969, when the New Left feminists began to speak out publicly, their ideas were spreading rapidly among movement women. From the beginning meetings planned as political discussions tended to "degenerate" into "bitch sessions," where women shared ideas about their social status and experienced individual consciousness raising. The transition from such discussions to groups explicitly organized for "consciousness raising" was gradual; we cannot date the start of "consciousness raising" because the transition is so poorly defined. Robins states that the first groups deliberately aimed at raising women's consciousness of their oppression were formed in 1966 and 1967,[13] but I am unable to substantiate her statement. It is clear that Jo Freeman and other Chicago women were active as feminists by September 1967, but within the political movement, not as consciousness-raising group organizers. Soon after, Shulamith Firestone moved from Chicago to New York City, where she joined Pamela Allen and others founding feminist groups. Kathie Sarachild (Amatniek) and other New York feminists, in contact with a group in Gainesville, Florida, worked out a theory of consciousness raising, which Sarachild presented as "A Program for Feminist Consciousness Raising"[14] at the Chicago conference in November 1968. Within a short time, the idea of the consciousness-raising group had become an integral part of the movement.

When the consciousness-raising paper was given Women's Liberation was still growing slowly. During the second half of 1969, however, the number of groups increased rapidly. Approximately once a month movement members in Chicago, New York, and Boston organized "mass meetings" of from 30 to 300 women who were interested in learning about Women's Liberation. About one-third of the women attending were recruited to new consciousness-raising groups.

By the end of 1969 groups had been founded in at least forty American cities. Many of these were large, cosmopolitan centers like Chicago or San Francisco, but groups were also founded in university towns like New Haven, Connecticut, and in more conservative places like New Orleans, Durham (North Carolina), Iowa City, and Minneapolis.[15] By the end of 1970, Robins reports, New York City had at least fifty consciousness raising groups, Chicago had thirty, and Boston, twenty-five.[16]

Other figures illustrate the continued growth of the movement. At the end of 1969 the San Francisco area had five or six small groups, Cleveland had one group of about ten, and New Haven had about twenty movement participants. By the end of 1970, the San Francisco area had thirty-five groups with several hundred participants, Cleveland had ten to twelve groups with a total of over a hundred members, and New Haven had over eighty participants. While membership continued to increase in cities with established groups, consciousness-raising groups were introduced into other cities and smaller towns. For example, by the end of 1970, over 100 participants were reported on Cape Cod, over 200 in Amherst, Massachusetts, and about 250 in thiry-one groups scattered around Ohio (in addition to the 100 or so in the Cleveland groups).

The estimates of group members themselves upon which almost all of the above statements are based are the most accurate available measure of movement growth. Another such measure, however, lies in the total number of newsletters and other periodicals being produced. In 1968 there were only two such publications: *Voice of the Women's Liberation Movement* (Chicago, with a circulation of 2,000), and *No More Fun and Games* (Boston, circulation unknown). The number of newsletters, magazines, and newspapers[17] increased to ten in 1969, thirty in 1970, and sixty in 1971. The growth appeared to stabilize at that point, with fourteen new periodicals founded in 1972 while thirteen ceased publication. By the spring of 1973, according to my subscription records, eighty-three such periodicals had been published (including five which appealed equally to Women's Liberation and Women's Rights readers, but excluding forty with a distinctly Women's Rights orientation). Twenty-nine of the eighty-three Women's Liberation periodicals had ceased publication by 1973 and the status of six more was uncertain.

Another indirect measure of the movement's growth is given by the periodicals' distribution figures. These figures usually total three or four times the number of women known to be participating in consciousness-raising groups in the city where they are published. Thus, when 100 women were involved in small groups in Cleveland, their joint newsletter was being sent out to 350 people. Changing subscription lists, therefore, measure proportional rather than absolute increases in both participation and interest. Participants report that early in 1970 the San Francisco newsletter was being sent to some 300 people; by the fall of that year subscriptions had jumped to 1,200; and by January 1971, 1,000 people in San Francisco and 500 outside the city were receiving it.

Distribution figures for such newsletters, when they are available, help to measure the movement's national scope as well as its local growth. Toward the end of 1971 Boston's biweekly *Female Liberation* (one of the few free newsletters) was being distributed to 900 people; Austin, Texas's monthly newspaper *The Second Coming* had 200 subscribers; and Philadelphia's bimonthly newspaper *Awake and Move* had 137 subscribers. In the spring of 1972, Seattle's biweekly newsletter *Pandora* reported 300 subscribers and additional street sales of 200 copies, while New Haven's newsletter *Sister*, published every two months, had 400 subscribers. The largest newsletter circulation is reported by the Los Angeles Women's Center, which sent out 2,700 copies of its January 1972 newsletter.[18]

THE STRUCTURE OF WOMEN'S LIBERATION

As the Women's Liberation movement increased in size, its informal local and national network dependent initially upon the New Left communication system was gradually elaborated independently. The small groups became linked by innumerable ties through the exchange of periodicals or other movement publications and through personal contacts among women who visited throughout the country or who attended conferences.[19]

Coalitions

On a local level, small groups from a particular city, state, or geographical region have often affiliated into "coalitions." By means of periodic meetings of the whole membership or of their representatives, the coalitions have tried to prevent members from feeling isolated, to inform women about events elsewhere in the movement and to help them become involved in activities outside of their consciousness-raising groups. That members genuinely want such broader contacts is evident from the interviews, in which respondents frequently reported that they felt isolated from the ongoing movement and complained about inadequate communication systems. Most felt that some form of central organization would have the advantages of bringing strength, unity, and a broader base for action to the movement. At the same time almost all were afraid that central leadership would infringe on the individual and small group autonomy they value so highly.

Coalitions have been formed in many areas of the country. Throughout 1970 and 1971 Bread and Roses was such an umbrella group in Boston; its member collectives held what movement members considered a radical stance, both in their feminism and in their New Left politics. Another example was Michigan's Women's Liberation Coalition, formed in 1970,

> for the purpose of bringing together existing small discussion groups and action groups of any other kind so we could share information and work together on large actions. . . . The newsletter goes all over the state . . . and even crosses the border to reach an active group in Windsor, Ontario.[20]

Similar coalitions have been formed (and sometimes later disintegrated) in such places as Detroit; Chicago; San Francisco; Los Angeles; Amherst, Massachusetts; South Bend, Indiana; Westchester County, New York; New York City; and New England.

Women's Centers

Movement members had founded at least fifty-five Women's Centers, serving as gathering places or as communication centers, by June 1972. These centers consist of an office, a storefront, a rented house, a member's apartment, a room in the local YWCA, a room in a church complex, or part of a university building. They have been founded in places ranging from Santa Barbara, California, to Iowa City and Bangor, Maine, to St. Louis University.

The Women's Centers have found themselves, often unexpectedly, playing an important role in the Liberation movement's communications network and action programs. The half-dozen or dozen women who assume responsibility for answering the telephone, coordinating the activities held in the center, and paying the rent[21] find that progressively more responsibility is thrust upon them. Because the centers provide a visible and accessible core for the movement in their area, outsiders and insiders alike look to them as the source of all information about Women's Liberation and about all women-related problems: they "become a switchboard for women's activities." "The phone rings every ten minutes."

Conferences

Like the Women's Centers, Women's Liberation conferences have served as occasions for the exchange of information and ideas, and for the provision of mutual support. The first such conference, attended by twenty women, was held in Sandy Springs, Maryland, in August 1968. Encouraged by its success, the participants (who included Marilyn Salzman-Webb, Charlotte Bunch-Weeks, and Shulamith Firestone) planned a larger three-day conference, or "Women's Convention," for Thanksgiving 1968. The organizers expected to attract about 50 women, mostly from the northest, but when the conference opened at the YMCA's Camp Hastings, in Lake Villa outside of Chicago, more than 200 women arrived from all over the United States and Canada. At a later date, one of these stated that they represented, informally, more than 5,000 members of Women's Liberation, and included women who were to become prominent figures in the larger new feminist movement: Ti-Grace Atkinson, Jacqueline Ceballos, Ann Forfreedom (Hershfang), Joreen (Jo Freeman), Naomi Weisstein, Heather Booth, and Marlene Dixon. Many women found that the workshops and informal discussions raised their consciousnesses significantly, helped them to clarify ideological principles, and convinced them that Women's Liberation had nationwide support. They feel that, for movement women, the Chicago conference marks the emergence of Women's Liberation on a national level.

Similar conferences soon were organized locally. By March 1969 two conferences had been held in the San Francisco Bay area, one in Boston, and one in Atlanta.[22] They were continued in the 1970s with, for example, five national and at least eight regional meetings being held between April and July 1971 in places ranging from Minot, North Dakota, to New York City. But, during the first years of the 1970s, and already by 1971, conferences were less concerned with consciousness raising, ideological discussion, and social support and, as has been characteristic of all movement activities, more concerned with specific topics, such as health, abortion, Chicano women, lesbianism, rape, and lower-class women.

Lesbians and Women's Liberation

Lesbianism, which subsequently became a topic around which whole conferences were organized, was initially a tabooed topic in Women's Liberation. Lesbians themselves were not involved in the movement during its first years: they were organizing independently. Prior to the 1960s the only lesbian organization was the Daughters of Bilitis (DOB) a national organization founded in 1955. When young gay women, encouraged by the tolerant youth culture, began to "come out" during the 1960s, they tried unsuccessfully to work with the DOB or with mixed homosexual organizations. Unfortunately for them, most DOB members (usually older women) wanted to make private adjustments to their situations, while their male contemporaries, who shared their interest in making the homosexual life style publicly accepted, dominated the mixed organizations. Affiliation with Women's Liberation seemed a viable alternative. Although at first rejected by most heterosexual Liberation groups, the lesbians have gradually been accepted as an integral part of the movement.

In 1970 they were participating actively in the less conservative Liberation groups. For example, in October of that year the Women's Caucus of the Los Angeles Gay Liberation Front had changed its name to the Lesbian Feminists and become affiliated with the Women's Liberation Center. Feminists on the west coast report that they were not so "up tight" about the issue as were women elsewhere. In San Francisco, "People were shy and nervous about it—uncomfortable. But there was never any question that the lesbians would not be in. . . . People here are far less surprised by something odd." By 1972, only the more conservative groups questioned the lesbians' participation. Lesbians in Kansas City, for example, have tried not to force the issue. "It has seemed more natural to confront attitudes towards it as they arise as a natural part of other matters, and as a gay woman I myself have been satisfied with that;

I have seen many sisters grow in awareness and show great openness and eagerness to understand the unique nature of gay oppression."[23]

On the whole, by 1972 gay women had become one segment of the multisegmented Women's Liberation movement. Locally and nationally they supported the movement's general ideology while concentrating upon those topics that were of particular interest to themselves—mutual support, aid to women who were trying to come to terms with their lesbianism, and the achievement of social acceptance.

Women's Liberation Literature

Communication along the Women's Liberation movement's informal network of groups is by personal contact and movement literature. Before 1968 the women published their ideas in New Left periodicals. One of the earliest and most influential articles was Juliet Mitchell's "Women: The Longest Revolution," printed in the *New Left Review*, November–December issue, 1966. Few such pieces were circulated prior to 1968 but, soon after the consciousness-raising group idea had taken hold and shortly before the schism within the New Left became generally recognized, the women's movement began to publish independently. The seminal articles were distributed primarily in leaflet and pamphlet form. Among them are: Margaret Benston, "The Political Economy of Women's Liberation,"[24] Beverly Jones and Judith Brown, "Toward a Female Liberation Movement," Anne Koedt, "The Myth of the Vaginal Orgasm," Pat Mainardi, "The Politics of Housework," early selections from Kate Millet's *Sexual Politics*, Naomi Weisstein, "Kinde, Kuche, Kirche as Scientific Law: Psychology Constructs the Female," and Lyn Wells, "American Women: Their Use and Abuse."[25] By the end of 1968 such New Left groups as the New England Free Press were reprinting these and other Women's Liberation articles and distributing them throughout the country. Since then movement members themselves have taken over the job: inexpensive reproduction processes have enabled them to put out far greater quantities of literature than was possible for the nineteenth-century feminists.

Since 1969, the relative importance of articles distributed in pamphlet form has decreased, as the number of movement periodicals increased from two in 1968 to a high of sixty-one in 1972 and the commercial presses published a large number of books and compilations. These periodicals, aided by personal contacts, form a relatively unstructured national communication network whose efficiency is illustrated by the speed with which important articles are reprinted and news is spread. For example, the October 1972 newsletter of the North Shore (Massachusetts) Feminists[26] published the news that women from the Los Angeles Women's

Liberation Self-Help Clinic had been arrested on 20 September 1972 for practicing medicine without a license.

It is difficult for me to evaluate the relative importance of the movement literature and personal contacts in transmitting ideas to the individual members; the problem is complicated because the bulk of my interviewing was done in 1969-71, the period when the volume of movement literature was increasing most rapidly. A clear majority of my respondents had read very few books and only occasional articles about the movement, but they had learned through personal contacts the basic ideas presented in these publications. This suggests a two-step model for the movement communication system,[27] in which a relatively few members read and digest the literature, and then pass the ideas on in private conversations and group meetings.

When, by the end of 1969, Women's Liberation became nationally known, it was an established movement with its own ideology, a growing membership, and an informal but defined organizational structure. Its origins lay several years earlier within the civil rights and later New Left movements. At first new feminist ideas, partially formulated, spread along the communication networks established by these other movements. Subsequently Women's Liberation developed a similarly complex, informal, and often highly personal communication network. The credit for piecing ideas together and "inventing" Women's Liberation belongs to no one person or group. Instead, through the process of constant interchange, groups as far apart as New York, Chicago, and Seattle developed basically similar formulations and Women's Liberation became a coherent if many-faceted movement, with its own ideological base and organizational principles.

CHAPTER SIX

WOMEN'S LIBERATION: ACTIONS

B y the early 1970s Women's Liberation consciousness-raising groups were to be found in large cities and small towns throughout the United States. Many of these groups had been formed at the initiative of movement members but, increasingly, women who had had no contact with the informal network of women composing the Liberation movement were forming consciousness-raising groups for example, from among occupants of a particular apartment building, or among mothers whose children attended the same play school. The consciousness-raising group idea had spread also into the National Organization for Women where many chapters found enthusiasts among their recruits.

THE WOMEN'S LIBERATION NETWORK

Although many consciousness-raising groups disintegrate within a few weeks or months and some survive for two or more years, the typical group lasts for about nine months. During this time it passes through two stages of development. First, participants gradually reconceptualize their personal situations in terms of the new feminist ideology. The degree of reconceptualization reached does not depend upon the group's life span but upon its members' openness to radical ideas and their prior commitment to a traditional or nontraditional life style. For some women, the experience marks a complete rejection of the traditional role: they decide never to become legally married, to have children only if they can find some cooperative day-care arrangement, to reject the social pressures to become "supermothers" who manage all roles—wife, mother, and paid worker—at the cost of personal exhaustion, to reject also the pressures to create an elegant but time-consuming home and an extensive but superficial social life. One example is a woman whose "second" child turned out to be twins. She and her husband decided that they should share equally all the responsibilities of child care, housekeeping, and earning a living. A few women have decided to have children without being married, have moved into women's communes (or semi-communes), have openly declared their lesbianism, or have, on principle, decided to be celibate for a year.

More conservative women, however, have found that the consciousness-raising group experience does not move them this far from the traditional role. One such person reported that her husband now put the children to bed each night and helped take care of them over the weekend. "It took me a year to get this far," she added. Another shared with her husband the responsibility for cooking dinner and for putting the children to bed but reported that it was still hard to tell her husband, " 'Honey you forgot the napkins.' I am uneasy that this man is waiting on me." Yet another, whose husband always insisted that she be home whenever he was, found that only "after six months [in the movement] am I getting to the point when I can insist on going to a Women's Liberation meeting of 'mine' on one of the few evenings when my husband is home." Many women, encouraged by their groups, change jobs, go back to college, or return to paid employment. One woman, for example, gave up teaching to establish a business as a professional dressmaker.

However much or however little participants change their ideas as a consequence of participation, they generally reach a point at which the consciousness-raising group itself can contribute little more; it has "served its purpose." Members' realization of this fact marks the group's second stage of development—one in which they try to redefine their common objectives. Suggestions range from proselytizing for and organizing new groups to doing research on women's history, from writing nonsexist children's books to founding a child-care center. Only rarely do members agree on what they would like to do. Consequently, only rarely does the group continue through this second stage. Most commonly it disintegrates: "Everyone went away for the summer and, when we came back, we couldn't seem to get started again."

Such disintegration contributes to the general reshuffling which goes on constantly within Women's Liberation. When their group breaks up, many women, although they remain committed feminists, cease active participation. With their outlook and attitudes changed, they revise their way of life and, thereby, revise the lives of people around them; but they do so as part of the broader feminist movement, not as part of Women's Liberation. Participants estimate that between 5 and 15 percent remain active in Women's Liberation: they seek out others like themselves and become involved in a wide range of social action projects through which they try to change society, not simply their own lives or the lives of people immediately around them.

The typical Women's Liberation activist has experienced a more thoroughgoing reconceptualization of her role than the woman whose involvement ceases with the disintegration of her consciousness-raising group. Her commitment to feminism is, therefore, a major factor in her decision to remain. But it is not her only reason. She may be particularly interested in some application of the ideology such as the medical profession's treatment of women or, "unwilling to join the larger society which is on an ego trip or a machismo trip," she remains in the reassuring movement environment. Most participants continue to enjoy a sense of "belonging"—a few to the point of realizing that the movement substitutes for other social relationships. They have available time and they enjoy the sorts of work demanded of someone who is trying to initiate social change. The conflicts associated with the feminine role which brought them to feminism still motivate them but these additional rewards, plus an increased sense of dedication to the cause learned within the movement, are important considerations in their decision to remain active.

Women's Liberation, therefore, has a relatively stable structure but a changing membership. A deeply involved group of social-action-oriented women are linked together in the basic nationwide Liberation network. A secondary network, closely tied to the first, consists of the numerous consciousness-raising groups which have been formed under the auspices of the social activist women. These relatively short-lived groups provide a constant supply of recruits to the movement's social activist core. A third part of the movement consists of women who belong to independent consciousness-raising groups which have little if any connection with the primary and secondary Liberation networks; usually, neither they nor women in the other groups define these independent groups as a part of Women's Liberation.

SOCIAL ACTIVISM: EARLY EXPERIMENTS

Social activists within Women's Liberation have, from the beginning, grappled with the problem of translating an ideology which all agreed should be general and flexible into concrete goals and projects. Until about 1970, the only sustained activities were proselytizing by means of organizing new consciousness-raising groups and of publishing feminist literature. All other activities, though eye-catching, were spontaneous and small-scale. Such "zap" actions included guerrilla theater in the streets, sit-ins at male-only luncheon facilities, and a variety of demonstrations. One small group in San Francisco held a "hairy legs" demonstration to protest the action of a local pet store owner who dismissed a newly hired employee because, he said, she had hairy legs. After watching a half-dozen or so women demonstrate outside his store for a day, the owner capitulated, publicly retracted his accusation (made after the firing) that he had mysteriously lost $20.00, and offered to rehire the woman. Had he known that "the group did not have the strength to go on [picketing] for a long time" he might not have given in so easily, a demonstrator reported later.

Actions of this sort, carried out by from six to twenty people, may have gained publicity for the movement, but they did little to change what the feminists believed were the major problems confronting them and all other American women. Consequently, in addition to the almost universal effort to found more consciousness-raising groups, many activist groups began to specialize in particular areas. Classes in "women's history" were introduced very early. The women felt that they, like blacks, had been neglected by white male historians. Usually taught by a movement member who had been doing research on the subject, these classes were intended to help women attain a sense of identity and pride comparable to that sought by the black separatist groups.

Other classes that were introduced at an early date contributed to women's independence. They included bicycle repair, car maintenance, plumbing, carpentry, how to organize demonstrations, physical exercise, and the much publicized self-defense. (Self-defense classes, like articles on "how to protect yourself from rapists while you're hitchhiking," epitomize the movement members' desire to step out of the traditional "need-to-be-protected" role.) New topics are introduced constantly. In 1972, for example, we find a sudden enthusiasm for such subjects as children's liberation,[1] vasectomy, women and the arts, women and the law, lesbianism, divorce procedures, and prostitution.

While such activities encouraged participants to develop the highly valued personal autonomy, the work was not enough to satisfy their desire for social change: except insofar as they set an example, class participants only helped themselves; they did not help other women to become self-reliant. In order that other women could profit, some groups, therefore, began to publish the information which their members compiled. They wrote booklets on "Women and Their Bodies,"[2] produced lists of "nonsexist" children's books,[3] wrote such books for themselves,[4] or put together feminist bibliographies.

Implicit, and occasionally explicit, in these activities was the notion that the women's movement could operate as a system, independent of the larger society, and using its own economic resources, communication network, educational and welfare institutions. To the most idealistic among the feminists, this system of independent economic institutions was to be "comparable to the old utopian communities, but not isolated."

UNINTENTIONAL PERPETUATION OF THE STATUS QUO

Ironically, in its efforts to bring about its vision of societal transformation, Women's Liberation often inadvertently succeeded in bolstering what it considers the gross inadequacies of modern society. It has treated some of America's most pressing problems with palliative rather than curative measures.

One such problem is the issue of abortion. While many women worked through small groups or coalitions to change abortion laws, thereby changing the "system," many others created abortion referral services which implicitly accepted the inadequacies of the system and concentrated upon helping women to get around those inadequacies. Although the referral services generally do a good job and certainly help many individual women, they may actually have reduced the social pressure both for reform of abortion statutes in line with the 1973 Supreme Court decision on abortion and for the creation of appropriate medical facilities in states where the old statutes have been struck down.

As regards other parts of the medical-care system, particularly the areas of birth control, pregnancy, and childbirth, the movement is also filling a role which it believes ought, ideally, to be filled by the medical people themselves. Members object strenuously to the brusque treatment and impersonal care that physicians offer gynecological and obstetrical patients. They complain, for example, about a physician who refused to examine a woman patient who had not menstruated for two months, was chronically tired, and had swollen legs. "Are you sure you're not pregnant?" he asked, and simply would not believe her reply, "I know when I get laid." She was not, in fact, pregnant. Another woman reported in a movement periodical:

> A week before I had the baby, [the doctor] said I was gaining too much weight and my ankles were swelling. He asked me if I had ever seen anybody in a convulsion and said, "If you don't do what I tell you you're going to die." He put me on a 1,200 calorie diet. He just tried to frighten me and never explained anything to me.[5]

To cope with these sorts of problems, a number of Liberation groups specializing in medical matters have instituted such procedures as arranging that a member of the group accompany women on visits to a physician or hospital to oversee the quality of the care. They arrange pregnancy tests and provide the pregnancy counseling that gynecologists have no time to offer their patients; they recommend gynecologists and physicians who, they feel, are sympathetic toward women's needs; they refer women to birth control clinics or venereal disease clinics; they form "health collectives" which, for example, show films on abortion, hold rap sessions on masturbation, or discuss psychosurgery and psychotherapy; they establish "self-help" or "free" clinics;[6] and they encourage women to prepare for "natural" childbirth. Whereas Betty Friedan in *The Feminine Mystique* saw the glorification of natural childbirth as another example of the overemphasis on motherhood, these women, instead, see it as a way for women to be "in control of their own bodies" instead of being manipulated by unsympathetic physicians and hospital staffs.

However much such programs may help individual women, they leave untouched the essential problem. Today's physicians frequently view their job as one of identifying and avoiding crises; when overworked, as many are, they are especially likely to take this attitude. Pregnancy is a natural process, and for the physician at least, its varied symptoms are commonplace. For the woman, however, such symptoms are often associated with personal discomfort and with considerable anxiety about the unknowns of pregnancy. She tends to view her gynecologist in the ideal terms of the family physician—he ought to be professionally concerned with these real, if minor, problems, to offer advice, and to reassure her. Whether or not physicians ought to or can provide such attention is irrelevant to the present argument. The fact is that they do not and that many women perceive their behavior as condescending and derogatory.

The problem of differing expectations of obstetrician and pregnant woman is aggravated by two other conditions common among young middle- and upper middle-class participants in the new feminist movement. First, the women involved are generally healthy. Obstetricians, therefore, are usually the first physicians on whom they have been dependent since childhood. It is on them, therefore, that the brunt of the woman's disillusion with the impersonality of modern medicine falls.

Second, although she rarely sees it in these terms, pregnancy often symbolizes for the contemporary feminist her lack of integration in any community. She usually lives far away from her relatives and from the close friends she made at college. If she has not managed to make friends in a new city, she has no one with whom to share the minor (and major) worries of pregnancy. Women's Liberation finds itself fulfilling such a person's need for friendship and her demands for more knowledge about the details of pregnancy and birth.[7]

The ways the movement tackles these problems associated with abortion, pregnancy, and childbirth exemplify the ways it, at first, treated most social problems. Its efforts to work outside the established social structure become stopgap measures that substitute for needed social change. The activist groups that were most likely to be pressured into performing ameliorative functions have often been associated with a Women's Center. Once any such group became known, requests for information and help filtered in from all quarters. Thus we find from the Women's Center notice boards and newsletters that the groups offer information about possible jobs; list "sympathetic" physicians and even psychiatrists; organize babysitting services for fees or for exchange of help; offer advice and group support to single mothers; appeal for bail money for women prisoners; advertise lessons in French, Hebrew, guitar, or modern dance; list available apartments; request volunteers to attend a demonstration; offer baby clothes for sale; and give advice on "figuring your income tax."

Across the country Women's Liberation groups have organized dance collectives, "older women's liberation" (OWL) groups, women's rock bands, graphics collectives, drama groups, committees on equal employment, health collectives, "survival phones," "Women's Crisis Centers," book clubs and book stores, "Women's Yellow Pages" (i.e. directories of services of use to women), and conferences on rape and even "rape squads" to aid rape victims. They frequently list or hand out telephone numbers of other volunteer groups which deal with such matters as drug problems, immigration counseling, legal aid, suicide prevention, students' rights, "political prisoners," and antiwar activities. In the long run, however, all these activities result in temporary self-help, rather than permanent reform.

The same limitations apply to the middle-class movement members' efforts to work in the interests of minority group and poor women. The feminists have neither the money nor the personnel to institute sweeping social change. Instead, they have counseled poor women on how to get maximum welfare benefits, and protested cutbacks in welfare and food-stamp programs; they have planned exercise classes for women prisoners, arranged transportation so that families can visit prisoners, joined striking waitresses on a picket line, and organized clinics for Asian women. In law as in medicine, they have trained women as paraprofessionals—precisely the sort of jobs that will leave women in subordinate, powerless positions. The People's Law Institute, of Washington, D. C., taught free courses for neither grades nor degrees. One could learn about "women and the law," welfare law, juvenile law, and prison law, or the military and the draft. Similarly, Philadelphia Women's Liberation trained volunteers to be paralegal counselors on separation and divorce.[8] Other groups have taught women how to file and carry through their own divorce cases.

The total effect of such actions is comparable to that of the Lady Bountiful of earlier centuries. Individual women's problems will be alleviated for the time being, but no lasting change is produced. During 1971 more and more activist women recognized this danger and, in order to avert it, initiated new types of protest actions.

TOWARD CHANGE IN THE SOCIAL STRUCTURE

Throughout 1971, and even as early as 1970, activist members of Women's Liberation asked with increasing frequency, "Where is Women's Liberation going?" Although dissatisfied with their previous attempts to introduce social change, they were hindered in their search for a new sense of direction by the generality and flexibility of their ideology. Yet radical and conservative women from all parts of the country voiced similar concerns. One person made a particularly violent attack on the activities of Women's Liberation groups in San Francisco:

> A lot of projects faded as they began—day care, abortion. They were completely unsuccessful. No one had enough stake in what they were doing. There was no place in the women's movement where women could gather to discuss strategic questions about what the movement was doing. Only the orientation meetings could go on effectively. . . . [The other activities] were bullshit—fantasies in the hearts of the people who created them. Given what power we have, what can you do about day care and abortion? For example, in San Francisco, people wanted to do something with Planned Parenthood; but what could they do that Planned Parenthood was not doing?

One woman complained that the movement had no "concrete common purposes" around which people could "focus their energies." Another said, "We have no strategy. Until we have a strategy we will be in a state of limbo." The handful of women who edited the Austin, Texas, newsletter *Second Coming* editorialized:

> Last year as more and more women's publications appeared, we eagerly read all that we could find—excited and delighted about . . . the myriad of new ideas and alternatives generated from it. And now it seems that many of us are bored with much of women's literature—we have assimilated the thoughts and ideas, and it no longer presents us with anything new. . . .

We had originally hoped to orient S[econd] C[oming] toward alternatives. . . .

But we still have no idea as to the general reaction to [what we have written].[9]

In their efforts to resolve the "lack of overall direction," to overcome their sense of "floundering," and to escape from their despair, the activist members of Women's Liberation began, either independently or in cooperation with reformist groups, to work for change within the established system.

Their work in a few areas, such as abortion law repeal, where they were already cooperating with other groups to promote institutionalized change, provided an example. Adding their special brand of fiery support at legislative hearings, they gave statistics of the number of deaths from illegal "botched" abortions, added gory details of the horrors of the experience, and demonstrated their concern simply by their presence.

Abortion law repeal or reform was supported by groups ranging from Zero Population Growth to some Protestant churches. Women's Liberation has done proportionally more of the work promoting institutionalized legal reform in another area related to sexual mores—prostitution. For the present, at least, it is joined only by the more radical of the Women's Rights groups in the defense of prostitutes. Early demands for institutional reform in the treatment of prostitutes were multiplied in the summer of 1971 during the police "crackdowns" on New York prostitutes. The more radical feminist position was made clear at a Forum on Prostitution organized by The Feminists and attended by about 300 people. Prostitutes were described as "victims" of their male customers, not "criminals." Society forced them into prostitution because they had nowhere else to get money—especially if they were drug addicts and needed large sums to sustain their habit. Why, asked the forum's participants, did the city not provide drug rehabiliation for women addicts, as it did for male addicts? And why were prostitutes arrested when their customers almost invariably went free?

In contrast to prostitution, the child-care issue has attracted the attention of many feminist and nonfeminist organizations. After trying largely unsuccessfully to create their own facilities, the Liberation groups have recognized the need for larger support in terms of funds, knowledge, and personnel. Some have organized drives to press companies, universities, and government facilities into establishing their own centers. One periodical urged women to take advantage of the money which New York City had available for nursery schools "if you fight for it."[10] A Boston-based group, Female Liberation, turned to the local political system. It was instrumental in getting a referendum passed in favor of community-sponsored child care in Cambridge, Massachusetts, in the fall of 1971. (As of 1973, no funds were available to implement this decision.)

In the legal area, a number of Women's Liberation groups have ceased training their own legal counselors and have arranged for experts, including lawyers and government officials, to lecture on subjects like how to file suit against a discriminating employer. Many are urging lawyers, law students, and others to help work on antidiscrimination cases. Others are pressing to get more women admitted to law schools and medical schools. Whereas in the past they disapproved of NOW's "reform-oriented" activities such as working toward the elimination of "male" and "female" categories over newspaper help-wanted columns, more recently, for example, the Women's Liberation Union of Rhode Island has filed an official complaint against the Providence *Journal Bulletin* for listing advertisements for jobs under the headings "Help Wanted: Male" and "Help Wanted: Female."[11]

Independently and in cooperation with local Welfare Rights Organizations (WRO), Women's Liberation activists are pressing federal and local government authorities to improve the training facilities and financial aid available for welfare recipients. Many Liberation groups sent representatives to the WRO-organized Children's March for Survival held in Washington, D. C., in March 1972, to protest the government's proposed Family Assistance Plan, President Nixon's veto of the Child Development Bill, and cutbacks in federal food-provision programs.

A number of women's unions or women's caucuses within trade unions, which have sprung up in the last few years, have received support from members of Women's Liberation. Undoubtedly the major thrust has come from the union women themselves, but the feminists have begun to offer practical help instead of simply publishing accounts of the unpleasant conditions under which such women work. In Berkeley the Militant Action Caucus formed from Women's Liberation groups joined with the Communication Workers of America to demand such benefits as sick pay and child care for the 223 operators in the Berkeley Bell Telephone office. (All but eight of the operators were women.)[12] Other women from the Liberation movement were pressuring California legislators to pass bills improving working women's pay, job security, and working conditions. In Boston and Cambridge, the coalition Bread and Roses helped sponsor attempts to organize secretaries at the Massachusetts Institute of Technology and other institutions.

Many Liberation groups' decision that they should work to change established institutions was marked by their support for the Equal Rights Amendment to the Federal Constitution. Although the number of women actively working for the legislation is small, the movement as a whole looks upon it favorably. [13]

By 1972 members of Women's Liberation were commenting sympathetically on the achievements of Women's Rights and other reformist groups. For example, a Boston group reported that the New York State Human Rights Commission ordered a Long Island School district to give seven weeks' back pay to the woman teacher who was forced to begin pregnancy leave before she wished.[14] San Diego women reported on fifty bills "that would enhance women's rights and freedoms that were introduced in the California state legislature in 1972."[15] Others urged women to register to vote, even noting without comment that registrations under the title "Ms." are invalid in some states.

A few Women's Liberation groups have not only cooperated with reformist organizations, they have cooperated with established institutions, even to the point of abandoning their adversary role. They have sent student representatives to a Governor's Commission on the Status of Women;[16] represented the movement at physicians' conferences on obstetrics and gynecology where, they reported "doctors . . . were really trying to learn and change";[17] established job referral systems; cooperated with local church groups in efforts to improve the status of women in religion; and supported local, state, and national political party candidates who represent the interests of women and poor people.

LESBIANS WITHIN WOMEN'S LIBERATION

The lesbians who joined Women's Liberation primarily because they wished to gain acceptance as lesbians have been concerned mostly with consciousness raising. Shared discussion and social support is probably even more important to them than to other participants in Women's Liberation. As in other Liberation groups, the topics discussed in gay groups follow a particular pattern over time. At first the members talk about what it is like to be a lesbian, and the problem of "coming out" (that is, either admitting their lesbianism to themselves, or revealing it publicly). Later they move on to discuss the problems of lesbian mothers, working lesbians, Third World lesbians, lesbians in history, lesbians and the Vietnam war, lesbians and the arts, and bisexuality. For lesbians, as for other movement members, the sense of shared understanding and mutual trust in an alien world is an important by-product of participation.

Those lesbians who turn from consciousness raising to action have even more difficulty than their straight sisters in deciding how best to use their energies. Ideally, they would like the society at large to accept and respect lesbians. In fact, they know that, alone, they can do very little to achieve this change. So far they have mostly confined themselves to describing to other women inside and outside the movement what it is like to be a lesbian and why they also have a right to assert their individuality and lead free, creative lives.

Most commonly, they have tried to achieve this understanding through their writings and in their appearances at conferences. By 1970 and 1971 most Women's Liberation conferences included in their workshops discussions of the "gay experience," "alternative life styles," or "types of gay relationships." Later, lesbians began making demands. Thus, a July 1971 conference on abortion in New York City was forced to debate and eventually decided to vote down the gay women's demands that "freedom of sexual expression" be included in the conference resolutions.[18]

A few lesbians are moving into more direct social action: they have argued to family service agencies that lesbian mothers should be allowed to keep their children; they have volunteered to help parents who find that their children are homosexuals; and they have worked to change state laws which ban homosexual acts between consenting adults.

The lesbians in Women's Liberation are, therefore, passing through the same stages as the heterosexual women—from consciousness raising to social activism. But throughout this development their focal concern has been to gain social acceptance for their lesbianism. Because their interests are often different from those of heterosexual women, they have tended to form such independent segments within the movement as the "Radicalesbians" of Antioch, Ohio, and the "Gay Women of Denver," Colorado. It is likely that although the groups will continue to work together in certain areas, lesbians will retain their relatively independent status within the general movement.

While most Women's Liberation groups remain concerned primarily with consciousness raising and while the movement still considers theoretical ideological analysis a major function, a few highly visible groups are working diligently for a wide range of social changes which they hope will improve the lives of all women. The members of these activist segments of the movement at first believed that they could change existing institutions without becoming involved in the ongoing operation of these institutions. Later, they concluded that the only way to achieve their objective of drastic social change was to work through established channels of social reform and to revise rather than to re-create the existing social system. While their goals and the means they use to achieve these goals are, therefore, now nearer those of the Women's Rights organizations, they are still distinct. The Women's Liberation activists' view of social change is broad and visionary. Of all the new feminist groups, they are most likely to see themselves as adversaries of the status quo, and they are the most willing to try new, even unknown, paths in their far-reaching efforts to improve both the woman's role and the condition of society as a whole.

CHAPTER SEVEN

WOMEN'S LIBERATION: ORGANIZATION

The network of varied, informal, and loosely structured Women's Liberation groups is no exception to the generalization that protest movements generate considerable intergroup and intragroup conflict. In the case of Women's Liberation two conditions (frequently found in other movements) encourage this conflict: members disagree over how to translate their ideology in terms of specific goals and they experience considerable frustration in trying to implement idealistic principles for organizational operation.

The varied interpretations of the movement ideology are themselves being changed constantly as participants experience progressive consciousness raising. Justification for this ongoing development of theory is found in the idea that theory must derive from personal feelings; theory leads to action which, in turn, leads to new feelings, and new theory. Theory, actions, and feelings are thus constantly developing.[1]

The ideological diversity which the movement has, as a matter of principle, encouraged in this way can and does foster individual enthusiasm, encourage members to experiment with new ideas, increase the total number of women who are attracted to the movement, and insure that any social problem is tackled from several different directions, thereby increasing the probability that some resolution will be found. Ideological diversity can, however, also cause organizational paralysis when members cannot find sufficient common ground to serve as a basis for social action. Women's Liberation has faced and is facing precisely this danger, although it has not succumbed to the threat of paralysis.

One of the few areas in which Women's Liberation has specified the applications of its ideology is in the principles by which its groups operate. These principles include: (1) self-realization—all participants shall be encouraged to develop or realize their full human potential, both intellectually and emotionally; (2) equality or antielitism—no person or persons shall dominate over the other group members after the fashion of the "male chauvinist" outside world; (3) sisterhood—the genuine attempt to understand and to establish common bonds with other women; and (4) authority of personal experience—one's own experience, rather than the abstract formulation of some "expert," shall be the primary source of new ideas.

All these principles are, of course, derivative of ideas present in the remainder of the society. Emphasis upon self-development, upon the validity of personal experience, upon increased social responsibility, and upon the rewards of group participation are common not only in the radical subculture, but also in the more progressive or radical segments of institutionalized religion, education, the arts, and politics. The women's movement has selected and emphasized some of these principles both because feminists tend to be either liberal or radical as regards social change and because these principles underscore precisely those elements of the traditional feminine role which they admire and have no intention of abandoning—a concern for interpersonal relationships, rejection of dispassionate dealings with other people, and the ready admission, even expression, of individual emotions.

The consciousness-raising groups, in contrast to the activist groups, are the one major part of Women's Liberation that has not encountered persistent organizational conflicts. Their objective—consciousness raising —has been specified; and the organizational principles of sisterhood, equality, reliance on personal experience, and emphasis upon personal growth have been realistic bases for operation. When members create an atmosphere of mutual trust, or sisterhood, and talk freely about their personal experiences, they can best encourage each other in their personal development or self-realization. Since domination by one or more persons would discourage this sort of trust, it is advantageous to avoid so-called elitism in favor of equality. So long as the group serves primarily as a forum for discussion and a place for social support, the members can continue to pursue their shared objective of consciousness raising. Problems arise, however, when the group considers extending its objectives to include some form of social action. Usually it continues with its consciousness-raising functions at the same time as it branches out into new activities, but it ceases to operate so successfully once members have become involved in social action either independently or as a body.

ORGANIZATIONAL CONFLICTS

Disagreement over Objectives

Once individuals and groups move beyond the stage of exclusive pre-occupation with consciousness raising into social action, failure to agree on new organizational objectives creates internal conflicts. The resulting disagreements have been one of the major causes of the contemporary movement's constant fragmentation. The first New York City Women's Liberation group, New York Radical Women, is an example. Founded in the last months of 1967, it soon had twelve to twenty core members who had helped up to a hundred more women to organize into consciousness-raising groups. Problems arose chiefly among the action-oriented core members. Early in 1968 differences of opinion among the politicos, feminists, and a less ideological intermediate group caused the New York Radical Women to break up. Former members, joined by women recruited from elsewhere, created three new groups: WITCH, composed of a few women concerned with consciousness-raising for the general public through guerrilla theater; Redstockings, originally intended as an activist group; and The Feminists. WITCH continued on a small scale for several years. Redstockings was transformed into a series of consciousness-raising groups while its founders, Shulamith Firestone and Ellen Willis, were eased out. The Feminists became a small, select, regimented group of from ten to twenty women.

In 1969 some dissatisfied women from Redstockings joined by a few dissidents from The Feminists formed the New York Radical Feminists (as opposed to the earlier group the New York Radical *Women*). By the time this group's membership had grown to about 200 women, divided into independent consciousness-raising groups but loosely affiliated with the larger organization, it was suffering severely from a lack of direction. After several months of fruitless discussion, a few women privately composed an ideological manifesto and devised a special form of organizational structure. A majority of members accepted these at an open membership meeting. Thus the New York Radical Feminists were divided into a series of semiautonomous "brigades" that would each, after a period of consciousness raising, supposedly vote to accept the manifesto and thereby become fully fledged members of the federated group. Before the brigade system was fully established, another power block called a general membership meeting and voted out the whole idea. During 1970 the preexisting brigades gradually lost contact with each other. The New York Radical Feminists reemerged as an active group in 1972 but neither it nor any other group has managed to coordinate the activities of the multifaceted New York City Women's Liberation.

In San Francisco groups formed and re-formed in a similar way. About ten women founded Sudso'floppen—a pure fanciful name—in the fall of 1968. Out of it came both an ideology workshop, which for a few months ran a Women's Liberation office, and a group named Gallstones. In the spring of 1969 an intergroup council of about eight newly formed small groups was established, and more orientation sessions were held so that new groups could be created. In the succeeding two years, two new Women's Liberation offices were opened and closed; and many new groups were founded. By 1973 most of these survived in name only —Bay Area Radical Teachers, Leviathan (which became the 25th Street Collective), Women's Free Press, Uppity Women's Fishing Boat, Mother Jones Collective, Independent Campus Women, San Francisco Breakaway, and Berkeley Breakaway. Few of these groups ever had more than a dozen members.

Another form of realignment based upon ideological differences that has worried members of Women's Liberation, particularly during 1970-71, is the Socialist Workers' Party/Young Socialist Alliance (SWP/YSA) take-overs of their groups. It is generally felt in the movement that the socialist women who become involved are primarily committed to socialism not feminism and are using the women's movement as a means to promote the socialist cause at the expense of the women's cause. For example, a group of YSA women did much of the organizing for the New England Congress to Unite Women (now defunct) conference held in Cambridge in March 1971. The conference was supposedly representative of regional Women's Liberation and some Women's Rights groups. A few of the non-YSA women became aware of the socialist women's role. They were furious that the YSA people should try to push through a motion that a feminist contingent from that conference coalition participate in an antiwar rally. They argued, in private, that they were objecting not to feminists' antiwar activity, but to manipulation in the interest of the SWP. They were even more angry to discover that the YSA women had organized a press conference to report on the meeting's resolutions precisely halfway through the time allotted for voting on them.[2]

YSA women are often in a strategic position to take control of any structured group such as a coalition or a Women's Center: their politics unite them behind common goals and actions, while the other feminists are split into several ill-defined interest groups. Thus, the feminist element in such a coalition or center may suddenly find that most of the group's hardest workers belong to the Young Socialist Alliance division of the Socialist Workers' Party.

Participants' fears of SWP/YSA influence in the women's movement probably are exaggerated. Some half-dozen or a dozen Women's Centers or coalition bodies have been dominated by party members. These groups are visible because they are well-organized and because they frequently publish newsletters or periodicals. Even where a YSA group has taken control of one segment of a citywide movement, however, Women's Liberation's organizational structure is so loose that other groups continue with their own concerns. They may, of course, be deceived into working for the YSA through such items as a child-care referendum, but they will rarely knowingly work with YSA women even on feminist projects and will stop working through Women's Centers that have been taken over by YSA women.

Despite the periodic furors over YSA infiltration, or attempted infiltration, the majority of "take-overs" occurring within Women's Liberation have involved purely feminist factions. After the middle of 1970 such reorganizations were frequently followed by attempts to create more formally organized groups. No one would suggest that even the reorganized groups were highly structured. However, a majority of them were moving in the direction of a narrower definition of their objectives and a more formal statement of their organization's structure.

Disagreements over Organizational Procedures

In contrast to disagreements over ideology, the second major cause of organizational conflict operates at a very different level: members disagree not only over what should be done, but on how they should be working together. Activist groups have found the movement's idealistic organizational principles a continuing source of frustration. Except for consciousness raising, they hamper the achievement of almost all goals because if a person works according to one principle, she frequently finds she is contravening another.[3]

One of the most common criticisms made of a movement member is that she is assuming a leadership role by organizing others, by speaking about the movement, or by writing about it. By being an "elitist" leader, she prevents her sisters from learning how to organize, give lectures, and write articles. Yet from another viewpoint she is being denied the opportunity for self-development. For example, one movement member canceled a challenging speaking engagement in a distant city because her collective (that is, small group) said that she had already done more than her share of public speaking. An early statement of these organizational principles and of the members' failure to observe them was stimulated by a Boston conference of some 300 women early in 1969:

> What became clear to me after talking to people from several workshops is that the conference was being controlled by one group from Boston, and that one analysis and strategy was being set up for everyone else to absorb. It was very manipulative—one group had chosen to be teachers while the rest of us learned. . . .
>
> This kind of manipulation is destructive; it divides us, it keeps us from learning and sharing in the analysis which must come from the experiences of all of us. Because no one is going to analyze the oppression of women in our society, or demand our liberation, unless we do it. . . .
>
> We have to find new ways of working together, and I think we have the means to do that. Women have been programmed in this society to listen instead of speak, to comfort and maintain instead of asserting our own ideas. That kind of programming is destructive to selfhood; but what I think we can retain as we break out of old patterns is our ability to listen and be sensitive to one another. I have been meeting with the upper west side W.I.T.C.H. group and the rapport there has given us the freedom to work efficiently as well as give support to one another.[4]

The strongest statement of this position accuses "elitist stars" of working for their own aggrandizement rather than for the welfare of the movement as a whole. Women who have been criticized on this score include members of Women's Rights groups. Many are well-known outside of the movement—Kate Millett, Gloria Steinem, Ti-Grace Atkinson, and Betty Friedan—while others stand out within the movement—Marlene Dixon, Roxanne Dunbar, Anne Koedt, Kathy Sarachild (Amatniek), and Joreen (Jo Freeman).

The unknown person is equally vulnerable. One woman found that her consciousness-raising group interpreted her efforts to organize a local conference as a power play. As she put it, "They said I was out for myself and not for the movement." A fellow member told her, "You are not going to be a success on my blood." Anyone who exercises initiative, who talks a good deal, who knows more than the other group members, or even who is especially liked by other members is vulnerable to such attacks. To protect themselves these women often back off from assuming any sort of responsibility, thereby stifling group action.[5] For its part, the group tries to prevent the emergence of stars by demanding that all members share jobs equally. A specific application of this rule is the common insistence that no one person act as spokeswoman for a group, whether it consists of 6 or 600 persons. Thus, almost all groups which provide public speakers insist that two or more of their members be present. While officially this procedure exemplifies the group's democratic operation, reassures inexperienced speakers, and insures that listeners receive the most complete account possible of the movement, it also insures that all speakers are under constant group surveillance.[6]

The Women's Liberation groups' emphasis upon self-development and their objection to elitism are consistent with their firm belief in the authority of personal experience. When they speak about women's experiences, they repeat the blacks' argument that the outsider can never really empathize with their oppression. Within the movement the argument is taken a step further: each individual is the only person who can truly appreciate her own situation; she must rely upon the authority of her own feelings. Thus, when a participant is asked a question that she has not previously thought about, she will often reply, "I have no gut reaction to that idea. I have not yet worked out how I feel about it." Any expression of "expert" authority, such as an explanation of how to organize a demonstration, can be interpreted as an elitist put-down of the other women and is frequently attacked on that basis.

Women occasionally intrepret the organizational ideals in self-interested terms: specifically they use the ideals as a means to vent interpersonal hostilities. It is easy to accuse someone of being elitist or of refusing to allow others an opportunity for self-development or of denying the validity of another's experience. On the grounds that frankness helps create interpersonal trust, someone can express her annoyance at a fellow member by saying something like "I get bad vibes from you. I don't know why, but I just don't seem to be able to get along with you." Alternatively a participant can be accused of failing to take into account the feelings of another. "I feel that you are being hostile, and so you refuse to share my experience." When a person is attacked for falling short of the very principles she espouses, she is put in a particularly defensive position. The open expression of hostility is supposed to clear the air; in cases such as this, it is more than likely to make the person attacked defensive and hostile.

In the eyes of outsiders and an increasing proportion of insiders, the Liberation movement members' determined commitment to their idealistic organizational principles not only creates these interpersonal conflicts but also greatly reduces opportunities for effective action. Absolute equality and the rejection of "expert" authority preclude the possibility of any lasting division of labor. For example, women producing the many leaflets, pamphlets, newsletters, and periodicals typical of the movement frequently insist that each person in a small group learn every step in the production process—from writing articles to designing layout to mailing the finished product. Such a procedure may increase the total amount of personal enjoyment of the work, but it also takes up a great deal of time, nervous energy, patience, and sometimes money. Whether the total rewards outweigh the total costs depends upon the evaluator's system of values.

A similar practical problem occurs when group members insist that nonelitism, self-expression, and sisterhood require that all problems be thoroughly discussed by the whole group before a decision (preferably by consensus) is reached. A tongue-in-cheek report of a National Women's Political Caucus Workshop illustrates the frustrations of the decision-making process. After a radical Women's Liberation contingent disrupted the procedures planned for the workshop a more conservative feminist wrote:

> The Grass Roots Workshop opened on an orderly note with selection of facilitators and introduction of members. We immediately moved into political techniques with a specific case history of a group from Nassau County, New York, who had initiated a functioning political women's power bloc. Another case history from Pittsburgh was related. This lowered the threshold of frustration for about half the group and after some creative infighting, it was agreed to splinter into two groups—the Philosophical Group and the Specific Group. Many of us in the (grass roots) philosophical group felt a need to understand each other and ourselves better before we could discuss the specifics of grass roots organization. We started with the root of ourselves. Each one of us communicated her own personal feelings, philosophy and frustrations instead of her specific experiences or achievements. We began to understand the philosophical process of grass roots organization. We felt the need for a collective understanding in any group before it could attempt to organize others. We felt that this was a process that must be renewed with each group. We felt that our group's original desire to explore "grass roots" strategy from a different point of view, and our frustrations, represented a microcosm of the political process where many who are not reached are left behind.[7]

The frustrations experienced by the Women's Rights group member who wrote this report are also felt by many members of Women's Liberation. Nonetheless, the typical participant in a Women's Liberation group is willing in the interests of group ideals to tolerate what others consider to be a great deal of such frustration. She wants everyone to have her say, listens seriously to all participants' ideas and accounts of their experiences, sympathizes with the person who cannot express herself in public, and tries to join her sisters in reaching a decision by consensus. Participants have devised norms to implement these ideals. An example occurred at a conference workshop where one woman was dominating the discussion. Other participants grew impatient and one said to the offender in exasperation, "Could you learn how to listen?" She then addressed the group, "I don't like it that she raises her hand every minute while someone else is speaking." No one needed to say more. The other participants merely nodded in agreement and continued the discussion. The talkative person did, indeed, restrain herself for the rest of the meeting. Expression of one's personal or "gut" feelings is still encouraged but participants are more likely to insist that these should have direct relevance to the particular problems under discussion. The woman who brings up extraneous gripes or personal "hangups" is reproved for distracting the group from the issues at hand, and therefore being inconsiderate of her sisters.

Most Women's Liberation groups have made a basic compromise in accepting a certain amount of leadership. Simultaneously they have been working out normative patterns that limit the leaders' power. They insist that authority lies in the group as a whole and view their leaders as people who help the group make its own decisions rather than as people to whom they delegate responsibility—and authority. The leaders themselves encourage a great deal of individual participation.

Ideas are discussed at length with the serious objective of reaching group consensus. Each person is expected to discuss more than one side of a particular issue. And it is believed that when all have understood all the aspects of the question at hand, they will arrive at the same conclusion.[8]

These procedures whereby new feminist groups attempt to create participatory democracies will be described and discussed in more detail in Chapter Nine. Here, however, we should note that, in adopting unorthodox as well as orthodox organizational norms, Women's Libration has set an important example for many other groups: they have tried to show that the traditional bureaucratic procedures are not the only practical ways of running an organization.

We should also note that such unconventional means of group operation do, in fact, have the desired positive effect upon participants. My observations confirm those of many members of Women's Liberation: women who prior to involvement were withdrawn, timid, dependent, and quite unsure of themselves have attained the self-confidence, the ability to develop their individual capacities, and the sense of personal integrity which people inside and outside the movement view as desirable human traits.

INSTITUTIONALIZATION

The activist Women's Liberation groups have in general responded to their organizational problems by becoming more institutionalized. In contrast, the non-activist consciousness-raising groups (which also are usually less radical) have remained loosely structured. While these latter groups include by far the greater proportion of Women's Liberation participants, they are far less visible to the outsider and, more important, being less socially involved, have far less influence on the movement's development.

The process of institutionalization, which began in 1971, has involved changes in both the structure of the groups concerned and changes in the way the structure works.

In the course of frequent schisms and reorganizations, almost all the activist groups have gone through some informal and occasionally formal processes comparable to incorporation. The Twin Cities (Minneapolis-St. Paul) Female Liberation Group is an example. It was founded in January 1970 as an impartial umbrella group that would coordinate Liberation activities in the area but, by default, soon became represented by about a dozen women who ran its office and produced its newsletter. Other women, officially members of the umbrella group, objected to what they called the inefficiency and ideological inflexibility of the office staff and asked for "Committment [sic] to stable, underlying ideas about goals of the organization with a system of accountability for accomplishing them and out-front access to policy making."[9] At two general membership meetings attended by less than twenty-five people, the group adopted a founding charter for the newly named "Twin Cities Female Liberation Communication Center." The charter was complete with separate articles stating the group's name, purposes, structure, composition of its policy board, conditions of membership, arrangements for meetings, grievance procedures, and means to introduce charter amendments.[10]

Similar modifications have been informally instituted in many groups. Members commonly take minutes at meetings, designate specific offices, hold elections to fill those offices, select chairpersons to run meetings (generally rotating the job), and frequently make decisions by vote rather than trying to work exclusively by a consensus system.

Other groups have divided work among several committees such as "child care" or "abortion referral," thereby sacrificing the original ideal of sharing equally in every responsibility. Iowa City's Women's Liberation worked out a slightly different system. After trying, unsuccessfully, to operate as one large organization derived from consciousness-raising groups, the organization turned

> to a structure of small [specialized] collectives. Because the large group was unwieldy, we couldn't talk to each other, and we couldn't get anything done. The collectives we developed centered around proposed action such as beginning a paper, a political study group, medical cell, revolutionary art cell, daycare center, and a gay cell.[11]

Groups which have adopted a more structured form of organization have generally proved more stable and able to become seriously involved in social action. Any such group nevertheless exposes itself to accusations of "selling out" the principles of Women's Liberation. It is true that the new groups are not obliged to make decisions by the old consensus procedures and that greater structure reduces members' freedom of action. However, participants are gratified at their ability to "get things done" and at their relative freedom from the emotional and practical strains associated with less structured government.

By the middle of 1972 many members of Women's Liberation had come to accept the idea that it was best to work in structured groups. An article entitled "The Tyranny of Structurelessness," by the respected, middle-of-the-road Liberation movement member Jo Freeman, was referred to favorably and reprinted in several periodicals. Its author argues that "Contrary to what we would like to believe, there is no such thing as a structureless group." A group's structure may be flexible or inflexible; it may vary over time; tasks may or may not be distributed evenly. But structure will be found. Even informal groups have a covert structure. The idea of structurelessness was a "natural reaction against the overstructured society in which most of us found ourselves." However, it has moved from being a healthy countertendency "to becoming a goddess in its own right."[12]

Not only in their organizational structure but also in many other aspects of their day-to-day operations the Liberation groups have begun to follow the previously rejected practices of the larger American society. For a long time, the notion of paying anyone to do such routine chores as typing, or answering the telephone, was totally alien to women who are deeply committed to the ideas that all members are sisters and that none should be treated differently from any other. In particular, it has been argued that no one person, paid or unpaid, should have to be solely responsible for the "shitwork" traditionally delegated to women. Yet an occasional group, such as that composing Philadelphia's Women's Liberation Center, has gone so far as to suggest hiring movement people to do some of this work. Early in 1972 the Women's Liberation Union in Chicago hired two part-time staff workers at $50 a week,[13] and about the same time *Pandora*, a periodical published in Seattle, was planning to employ a paid staff of women who would be trained in "reporting, newspaper publishing, etc." and a distribution manager "with an organized mind to coordinate street sellers and distribution to centers and businesses."[14] By that date many groups were paying mailing list firms to keep their subscription lists up to date and to address their newsletters and periodicals.

During 1971 and 1972 many members reevaluated the question of organization funding. Previously they had explicitly rejected the idea of "making money off one's sisters," saying that any woman, black or white, rich or poor, young or old, should be free to participate without cost. Groups refused to solicit donations at the introductory meetings they organized, speakers did not charge for their appearances, almost all groups refused to collect membership dues, slide shows illustrating movement ideas about restrictive female socialization were presented free of charge, and although most publications had to be paid for, they were generally distributed at cost.

Participants have changed their behavior on this point for two reasons. First, the movement is now well known; speakers, publications, and the like are in such demand that Liberation groups can afford to charge for them. Second and far more important, group after group has found itself in severe financial straits as members tried to pay for supplies, equipment, mailings, rental of offices and meeting rooms, telephones, and so forth.[15]

By 1973 Liberation groups had devised a variety of means for financial support. Appeals for money were commonplace. For example, San Francisco's Women's Center received $336.30 in response to an appeal in November 1971, and although "several women" criticized the "strongly worded request" the newsletter staff was obviously more gratified by the donations than troubled by the criticisms.[16] In October of that year the *Scarlet Letter* published in Madison, Wisconsin, appealed to readers for special donations to supplement their regular subscriptions.

Appeals to members for donations, however, began to annoy both those who solicited and those who were solicited. As one person put it, "Poverty is not ennobling to people or organizations." Consequently, many groups began to look for outside sources of funds. The East Lansing Women's Center has pressed (unsuccessfully so far) both the city government and Michigan State University for funding. Some groups felt that philanthropic foundations would be helpful, but experience has proved them notably unhelpful. Women's Liberation groups are not eligible for monies set aside for charity, and their applications for funding of action programs or research programs have not been up to the high standard required for this highly specialized task. Furthermore, foundations are wary of giving money to small, unestablished protest groups. Occasionally a university's student activities committee, a local religious group, or a local social-service organization has contributed a few hundred dollars. The United Presbyterian Church Women and a number of local philanthropic foundations together awarded approximately $2,500 to Women in Transition, a group within the Philadelphia Women's Center which offered referral, volunteer professional help, and social support to women in the midst of separation or divorce.[17] It is significant that the

Presbyterian women made the award for work which, by movement standards, was essentially conservative and thoroughly within the functions defined by the traditional feminine role.[18]

Soon after the Liberation groups realized that their members were in demand as speakers before high school classes, college groups, women's clubs, the Rotary, Lions Clubs, workingmen's clubs, university alumnae, or local religious organizations, they began to charge fees to any group that could afford to pay. Fees range from $5 to $100 but most commonly are between $10 and $15. In keeping with the belief that participants should not deprive their sisters by making a profit from movement activities, Women's Liberation speakers usually keep only their traveling expenses and turn over to the group any money which remains. The number of talks given varies considerably, but even the most active speakers' bureaus make little money. For example, one of the New York City Women's Liberation Centers received about thirty requests for speakers for the last week in November and the first three weeks of December 1971. Probably only about half of these requests were filled because speakers were in short supply and because the women felt that some groups were motivated by a desire to be entertained by these "women's libbers." Thus, I estimate the center would gain about $100 from four week's worth of speaking engagements. A few months later, Kansas City's Women's Liberation was in a similar situation. Between February 3 and March 7, 1972 its speakers' bureau had eleven engagements.[19]

Other efforts to raise money have included charging participants "who can afford it" for classes, soliciting previous contributors by telephone, holding parties at which participants make donations, benefit concerts, a "Women's Weekend" of films, flea markets, rummage sales, "women's (usually lesbians') dances," and even that most traditional source of funds—a bake sale (on one such occasion, at least, men did the baking).

The more visible the social-activist groups become, the more likely they are to have found a regular source of funds. Some, like the Philadelphia Women's Center, ask for monthly pledges from people who use the center and from others who have shown some sympathetic interest. Boston's Female Liberation, which is one of the few groups with a formal membership, asked members for regular contributions, large enough to at least pay the rent for its Women's Center.[20] New Haven's Women's Liberation has stated flatly that the "old informal finance system" is "outdated," and has asked sisters to pledge a certain amount each month.[21] The group subsequently sent reminders to women who did not follow through on their commitment. While the Philadelphia and

New Haven groups have asked for sums on the order of $5, the Women's Center of Washington, D. C., was much more ambitious. Perhaps because the organization was planning to buy a house from which to run the center, it asked for donations ranging from $5 to $5,000.

Periodicals have started to charge for advertisements. For example, early in 1972, the magazine *Off Our Backs* charged $15 for a three-inch-by-two-inch box.[22] *The Feminist Voice*, with a tabloid-size newspaper format, charged $50 for a full-page advertisement.[23] At that date *Everywoman* was already charging for advertisements, *Pandora* was planning to, and so, throughout the Women's Liberation segment of the movement, periodicals were beginning to support themselves in the traditional "establishment" fashion. A few periodicals, particularly those nationally distributed, have become self-sustaining but their financial base, which still depends almost entirely on subscriptions, is never very sound.

A final change, minor in itself but symbolic of Women's Liberation's partial return to the establishment, is found in the way members are beginning to question the movement practice of reprinting articles without attention to copyright or sometimes even authorship attribution. During 1972 such periodicals as *The Feminist Voice* and *The Furies* copyrighted their publications. Others began to add notes to the effect that movement media were free to reprint material with appropriate credits. Thus the movement's rapid semiunderground communication network remains intact, but creative members receive credit for their ideas.

Many participants have opposed the trend toward increased formality in the structure and operation of their Liberation groups. They feel that in adopting the ways of the outside society, the movement is accepting an essentially masculine way of working. Yet many of the most radical groups are among those which have moved toward institutionalization: having adopted radical ideas and (relatively speaking) isolated themselves from the outside society, they find that organizational problems are best resolved by adopting more conventional procedures. In contrast, the less radical groups, oriented more specifically toward consciousness raising, can operate effectively within the idealistic framework espoused by the radicals: even if they wanted to become institutionalized, their loose communication network would greatly hinder the process.

Although by adopting a more formal structure the activist segment of Women's Liberation is retracing the path typically taken by all kinds of voluntary organizations, it retains (and may in the future still retain) distinctive organizational characteristics: it is continually experimenting with means to increase members' real sense of involvement—that is, to create a truly participatory democracy. Regardless of whether these efforts succeed, the organizational changes described above have the effect of keeping the more radical (and therefore the most change-oriented) Women's Liberation ideas before the general public. The action-oriented, radical, encapsulated group is able to develop and publicize feminist ideas far more readily than is the average consciousness-raising group. So long as the action-oriented groups do not succumb to the danger of too much encapsulation, they can continue to explore new ideological and behavioral paths which the rest of Women's Liberation—and other feminist groups—may take in the future.

PART FOUR

THE NEW FEMINIST GROUPS: WOMEN'S RIGHTS

CHAPTER EIGHT

NATIONAL ORGANIZATION FOR WOMEN: EMERGENCE AND GROWTH

The National Organization for Women (NOW) is the oldest and (with the exception of the Women's Political Caucus) also the largest of the Women's Rights Groups. With its varied membership, its wide network of chapters, and its broad range of activities, NOW represents the spectrum of characteristics found, in different proportions, within the other groups, and reveals developmental trends which are less easily identifiable in the shorter-lived groups. Because NOW is in such respects the most important and the most representative of the Women's Rights organizations, it will be the subject of the following two chapters.

EMERGENCE OF THE NATIONAL ORGANIZATION FOR WOMEN

The National Organization for Women's organizing meeting was held on October 29, 1966. The twenty-eight women who arranged this meeting had been brought together by their work on or with the state Commissions on the Status of Women. Four months earlier they had attended, as representatives or observers, the annual national conference of the state commissions in Washington, D. C. Already frustrated at the federal government's unenthusiastic approach to the problems of women, they became even more frustrated at this meeting. One part of the group arrived at the conference convinced that an "NAACP for women" was needed; another part was not convinced until, at the end of the conference, the organizers prevented them from submitting a formal motion that would have had the effect of urging government implementation of legislation forbidding sex discrimination. After this rebuff, the more conservative faction was won over. Some of the 28 founders sat together at the conference's final luncheon to outline plans for the organization which Betty Friedan, its principal organizer, christened the National Organization for Women.

At the first meeting of NOW in October of that year, 300 women and men adopted bylaws, elected officers, and formally accepted NOW's broad Statement of Purpose. The organization's central goal was to "take action to bring women into full participation in the mainstream of American society NOW, exercising all the privileges and responsibilities thereof in truly equal partnership with men." Its Statement of Purpose attacked "the traditional assumption that a woman has to choose between marriage and motherhood on the one hand and serious participation in industry or the professions on the other," and expressed alarm at the increasing concentration of women "on the bottom of the job ladder." NOW, it declared, would work for women's interests inside and outside of the home: it would "press for enforcement of laws which prohibit discrimination on the basis of sex" and would work for "true partnership" in marriage.[1]

Among the first officials elected were Betty Friedan as president; Kathryn Clarenbach as chairman of the board; Aileen Hernandez as vice-president West; Richard Graham as vice-president East; and Caroline Davis as secretary-treasurer. They and the other twenty-four board members formed a distinguished group which included seven university professors or administrators, four federal and local government officials, five state and national labor union officials, and four business executives. Seven of these board members had Ph.D.'s, and one held an M.D.; two were nuns and one was a minister; four members had served or were serving on state Commissions on the Status of Women; four of the board members were men.[2]

NOW's charter members, like the board which represented them, were in the main highly educated professional people. Although the composition of the board and the membership at large has changed in the ensuing years so that the proportion of high-powered professionals is considerably lower, most members are still middle- and upper middle-class. Men have become less evident in the organization. The national board elected in September 1971 contained one man as did the board elected at the next national conference in February 1973. Locally, men usually comprise between 1 and 5 percent of the membership, but only an occasional male participates actively. (It is nonetheless noteworthy that, in contrast to Women's Liberation, NOW encourages men to participate, as do most other Women's Rights organizations.)

Soon after they had founded NOW, the charter members realized that their influence would be greater if they organized on a local as well as a national level. They believed that corporations, school boards, political organizations, and other interest groups would be far more responsive to the demands of local feminists than to pressures from a distant, national group. Further, the national organization lacked personnel, funds, knowledge, and even interest in working at local levels. Finally, national NOW realized that it would attract far more attention if many subgroups were speaking and acting for the organization. By the end of 1967, therefore, a little over a year after NOW's founding, it had 14 local chapters. By the middle of 1972, it had over 200 chapters and by February 1973, 365 chapters. Some of these serve whole cities, some serve small towns, and occasionally a chapter has represented a whole state. The majority of chapters have from 25 to 100 members although an occasional one has a membership of several hundred. In all, 5,800 people were members by December 1971 and over 20,000 by the spring of 1973.[3]

NOW's approach to social problems is pragmatic. Ideally many NOW members would like to transform or even eliminate societal role expectations for women and men but they do not believe they can achieve this goal directly: instead, they work for change by exerting pressure on the existing social structure. This pragmatic approach (which is shared by other Women's Rights groups) is commonly misinterpreted. Many people believe that NOW and similar groups want to modify the present society, not to restructure it. One member of Women's Liberation described her ideas about the differences between NOW and Women's Liberation:

> NOW is for legal reform. It has no critique of the family. It is not conscious of changing social relationships within the family, in new collectives, in physical intimate relationships with women. Many more professional women belong. . . . They are more concerned with legal rights. That seems absurd to us because these actions assume the society is right. They are comparable to the NAACP—to change society you change a few laws.

Most members of NOW react vigorously to such comments, pointing out that while NOW is in favor of legal reform, it expects such reforms to be combined with other changes in behavior and attitudes until, eventually, significant change in the social structure is achieved. They also argue that, while few of their members are willing or able to experiment with drastically new life styles, they approve of such experiments and are demanding equality in their own marriages. They go on to say that in 1971 NOW came out in favor of women's right to choose their sexual orientation—heterosexual, bisexual, or lesbian; and that they are not satisfied with improving only the position of middle-class women but are working through a wide range of means (of which legal cases are only one) to improve the position of all women.

One typical NOW member states that she wants women to be able to "aspire to anything they want" and "not be second-class in any way." She wants "a redefinition of male and female roles" but can

> still see the nuclear family as the practical thing. There will be a certain number living in a community setting, but I'm not especially interested in other styles of living. It's hard enough to relate to one person, let alone a whole group. . . . Family responsibility should be viewed as a fifty-fifty thing; so should careers. . . . I should like to see it possible for industry to run on a part-time basis, for men as well as women. . . . I would like to see day-care centers become common . . . I think we'll see socialized medicine before very long. . . . [But] I think such changes are possible within the system.

Another person, also commenting on the scope of social reform she envisioned, said,

> The only solution is some form of communalism. I don't want to give up privacy, but we need some form of group ways of caring for children —possibly through housing setups. Men's jobs have to change so they don't have to work so hard and so long at them.

Thus, while typical NOW members are more conservative than the more vocal participants in Women's Liberation, they support the status quo only insofar as they can see no alternative. The NOW Campus Organizing Circular summarizes their view of social change: "Organizing against discriminatory action may be the legs of a group, but developing new life styles as women and experiencing group solidarity are the lifeblood that keep the collective individuals moving and alive."

CHANGES IN MEMBERSHIP

New Members

Toward the end of 1970 two new types of women began to join the Women's Rights groups. First were what other movement members would call "ultrarespectable," conservative, but nonetheless feminist women who until that time had avoided the movement because of its radical image. They started to join when the cause itself became more socially acceptable and when the more conservative groups, such as WEAL, were making headway. Many of these new members are so involved with their work and so disinclined to picture themselves as "protesters," that they contribute little more to the organizations than their names and their dues.

The second new type of member resembles the recent converts to the Women's Liberation groups. While not confirmed feminists, these women have become aware of conflicts in their social roles, and they join NOW hoping to resolve these conflicts. Often they are suburban housewives, rather younger than previous members, with growing children and generalized worries about what to do with the rest of their lives. Such people select a Women's Rights group over Women's Liberation because they prefer these groups' relatively conservative image and because they will find there other women who are at a similar stage in their life cycles. Of all the Women's Rights groups, they are most likely to join NOW because they are most likely to come into contact with one of its many chapters and because these chapters are involved in a wide range of potentially interesting projects.

Despite their action-projects' appeal, the NOW chapters found that this new type of participant was unwilling to become involved in social action without prior consideration of the whole feminist issue. They therefore began to organize "discussion groups," "rap sessions," or "consciousness-raising groups" to cater to these new participants' needs and to prepare them for an activist role in the future. Chapters from Los Angeles to Wayne, Pennsylvania, from Parma, Ohio, to Washington, D. C., have organized such groups. Chicago's North Suburban chapter looked forward to attracting many active participants by this means: "The first rap session was exceedingly open and lively. This will obviously be the door through which many new members begin active membership."[4] A NOW member from the Boston area wrote in more detail about the advantage of consciousness-raising groups. They were a means to produce "self-confidence among the membership"—not an opportunity to "indulge in self-pity," but a chance for women to "discuss their lives with dignity," to discover "they share certain common dilemmas. . . . which require collective action for solution"; to learn "accurate information about their real potential"; to "explore new roles for social behavior and. . . . [provide] support for women who wish to break out of traditional female roles."[5] This account, like others, also emphasizes the benefits of "sisterhood"—the mutual support which provides a sense of "community" or of "belonging" in an impersonal male-oriented world.

The consciousness-raising programs themselves vary a great deal. On the whole, they are more structured than those of the typical Women's Liberation consciousness-raising group. Generally, someone who is already an active member of NOW moderates at the meeting; she keeps the discussion on the topic selected, ensures that all the relevant ideas have been covered, and periodically sums up what has been said. Most chapters suggest a list of specific topics. The more radical chapters borrow their ideas from the more formally organized of the Women's Liberation groups such as a local Women's Center or the New York Radical Feminists; the more conservative ones plan a series of their own, generally more academic, topics—"'Women and the Law," "What Kind of Life Styles Are Available to Women?," "Stereotypes of Men," "How did Your Parents Influence You on Male and Female Roles?," and "Stereotyped Ideals of Women; Liberated Ideals of Women." A few topics are more action-oriented—for example, "How to Raise Daughters to Be Liberated"—and sometimes a group will discuss a particular book or listen to an invited speaker.

Within NOW, consciousness-raising meetings became increasingly popular after the latter part of 1971. By the end of 1972, perhaps as many as half of the NOW chapters made such sessions an integral part of their overall programs.

Long-term Members

Just as new members bring with them new reasons for joining, so the active long-term members often change their attitudes as the initial exhilaration gradually gives way to earnest, realistic commitment. One member described this change:

> It was almost exactly two years ago that NOW began in Massachusetts, in what seems to me looking back an almost innocent frenzy of activity and telephone conversations. We burned with righteous indignation, anger and frustration, and into NOW poured the sum total of our years of silently endured humiliation, wakeful nights, doubts and anxieties. . . .
> And we talked. . . . And we read. . . .
> Our second year has seen us come of age, I think, and if, in our growing process, we have regrettably lost a certain intimacy and intensity, we have gained a great deal more in balance than we have lost. Our early frantic and deeply personal rage has been transmuted into a quiet, utterly determined committment [sic] to END FOR ALL TIME THE OPPRESSION OF WOMEN . . . and we are rapidly acquiring the skills, tools and knowledge to do it.[6]

For such people, participation in NOW can "cause disquieting thinking" and, once the old beliefs have broken down, make it "difficult to plan what to do with your own life"; but many members have been anxious and able to direct their energies into concrete social action. This personal investment not only helps confirm their commitment to the organization, it also leads to new, unanticipated gratifications. Members' comments about the pleasures of working with like-minded, supportive, and stimulating people have already been mentioned. Many people also commented on the practical experience they gained in the movement; they ran meetings, mediated conflicts among committee members, organized managerial work, and spoke in public.

In addition participants learn a good deal about the specific areas in which their chapter or task force is active. In organizing a child-care center, they root out the laws and local ordinances regarding such institutions and they cope with different interest groups within their community. In publicizing their chapter they devise strategies for persuading an unsympathetic local press to report their activities objectively. Members of an "image task force" devise pressure tactics to use against companies whose advertisements degrade women: they talk with advertising managers, television station representatives, and local store managers. When working on the issue of sex discrimination, members explore state and federal laws, executive orders, and the Equal Employment Opportunity Commission's guidelines regarding discrimination. One woman, who played a vital role in pressuring the Pennsylvania legislature into passing an equal rights amendment before the federal amendment was passed, described her rapid progress from political inactivity to skilled lobbying:

> I didn't know that you could look in the telephone book to find your local legislator. [Another woman] and I went to see a legislator who was a good friend of [her] boss. We prepared as much as for a dissertation defense . . . . [Later] we saw my representative. He asked how the unions felt. [My friend] went to the union office next door. . . . They were pro. She went straight back to the legislator and told him.

After more such interviews,

> we were beginning to realize the intricacy and complexity of politics and decided that [a legislator] . . . would be able to get more support. [He agreed to introduce the amendment.] After over a year I called him, though I was very diffident, to see what he was doing. He said there was still plenty of time. I had figured out from reading the constitution that there was scarcely time. He only needed telling. He had not realized the steps required for passage of a constitutional amendment. . . .

I discovered that politicians like to have their names in print. I would get it put in the NOW newsletter and send it to the legislator.

We made up voting records of people in the Pittsburgh area [regarding women's issues] . . . and sent evaluations to NOW members and to the legislators. . . . We did petitions, hundreds and hundreds. I telephoned the legislators every day to learn of the progress.

This sort of extensive experience has several effects upon the active participants. One of the most startling to the outsider is the evident increase in poise, willingness to try new ideas, and general ego strength. In the extreme cases, timid, retiring, and passive souls have blossomed into self-confident, vital women. These personal changes have been fostered also by NOW's commitment to organizational flexibility and to encouraging members to act upon their own initiative. Thus NOW, like Women's Liberation, provides participants with a way to that self-realization which they find excluded from the traditional role. Reassured by their achievements and by the scope of recent experience, they realize that working for the feminist cause is enjoyable. Indeed, many NOW chapters are notable for their cheerful *esprit*. "It's hectic, and we're always disagreeing with each other, but we enjoy it." Task force members like to talk over experiences after the official part of a committee meeting or during their frequent telephone conversations. In many chapters members gather informally for coffee after a general meeting. When such people enjoy their work, see it having real effects, and share the experience with other committed people, their own commitment grows. For the active participant, the circle of increased gratification leading to increased commitment continues to repeat itself.

Active members, however, often represent between 10 and 20 percent of the chapter membership. Among the less active members the process is not self-perpetuating. Yet, as with Women's Liberation, neither the member who becomes inactive nor the dropout is likely to have lost her commitment to feminism. Rather, she finds that, on balance, the total rewards of participation—including the sense of acting on some intensely personal issue—are not sufficient to offset other alternatives. The most common explanation of why women drop out or become inactive is that they have not found a personally satisfying way to contribute significantly to the group; they have no means to act upon their commitment to the movement. Many are tied down by family responsibilities; others are never really brought into the active core, perhaps because there is no area in which they are personally able to contribute; some take on outside jobs which leave no spare time for movement participation; a few transfer to other feminist groups, where they feel more at home. In general, therefore, the person who becomes or remains inactive has rarely ceased to be a feminist. Although there have been many cases where movement members have objected to specific tactics or actions and dropped out of the movement while retaining an ideological commitment to feminism, I have heard of only one case where a movement member became disillusioned with feminism as such and adopted an antifeminist ideology. This contrasts with the situation in other radical political or religious groups, where it appears that dropouts often switch to a reverse ideology.

Serious involvement in a Women's Rights or a Women's Liberation group may endanger a person's career outside the movement. Some feminists say that employers have refused them jobs, have failed to promote them, or have failed to renew their contracts because of their work in the movement. In the course of their movement activities some women have risked arrest by interrupting a state senate subcommittee's proceedings, by holding a sit-in at the Labor Secretary's office, or by taking over panel discussions or closed circuit television programs. Convinced that these were the only means to attain real changes in women's status they were willing, if necessary, to accept the punitive consequences of their actions.

In most of their actions, whether "conservative" or "radical," NOW members have established themselves as experienced, effective, and creative organizers, administrators and, above all, social activists. In the process many have made significant personal sacrifices. The story of these personal efforts, among NOW members as among all other contemporary feminists, must be told later in their biographies and autobiographies.

CHANGES IN ORGANIZATIONAL STRUCTURE AND GOALS

The organizational patterns of NOW and other Women's Rights groups are closely influenced by the participants' ideologies. These ideologies are more clearly defined than are those of Women's Liberation. They are specified through two main channels: the organizational charter and the elaboration of this charter by the participants at national meetings or by some form of representative board of directors.

Most individual members and subgroups, however, exercise considerable autonomy in their interpretations of organizational policy. Several conditions contribute to this situation. The organizational objectives are so general that they allow for considerable flexibility of interpretation; most members agree with Women's Liberation that, as women, they have been "put down" for too long to allow other members, even elected officials, to "impose" ideas upon them; the official organizational hierarchy has, in fact, little effective control because membership is entirely voluntary; the groups feel that they make the greatest gains if they encourage participants to work in areas where they personally feel most involved; and organizational flexibility allows the groups to adapt to changes in the social climate, thereby making maximum use of their resources.

Local Chapters' Autonomy

Prior to 1973, local chapters technically adopted a standard set of bylaws set by the national board, and supplemented these with non-conflicting implementing bylaws. However, since 1970, the national board has encouraged experiment so long as the chapter remained accountable to the national organization. As a result, some chapters which objected to what they felt was "sloppy" wording of the standard bylaws adopted their own versions. An even greater number of chapters felt that any bylaws concerning officers' elections, terms of office, criteria for membership, and so forth, were authoritarian. A few rewrote the provisions to suit their more egalitarian interests, but most simply disregarded their charters and informally adopted homemade organizational structures. Almost every chapter follows the basic pattern of dividing the work among a number of committees (or task forces) concerned with membership, legislation, job discrimination, and so forth. But they adapt the rest of the organizational structure freely. For instance, early in 1971 Berkeley NOW rejected the positions of president and vice-president and created instead the positions of meeting coordinator and organizer. The new names symbolized the incumbents' intention to divide more evenly the executive work and their dislike of formal hierarchies. The chapter was able to make this change without the prior approval of national NOW. Elsewhere, Eastern Massachusetts NOW, which consisted mostly of people from the Boston metropolitan area, decided that it could not operate a 500-member chapter efficiently, and its participants broke up into a number of semi-independent geographically based "units" while maintaining their right to participate in the large central chapter.

Individual chapters have been able not only to adapt the organizational structure proposed by national NOW but also have emphasized different aspects of its organizational goals. In accommodating to their individual situations, chapters based in large cities may lobby for feminist bills or evaluate and publicize the employment situation for women in local colleges, while chapters in suburban areas may use their energies more profitably by pressuring children's libraries to introduce nonsexist books or by ensuring that local schools give equal educational opportunities to girls and boys. All chapters must also take account of the prevailing social climate in the region they serve. It may be a waste of effort to encourage women to run for public office in a city where politics are controlled by local party machines or to organize women factory workers in a city with powerful male-dominated unions.

Many chapters have taken stands on issues upon which the national conference (where assembled members determine policy) has remained uncommitted. National NOW sanctions this sort of independence so long as a chapter does not take a stand directly contrary to existing policy. By officially encouraging local autonomy, the national body enables the chapters to adapt themselves to the interests and needs of their communities and their members.

A more general consequence of national NOW's nonauthoritarian policy is that the organization can explore on a small scale the implications of its more radical objectives before adopting them as national goals. The lesbian issue, for example, had been fermenting for years before it was brought before the 1971 national conference. Many members had feared that open recognition that the oppression of lesbians was a legitimate feminist concern would damage NOW's image. There was a sprinkling of lesbians in most chapters, but almost no one, lesbian or straight, discussed the fact publically.

In the years before 1971, many members feared any connection with the lesbian issue; this sensitivity makes it impossible to reconstruct the debates that must have occurred at both the national and local levels. Betty Friedan, NOW's president until March 1970, strongly opposed any public support for what she called the "lavender menace." The president of one of the far west chapters commented privately while attending the March 1970 national conference that one of the two questions her members wanted answered was how many of the national officers were lesbians. She could get no answer to this question because then, as now, most lesbians in NOW had not made their lesbianism public.

In 1971, some chapters brought the issue into the open. For example, in May 1971, Los Angeles NOW sponsored its first "Gay-Straight Workshop"[7] and in June the two founders of the Daughters of Bilitis, Del Martin and Phyllis Lyon, explained at a Berkeley NOW general membership meeting the sorts of problems lesbians face in a predominantly heterosexual society.[8] While the more conservative chapters, particularly in the central and southern states, still avoided the issue, a majority of the 750 NOW members who met at the September 1971 national conference had by then come to terms with it. They passed resolutions recognizing the double oppression of lesbians, asserting a woman's right "to define and express her own sexuality and to choose her own lifestyle," acknowledging "the oppression of lesbians as a legitimate concern of feminism," and supporting "child custody rights of mothers who are also lesbians."[9] These decisions, with which the national board agreed, exemplified the local chapters' potential for developing new ideas and, more particularly, evaluating members' and nonmembers' reactions to them before the national organization took a stand.

The issue of feminist support for lesbians also illustrates how Women's Liberation has led the way in developing the more radical parts of feminist ideology. Had Women's Liberation groups not shown that they could support gay women without being laughed out of existence, NOW's more conservative members' votes might have effectively prevented the organization from becoming involved in this radical topic.

Local chapters have initiated changes in the overall organizational goals in many other areas besides chapter organization and the rights of lesbians. One of the most recent of these changes has been a 1973 conference resolution originally proposed by the Boulder, Colorado chapter. The conference agreed that a special committee should study the "economic, social and political philosophy of our society to determine how or whether NOW's goals can be effectuated within the present framework." In passing this resolution, members recognized the possibility that if, as NOW proposes, women were to enter the work force without discrimination, child care facilities were to be provided on a significant scale, women were to be paid for housework, and so forth, such changes would have serious repercussions upon the whole societal structure. They felt that these repercussions should be carefully evaluated.

Organizational Goals

At both the local chapter and the national levels, NOW members have been guided in their work by the organization's general Statement of Purpose. Initially, NOW members' interpretations of this statement emphasized the need for legal action to combat discrimination thereby contributing to the typical Women's Liberation member's perception of NOW's goals. Soon after NOW was founded, however, its members at all levels in the organization began to interpret the statement more broadly so as to include what were, in fact, progressively more "radical" objectives. This change is illustrated by changes in the sorts of task forces working at both local and national levels. At first task forces were concerned with such topics as discrimination in employment and education, child care, and membership. Soon, new ones were established to work in broader or more controversial areas: abortion law repeal (as opposed to abortion law reform), revision of laws relating to marriage, discrimination against women in religion, the media's image of women, union women, nonsexist child raising, human reproduction, problems of women city planners, nonunion women workers, karate, women and poverty, women in prisons, Third-World women, lesbians, political action, minority women, volunteerism, and the "masculine mystique." By 1973 national NOW had a total of thirty task forces, and the larger local chapters each had between ten and fifteen task forces.

NOW members' activities in these task forces and elsewhere represent the same shift to a broader and more radical interpretation of feminist concerns through both legal and other strategies. By the end of the 1960s, NOW members were filing legal suits against newspapers and demonstrating outside of their offices because they listed jobs under the headings "Help Wanted: Male" and "Help Wanted: Female." They produced documented arguments that this practice discouraged women from considering jobs such as that of newspaper reporter or bookkeeper which were regularly listed in the "Help Wanted: Male" columns.[10] Other members organized letter-writing protests to companies which demeaned women in their advertising (for example, Bell Telephone's advertisement that "Three out of four housewives make that silly little mistake" of dialing the operator to place an out-of-town call). Women demonstrated or sat-in at "sexist" bars and restaurants (like McSorley's in New York City) until the management stopped reserving all or part of the facilities for men. They helped to change state, local, and federal laws to prohibit sex discrimination in public accommodations, housing, education, and employment; they testified at abortion law hearings. As early as 1967 NOW was instrumental in persuading President Johnson to issue Executive Order 11375 (banning sex-discrimination in the government and by federal contractors). Members have worked for passage of the Equal Rights Amendment at federal and state levels, lobbied successfully for passage of the EEOC Enforcement Act of 1972 which enabled the Commission to fight more effectively against sexual and racial discrimination, worked with EEOC in its moves against the AT&T Company (a NOW officer said, "A hell of a lot of work went into what went on with AT&T. We selected them deliberately because wealth was centered there and . . . [because we could make it] a concerted program for re-education" of the public). NOW members have pressured the Office of Federal Contract Compliance to rule that companies' affirmative action programs for women and minorities be made public. Via the lengthy NOW-appealed *Weeks* v. *Southern Bell* case they have established the legal precedent that an employer must open every job to women applicants unless it can be proved that all or substantially all women are not able to do the job in question.

NOW members have questioned why so few women held influential positions in religious groups and began to pressure local seminaries to accept more women applicants. They warned women of the rights they sacrificed on marriage and produced model bills for reform of divorce laws—including, for example, training and vocational guidance for separated and divorced persons, mutual consent as grounds for divorce, and legal recognition of marriage as an equal partnership.[11] They threatened the California State Welfare Board with a legal suit when it proposed an amendment to a state law that would have the effect of requiring a woman bearing her third illegitimate child to give up that child for adoption. Other NOW members have caused the administration of a women's prison to replace the prison physician and male nurse with a better-qualified part-time obstetrician-gynecologist and a female nurse. They have fought for improved pension plans for wage-earning women. They have persuaded companies to issue credit cards to divorced, single, and separated women; have convinced the same companies to issue married women credit cards in their own—not their husbands'—names, and have brought legal action against banks that would not grant mortgages to single women or would not consider a wife's income when evaluating a couple's eligibility for a mortgage. Some members ran for political office. (They were rarely successful, but few candidates of any kind succeed on their first try.) Others joined the demonstrations of women bank tellers who alleged discrimination and of waitresses who were dismissed for unionizing activities. They issued demands that the black political radical Angela Davis be given a just trial, joined welfare women when they sent delegations to local authorities to protest forced sterilization, and publicized the plight of a group of Chicano women who were unknowingly used in an experiment to test the side effects of birth control pills.[12] Most NOW members decided that rather than founding their own child-care centers, they should work for more lasting change by promoting the child-care movement on a national scale. National NOW began a stockholders' program through which members were asked to sign over their proxy rights so that representatives could attend stockholders' meetings to demand that companies treat all their employees equally and include women on boards of directors.

NOW's shift of organizational goals to cover broader and, on the average, more radical areas, is attributable to several conditions. First, objectives which members once considered radical became more acceptable to members and nonmembers alike as the general social climate became more favorable for feminists. Second, other groups have adopted some of NOW's more conservative objectives (together with some of its more conservative members) leaving NOW free to explore more radical areas. Abortion law repeal is an example: as organizations such as the National Association for the Repeal of Abortion Laws, Zero Population Growth, and the American Civil Liberties Union became more deeply involved in this issue, NOW allocated its seriously stretched resources of personnel and money to other areas. Third, individual members underwent consciousness-raising experiences in the course of their participation and, as was described in an earlier chapter, adopted progressively more radical positions. Fourth, members were self-conscious about their middle-class image and anxious that the organization work for the interests of women in all sectors of the society. A fifth reason for the change derives from the NOW members' changed perception of the relation between feminism and humanism.

Humanism and Feminism

For many members, NOW's increased involvement in such social problems as racial discrimination and prison reform has involved their reevaluation of the group's ideology. This reevaluation has brought them to the explicit belief that they cannot achieve feminist goals without also working for other humanist objectives and, ultimately, for fundamental changes in the structure of society. Many members were already stating this view privately in 1970. In September 1971 Aileen Hernandez, as NOW's retiring president, stated the case publicly:

> There are no such things as women's issues!! All issues are women's issues. The difference that we bring to the existing issues in our society —the issues of war and peace; the issues of poverty; the issues of child care; the issues of political power—is that we are going to bring the full, loud, clear, determined voice of women into deciding how those issues are going to be addressed. . . . [If] this movement is to be successful at all, . . . [it] must address itself . . . to every issue that not only faces the United States, but every issue that faces this world.[13]

While many NOW members and individual chapters already agreed with these ideas, it was not until the national meeting at which Hernandez gave the address from which the above extract is taken that they formally endorsed the idea of broader social involvement. This endorsement is shown in the conference resolutions concerning first, war and the "masculine mystique" and second, volunteerism. In a resolution opposing the Vietnam war it was argued that war was an expression of the masculine mystique which, historically, has used violence as a solution to problems and that in place of such violence, feminists should "create a society in which feminist, humanist values prevail."[14]

The members' enthusiastic support at that conference of a resolution on volunteer "service work" prepared by the Berkeley chapter measured their concern lest NOW allow itself to be coopted away from feminism and "used" both to make an existing inadequate social system work more smoothly and to encourage women to perform their traditional service role. Discussing a statement prepared by the Berkeley chapter, they agreed that traditional service work involving personal sacrifice by women with prosperous husbands only perpetuated women's dependent, secondary status. They accepted the resolution's preamble that traditional volunteerism by

> asking women to serve as the unpaid conscience of the nation only defers solutions to serious social problems. . . . [Traditional volunteerism] serves to assuage a housewife's discontent but rarely offers a realistic solution to her problems . . . [and has] greatly reinforced the feminine mystique. . . . [It] reinforces a woman's low self-image, by offering work which, because unpaid, confers little status.

With such ideas in mind, NOW members resolved to "distinguish between (1) voluntary activities which serve to maintain woman's dependent and secondary status on the one hand, and (2) change-directed activities which lead to more active participation in the decision-making process"; and, further, "to raise the consciousness of women engaged in these volunteer activities, so that they use their 'volunteer power' . . . to change policies detrimental to the interests of women."[15] Thus NOW, like Women's Liberation, argues for change in the social structure as opposed to palliative activities that help perpetuate the existing structure.

NOW's decision to become involved in a broader range of humanist concerns should not, therefore, be taken as a move toward becoming a social service organization. On the contrary, the change in emphasis represents members' determination to achieve even greater social change than, at first, they envisioned. Feminist objectives, they believe, cannot be achieved without fundamental change in the society as a whole. Thus, in recent years, NOW and Women's Liberation have grown closer together in their ideological positions. Women's Liberation still advocates "social revolution" (and the creation of independent feminist advisory and self-help groups) while NOW still advocates "significant social change" (and a relatively greater involvement in the establishment); but their interpretations of "social revolution" and "significant social change" are not so far apart as they were in the 1960s.

As other feminist and nonfeminist reform groups have taken over the more generally popular feminist ideas, NOW has moved toward progressively more radical goals. Balancing this change in NOW and parallel changes in other Women's Rights groups against the shift toward more conservative methods (though not goals) among the Women's Liberation groups, it is clear that the new feminist movement, taken as a whole, is adopting broader and more radical goals.

CHAPTER NINE

NATIONAL ORGANIZATION FOR WOMEN: INTERNAL ORGANIZATION

Many features of NOW's organization would be character-istic of any newly established voluntary organization. Other features are distinctly feminist and are the result of members' determination to run NOW according to certain idealistic principles characteristic of the feminist movement in general, rather than according to the impersonal fashion of the male establishment.

COMMUNICATION

NOW's national organizational network grew so rapidly that its founders, lacking staff, money, and basic secretarial help, were unable to keep up. Since the earliest days, it has been exceedingly difficult to keep communication channels operating smoothly.

The communication problem involved both communication between NOW and potential recruits and communication within NOW itself. As one member said in 1971, "It's horrendous." Potential members could not find "NOW" in the telephone book or any other source, even though there was an active local chapter; local "chapters" flourished without ever having been in contact with the national office. In at least one case, a small feminist group and a self-appointed organizer each started the "only" NOW chapter for the same city without either having heard of the other. Other organizers, who wanted to follow the procedures set down by the national office, had problems because they could not find out from national what specific steps were required of them.

The local communication problem has remained a severe one. In 1971 a member of a year-old chapter based in a suburb of Los Angeles said, "We are damn hard to get to. We hear hideous stories of potential members saying how hard it was to reach us."

Even when chapters were formed, a telephone number established, and meetings advertised, members had great difficulty staying in touch. Those people who worked on a specific task force generally saw or heard from each other often, but they knew little about activities in the rest of the chapter. They also knew little about what was occurring on a national scale. Chapters have duplicated each other's efforts in compiling lists of "nonsexist" children's books, in evaluating the merits of the Equal Rights Amendment, or in interpreting the 1965 and 1967 Executive Orders and Title VII of the 1964 Civil Rights Act as these apply to sex discrimination.

National NOW has faced the same sorts of communication problems as have the locals. Memos, long-distance telephone calls, and even conference telephone calls could not solve this problem. Indeed, this lack of contact is one of the reasons why the quarterly board meetings have taken on such importance.

In addition to keeping in touch with each other, board members of national NOW have faced the more difficult task of keeping in touch with the local chapters to inform them of what is going on at the national level and to coordinate the activities of the local groups. Keeping up with the first of these responsibilities ideally requires a large secretarial staff which the board has never had. The second task—a job which the original organization never envisioned for itself—is even more demanding. The one or two board members coordinating a particular program cannot stay in contact with all the interested NOW members, however hard they work. The chapters complain that it is impossible to reach the coordinators by letter or even by telephone, so that the locals must simply go ahead and work alone. Time and again chapter members have complained that they "don't know what national is doing." The national office has always been so seriously overburdened that it has never been able to answer its mail properly. The "severe communications gap" which Betty Friedan reported in 1967[1] remains today: many problems have been solved but, as NOW has grown, many new ones have appeared. In 1970 and 1971 my respondents knew little about national NOW.

"The national office is in Chicago, isn't it?" asked one newly elected chapter president. Her guess was right. "Contact with national NOW?" responded someone from another chapter, "None, except for the newsletter. They are badly organized. I'm sympathetic." And again, "National NOW is something out there that I hear from once in a while; or that I read about in the paper."

At the national conference in February 1973 members in all parts of the organization commented in public and private on the "communication problems top-to-bottom and bottom-to-top," on being "very much involved in the local/national communication issue," on the need for "more effective communication and support between national and the local chapters," and their concern for "more unity chapter to chapter and chapter to national board." While there was a good deal of feeling expressed, these difficulties were discussed openly and with humor.

Many of NOW's communication problems resulted from its inability to pay the basic operating costs of a national organization. Within the restrictions caused by its chronic shortage of funds, NOW, like Women's Liberation, has improved organizational efficiency by adopting the techniques of institutionalized voluntary organizations. Time-consuming technical work like the maintenance of mailing lists has been contracted out by the national office, so that by 1973 all "membership services" were done by a contractor.

While, at the local level, very few chapters can afford to have paid employees, they, like national NOW, have adopted a progressively more complex division of labor. More and more specific job assignments have been made: these include membership chairperson, treasurer, secretary, fund raiser, public-relations officer, and anywhere from one to fifteen task force chairpersons. In the early 1970s, some began to detail job specifications. In 1970 an attempt was made to bring local groups closer to the national board (and to cut down on the president's enormous work load) by creating four "regional directors." From the start the regional representatives were overworked; the obvious next step was to develop statewide organizations. By 1973 such groups have been proposed or initiated in at least half of the states.

Many groups within NOW have begun to circulate information they believe is useful to members. For example, by 1972 members of the national NOW board were distributing "kits" on how to form a NOW chapter, how to file complaints regarding sex discrimination in academia with the Department of Health, Education, and Welfare, and (on a system borrowed from the NAACP) how to monitor and evaluate "sexism" in TV programs and commercials. NOW informed members where to get a government pamphlet, "Guidelines on Discrimination Because of

Sex," advertised a NOW "Handbook for Effective Letter Writing," a "Press Handbook," and a "Handbook for the Corporate Suffragette."

Local and national groups began to make detailed suggestions for ways in which individual members could act. Whereas in the past suggestions had been few and general they became frequent and specific. Members realized that their colleagues were far more likely to "write their senator about the child development bill" and to influence the senator if they were told what were the relevant issues; who their senator was; where to address the letter; the bill's number; whether, given the bill's wording, the senator should be urged to vote for or against; and when the senate would be debating the issue. Similarly, when members were urged to write advertising agencies concerning their "demeaning" portrayals of women, the request included the agencies' names and addresses and carefully identified each of the offending advertisements.

More and more newsletters have appeared. At the national level, *NOW Acts*, the national newsletter published approximately every quarter, has been supplemented by a second monthly newsletter, *Do It NOW*. Started in the latter part of 1970 by the NOW board and originally written by a board member, its objective has been to suggest specific, timely actions through which NOW members could contribute to change on a local and national level. Another organization KNOW, Inc., of Pittsburgh, while independent, was initiated by Pittsburgh members. It operates a news service and prints or reprints feminist bibliographies, articles on feminism, books, and outlines of college and university courses in women's studies.

At the local level, newsletters have proved to be one of the more effective means of keeping chapter members informed. In contrast, general membership meetings (held perhaps once a month) have been less useful because they have frequently been attended only by between one-third and one-tenth of the members. Many chapters have devised telephone trees or grids through which to spread specific information about, say, the need for a large number of people to attend a public hearing on some proposed legislation; however, these have proved notably unsuccessful. Most chapters have tried to get the local press to report their activities, both as a means of keeping members' interest alive and as a means of spreading information about the chapter and recruiting new members. Although some newspapers have been very cooperative, most have given meager or distorted accounts of NOW activities, and a number which oppose NOW have refused to mention the organization in print. About a dozen chapters have been successful in founding NOW centers or NOW offices which, like the Women's Liberation centers, serve as a nexus in the local communication network.

FINANCES

Like Women's Liberation and the other Women's Rights groups, for years NOW subsisted almost exclusively upon its own resources— members' dues supplemented by a few small contributions and fund-raising efforts. National NOW's expenses for 1970 were $26,000; for 1971, $48,000; and for 1972, $100,000.[2] Estimates for 1973 approached $250,000. Local chapters' budgets ranged in 1971 and 1972 from a few dollars to $18,000 (varying primarily with chapter size), most often hovering between $200 to $600. In practice, however, the real budgets are many times larger than the stated amount: the difference is made up primarily of the unpaid time contributed by members.

At the chapter level, a committee member may devote one evening a week to addressing envelopes or making telephone calls and another evening each month to attending a committee meeting. Her chairperson puts in more time: she organizes meetings, writes letters, or arranges interviews with local government officials. Within the chapters, presidents are the most hard-pressed: when asked how much time they devote to NOW activities, those who are employed outside the home generally say that NOW takes up almost all the time that they are not at work; and those who are not employed outside the home say that it takes all the time they can afford to spend away from their families (very few chapter presidents have jobs *and* families). During a two-hour interview with such a person, the conversation may be interrupted four or five times by incoming telephone calls on NOW business. The cheerful but harassed life of such a chapter president is indicated by the introductory words of a memo one president sent out to the chapter's board members in July 1971. "Before leaving for [vacation] . . . . for the month of August (where I will be totally, completely, and *blissfully* unreachable), I would like to clarify some areas of concern and make a few suggestions. . . ."[3]

Most members of the national board of NOW devote at least as much time to the organization as chapter officials. In January 1971 one of the four regional directors, asked to give a job description to the national board, did so in a single sentence: "A regional director is someone who pours unlimited time and money into the region."

In addition to the donation of time, NOW members give unaccounted quantities of their own money to the organization because they pay for telephone calls, mailings, typing, occasional secretarial assistance, and travel. Estimates of national board members' expenses range from several hundred to several thousand dollars a year, of which no more than a few hundred dollars has been reimbursed to anyone except the president. (In 1972, for example, the president received $3,400 for expenses.) In the local chapters individual member's out-of-pocket expenses range from a few dollars to several hundred. Again, few of these expenses are covered by the chapter itself or even noted in its budget.

If members' contributions in time, goods and services, and out-of-pocket expenses were taken into account, then NOW's budget would increase by hundreds of thousands of dollars.[4] This fact further explains NOW's middle-class image. A person has to be relatively well off before she can afford to assume a position of responsibility. As a former west coast chapter president, a professional woman, put it, "Who can afford the money to be president? . . . NOW interferes with my attempts to earn a living."

Under the present dues system neither the local nor the national groups are adequately funded. Chapters collect individual dues of $10 to send to the national organization and charge additional local dues of from $2.50 to $15 for chapter needs. Both local chapters and national NOW have made serious efforts to find supplementary sources of ready cash. Like most other voluntary organizations, they use traditional strategies for fund raising. Chapters charge members and nonmembers for admission to lectures, demonstrations, and classes. They hold fund-raising parties (perhaps in honor of some nationally known feminist who happens to be in town). Some have tried soliciting funds through advertisements in local newspapers, but with little success. A number of chapters manufacture and/or retail such items as feminist stationery, posters (e.g., a "Women's Poem" and "Fuck Housework"), pendants, pins, or rings shaped in the form of the female symbol with an "equals" sign in the center, children's books, calendars, and even candles, coasters, or other consumer products. One chapter worked out an arrangement with local stores whereby it received 5 percent of the profits made on sales to NOW members and sympathizers who presented a special ticket on a specific day; but this effort failed.[5] Other chapters have tried art shows, garage sales, collecting trading stamps to buy an electric typewriter, and charging for advertisements in their newsletters. Most such sources have brought in a few hundred dollars at best, and unfortunately most of that money comes from the members themselves.

National NOW has had similar problems. Before 1971 board members were so preoccupied with action campaigns that they felt obliged to neglect fund-raising. Since that time national NOW has held a few specific fund-raising events, including the celebrations, speeches, and demonstrations commemorating the August 26 anniversary of women's suffrage, the rental (at $15 to NOW chapters and $25 to other groups) of an hour-and-a-half slide documentary on the origins of the new feminist movement and NOW, and a planned edition of selected writings and speeches of NOW members.[6] In 1972, $18,000, 11 percent of national NOW's gross income, came from contributions, fund-raising, and sale of publications.[7] The response to a fund-raising letter requesting money to support work for states' ratification of the Equal Rights Amendment measures the changing national-scale response to NOW's work. Signed by the president, Wilma Scott Heide, the direct mailing resulted in donations of $150,000 in a period of less than two months at the beginning of 1973.

In 1971, national NOW's "Legal and Educational Defense Fund" (LEDF) gained tax-exempt status. During 1972 and 1973 the LEDF began to get contributions of, for example, $10,000 from a foundation and of several thousand dollars worth of services from a broadcasting station and, clearly, was on its way to getting progressively larger amounts of money from such sources.

Throughout NOW, members have periodically raised the Women's Liberation groups' objections to "making money off members," but this complaint was far more common in 1969 and 1970 than in later years.

Another practice that some have protested is the effort by an occasional member to run a private or semiprivate business selling such items as calendars and stationery or operating a speakers' bureau. Most of these women split their profits with a local chapter or national NOW. Nonetheless the objection is made again that these women are profiting from other members. In response, the small-scale entrepreneurs claim that, rather than exploiting their local chapters, they contribute funds to the organization as a whole, and earn a subsistence living in the course of promoting feminism.

INTERNAL CONFLICTS

In the organization's first years and to a lesser extent in its later years, some but by no means all of NOW's local chapters have come into conflict with the national board. The conflicts are rarely voiced in terms of their real causes—shortage of money, communication problems, rapid increase in activities, and the other difficulties faced by a new voluntary organization that has to develop from scratch a complete set of organizational norms. Instead, members usually express any discontent in terms of the ideals generally accepted among the less conservative members of the new feminist movement. Of the two sides, the local groups are far more likely to complain. Some members feel that national NOW works too independently, failing to take account of the majority's interests or to draw upon the ideas and talents of the whole membership. These people believe that national NOW is an elitist clique, whose actions deny the organization's democratic principles. Their misperceptions include, for example, the idea that in 1971 "the slate for the new board of directors was almost the same as the previous year with people changing position." (In fact twenty-four of the thirty-eight members were new to the board, although only two of the nine officers were new.) A few believe that members of this central group are rich. In fact, only one or two of the national board members could be called "rich." Essentially all of them, however, are from financially secure middle-class families with incomes in the $10,000 to $20,000 range. As we have seen, it is hard if not impossible for someone to hold a leadership position in NOW unless she can personally pay her travel and other expenses.

Other members are less concerned with who belongs to the national board and more concerned that national NOW is so preoccupied with its own work that it fails to recognize the immense amount of activity at the local level. For example, from the local chapters' viewpoint it sometimes seems that some people on the national board treat their responsibilities in such areas as federal contract compliance, federal legislation, or child care as if they were the only people in the whole organization concerned with the issues when, of course, most local chapters have task forces or committees to deal with these and similar topics. They feel that "the national board works in a vacuum." Some task forces were particularly aggravated when members of the national board requested for example, that information describing all pending legal actions be sent to a national NOW coordinator before suits were filed locally or that all "Image of Women" task forces drop their current work to cooperate in a national project monitoring TV programs and commercials for sexist bias. "In the past, national's calls to action have sounded like orders to troops." Such requests that local groups report to or work under the direction of national NOW have sometimes been interpreted as attacks on local autonomy, rather than attempts to make NOW's actions more effective and coordinated, and to improve its internal communications. Members emphasize that national should "support the growth of strong grass-roots local chapters"; "the will of the membership is top priority"; and "we must break away the elitist values of the male world."

Complaints about national NOW's imposition on the local groups' autonomy frequently focus on the concrete issue of dues. A majority of chapter members feel that national NOW uses their annual contributions for its own purposes, and not in the chapters' interests. Members from all over the country make such comments as: "I wish the dues could be lower . . . I [am] . . . not sure what they do with it." "I object to the distribution of dues. It's like supporting the federal government while the state government goes broke. . . . You don't get enough back from national." "I think there is tremendous value in the national movement. . . . [But] I guess that every time we talk about the dues I get a little riled up at NOW national getting so much."

The causes of this intergroup conflict do not lie with a failure of members' idealism but with each side's misunderstanding of the other's situation. Neither side has thoroughly appreciated the other's role in the organization. Local chapters, preoccupied with their own activities, see national's function as one of providing information, advice, and support. For their part, the national board members have seen themselves primarily as activists and only secondarily as people who facilitate the operation of the whole organization.

Evidence that NOW's poor communications contribute substantially to local/national conflict lies in the observation that chapters which have a concerned local person sitting on the national board and chapters so located that the more grass-roots-oriented board members can often visit them usually are pleased with the national board's activities.

Many of the problems that emerge between local NOW chapters and the national board recur at the level of the local chapter. If a small group of hard-working people runs most of the chapter's activities (as is generally the case), the remaining members are apt to accuse the group of taking over the organization. Whenever an election is contested, one person or slate is likely to be closer to incumbent officials than the other—and is likely to be accused of being part of a ruling elite. Task forces compete with each other for the chapter's limited funds; if a president tries to oversee task-force actions too carefully, she is considered to be interfering; if she does not know exactly what a task force is doing, she may be accused of neglecting the chapter's concerns in favor of her own; some local chapter boards are accused of imposing their "too radical" or "too conservative" ideas upon the remaining members; and disagreements over issues are confused with personality conflicts.

The conflicts I have described are typical of the internal problems of rapidly expanding, activist, and idealistic voluntary organizations. It should be emphasized that these difficulties are minor when compared to the members' commitment to NOW and to the feminist cause in general— anyone who doubts this should note that over three-fourths of the 1971 members had renewed their memberships by December 1972.[8] What is interesting is that these conflicts shed light on NOW members' ideals for the operation of an organization: the complaining members legitimize their complaints, both to themselves and to other members, by expressing the complaints in terms of feminist ideals like sisterhood and anti-elitism.

THE ALLOCATION OF POWER AND PARTICIPATORY DEMOCRACY

Many members believe that NOW is unique in its aspiration toward humanism and participatory democracy. Most believe that no perfect democracy is possible so that, in practice, they must accept compromises in their ideals. Nonetheless, they aspire more or less deliberately toward the participatory ideal advocated so fervently in the counterculture.

Despite these expressed convictions, however, members have not specified what they mean by participatory democracy. A few espouse particular theories of democracy, while the majority (in keeping with NOW's pragmatism) are guided by an unsystematic set of ideas about how an ideal democracy should work. These ideas include the familiar feminist antiauthoritarian stance, the belief that all participants should be able to express their personal needs and to develop their individual talents in a sympathetic social environment, and an emphasis upon the sisterhood of all women—members and nonmembers. Implicitly and explicitly, such members adopt a consensus model of decision making in contrast to the adversary model of the "male world."

NOW members' efforts to institute these ideas are in some ways thoroughly conventional and in other ways distinctly unconventional. Among their more or less conventional actions have been their efforts to overcome a problem typical of voluntary organizations—only a small proportion of the membership is active at any one time.[9] Officials from local chapters estimate that in chapters with over 200 members this proportion is about 10 percent and that, below 200, the smaller the chapter the greater the proportion of active members. In all parts of NOW, locally and nationally, willing people who have the time and ability are thrust into positions of responsibility—and power. NOW chapters' adoption of the consciousness-raising idea has been, in part, an effort to bring more members into active participation. (Interestingly, the few social science theorists who have analyzed the problems of participatory democracy have emphasized the importance of training the participants to participate.[10]) Advocates of consciousness raising argue that many new members will remain inactive unless they learn more about the application of feminist ideology to their own and others' lives so that they have a base of facts and ideas to guide their future actions. "Consciousness-raising groups would help get people ready for action. We could have monthly meetings for discussion. Then participation would be a two-stage business; first discussion with other new members and second work in a task force."

One way in which NOW has differed from conventional voluntary organizations and resembles contemporary radical groups including Women's Liberation is the members' free expression of ideas *and* emotions: they give lengthy, and sometimes irrelevant, speeches, interject into the discussions many of their personal feelings, and in their enthusiasm for the discussion, they may frequently interrupt each other. When outsiders hear the heated discussions characteristic of many NOW meetings, see a conference ignore Robert's Rules, or hear members make personal comments from the floor, they sometimes conclude that the organization is composed of highly emotional, unstable people who are constantly quarreling with each other. "Aunt _____, *what* have you got us into?" asked one new member. Such observers, however, often perceive more conflict than actually exists because they do not recognize that many NOW groups accept as *normative* members' free expression of emotion. NOW members often perceive the disagreements in positive terms: at the 1973 national conference one person observed two board members arguing vigorously, "There were these two of them. . . . They had different positions, yet they were *helping* each other to make their points. I hope it stays that way."[11]

NOW has not introduced these modifications in group decision making without also modifying other traditional organizational norms. Ideally at least, all members learn that they have special responsibilities. They must exercise individual self-control rather than relying on the chairperson to check excessively long speeches and irrelevant emotional outbursts, or they must volunteer to leave a job for which they prove unsuitable. "They must realize they have got to help each other . . . and not be jealous." Yet, as a national board member and former chapter president put it, the "underlying kindness . . . characteristic of the movement . . . leads to a problem that recurs at all levels of NOW: we try so hard to treat people tenderly and thoughtfully [that it] . . . may ruin us. But I wouldn't like to see it changed." This underlying kindness is found throughout the organization. At a conference a member from a strictly conservative southern city, with numerous feminist buttons decorating her blouse, passed two chic, sophisticated northerners. "Buy a button! Buy a button!" When she had passed, the northerners exchanged deprecating looks which seconds later melted into sympathy and one said: "If *we* came from there, *we'd* have to behave like that to survive."

In NOW's day-to-day routine the negative effects of this kindness strategy are to some extent offset by the norm which advocates open expression of feelings and so allows the group to criticize a delinquent member. In addition, members are expected to sanction tactfully those people whose behavior or work is unsatisfactory. They must also assume responsibility for giving the chairperson visual clues (bored expressions, frowns, nods), in order that she can more readily grasp the sense of the meeting. When they find themselves involved in personality clashes, they must be willing to bring these into the open and, through frank discussion with their opponents, resolve their difficulties. "Yes, we have had personality clashes in the chapter. I suppose all chapters do. We try to solve them by bringing the two parties together to air their complaints. It seems to have worked." Such activities take up a great deal of time, emotional energy, and individual forbearance. Thus, boards of officers, committees, and task forces must all accept excessively long, tiring decision-making sessions. Finally, members must avoid the purely adversary role by always keeping in mind all sides of a question: "I really agree with you, but there is a need to consider . . . " or "I think the idea of a festival is great, but I fear the press will distort it. I'm trying to think of ideas to prevent this from happening."

Chairpersons and other leaders have comparable responsibilities. They learn to grasp the sense of a meeting and to present this in a way that emphasizes everyone's responsibility. They are sensitive to others' needs and avoid dominating. Consequently, when the group starts to pursue an irrelevant topic, they do not simply bring the meeting back to its agenda but, instead, point out that they are off the track and await a general expression that they should return to the agenda. If a particular subgroup wishes to do something "impossible," a leader may "let them talk themselves out. . . . After sufficient conversation in the whole group, they sometimes come around to other views."

The most highly regarded leaders are both talented and socially adept in these ways. People say of such a person, "She gives us a lift when she comes through," or "With her, leadership is a warm and friendly thing. She has turned people on. . . . She does not seek publicity. . . . She never gets rattled in any situation; she is always in control. And she's personally concerned too." "[NOW's] leaders need to be very sensitive to the problem of elitism. That's what's particularly bad about _____. I never detected [in her] the compassion that I see in _____."

One can argue correctly that any good executive practices these skills and that many groups within a wide range of modern organizations are considerate of others' feelings, make decisions by consensus, and so forth. No one in NOW would pretend that the association has a brand new normative system for organizational operation. Some argue that NOW differs little from other reformist or voluntary groups; others believe that differences exist but they cannot identify them.

In fact, NOW's unusual democratic qualities lie less in what its members do than in what they believe should be done. More than in other organizations, the NOW leader is seen as someone who helps the group reach its own decisions and who can *legitimately* be sanctioned for forcing her ideas on the group. Similarly, while NOW may make as many decisions by vote as does any normal committee or board of directors, in principle it rejects the assumption that "one side must win" for the assumption that, with sufficient effort invested, a compromise acceptable to all can be found.

Thus, regardless of whether idealistic members are correct in their assertions that NOW is more humanist than most other organizations, they are correct in their belief that NOW rates as more important the idealistic principles upon which this humanism is based.

However well intentioned its members may be, NOW is constantly pressured to solve individual problems by adopting the norms of established organizations. Some people want to sanction inefficient, lazy, or unqualified workers by holding them accountable to stated job descriptions instead of to potentially arbitrary group evaluations. Referring to NOW's lack of norms for allocation of power, one person said, "When people don't have traditions of power, they don't know how to use power." "Parliamentary procedure," she continued, "protects the majority." Together with other members, she also recognized that such changes would gradually mold NOW in the pattern of institutionalized voluntary organizations. There are indications, however, that NOW is trying to avoid this fate by defining what is meant by its humanist approach. A number of chapters have had special evaluative meetings to discuss, not just their future plans, but also the ways members wish to work together. In May 1972 the national board met in a "retreat" to discuss the questions: "Where are we going? How shall we get there?" They were not concerned with program development since that is officially the purpose of the national conference: instead, they were concerned with the areas of "Philosophy; Structure; Finances; Communications; Personal Growth and Development."[12] They were searching for what one board member called "a common *modus operandi*." NOW's Planning and Policy committee, originally created in the fall of 1971, has been making an on-going study of the issues raised at the retreat and, subsequently, by members at the February 1973 national conference.

The members' marked sense of confidence evinced at the 1973 conference epitomized the results of changes described in this chapter: NOW has come of age. Whereas some years ago members wondered if the organization would survive, now they are asking what directions will it take in the future. In the previous chapter I suggested that NOW's goals will probably remain "radical." Many members expect that its organizational operation will remain at least "different." Although NOW has moved steadily in the direction of greater institutionalization, some of its members remain self-consciously determined to avoid becoming an impersonal, bureaucratic organization and intend to combine the goal of organizational effectiveness with the goal of concern for the individual participant. Their efforts are not unique. In groups as different as the French communities of work, the Yugoslav workers' councils, American management consultants of the human relations school, and the New Left people are looking for strategies to increase group members' real participation in decision-making processes. The efforts of Women's Liberation and NOW have a two-fold significance: first, they are testing the theoretical assumption that members' experience in participatory decision-making is crucial to the creation of a truly participatory democracy and, second, they are seriously experimenting with specific normative strategies for making that democracy work.

CHAPTER TEN

THE RANGE OF WOMEN'S RIGHTS GROUPS

My objective in this chapter is to cover quickly the range of feminist organizations in the United States at the present time; to describe their internal organization by comparison with my previous analysis of NOW; and to describe communication and cooperation among feminist groups and between feminist groups and outside organizations. The traditional women's organizations, like the YWCA, the Business and Professional Women's Clubs, and the League of Women Voters, are well known and, despite their recent return to feminist issues, will not be discussed further here. The first half of this chapter covers women's interest groups, the Women's Equity Action League (WEAL), and the smaller Women's Rights organizations, a few representative examples of local Women's Rights organizations, and politically-oriented women's groups like the National Women's Political Caucus. The second half of the chapter discusses organizational operation.

WOMEN'S INTEREST GROUPS

With the rise of new feminist ideas, many women's caucuses and similar feminist interest groups have been formed by women brought together by their activity in larger nonfeminist social groupings. Among such interest groups is the Professional Women's Caucus (PWC). Chartered in 1970 with a membership limited to self-defined "professional" women, the PWC has the objectives of combating discrimination, pressuring the government and other organizations to appoint more women to responsible posts, and encouraging the election to political office of non-racist feminist women. An east-coast organization, primarily, the PWC had a couple of hundred members early in 1972. Other professional women have formed caucuses (with varying degrees of independence) within groups such as the American Library Association and the Modern Language Association. "Women Educators in Rhode Island" have got together to combat the "growing dominance" of males in educational administration. In Washington, D. C., several hundred female and male journalists have organized to oppose sex discrimination in journalism. In New York, journalists have joined with other interested women to form the "National Association of Media Women." Caucuses have been formed at *Newsweek*'s and *Time-Life*'s offices. "Stewardesses for Women's Rights" and the "Stewardesses Anti-Defamation League" represent women from the U.S. airlines. Religious groups, such as the United Presbyterian Church in the U.S.A. and the United Church of Christ have active Women's Task Forces.

"Federally Employed Women" (FEW) was founded in 1968 to represent the interests of women employed at all levels in the federal government. In August 1970 *FEW's News and Views* reported 600 women and men members, and in spring 1973, an official reported a nationwide membership of several thousand in over thirty chapters. Two similar, smaller groups are the "Organization for Women of the Social Security Administration" drawing its members from the Baltimore area, and the "Federal Women's Program" (not to be confused with the federal program of that name) representing government employees in the Chicago area. Women workers in the New York City financial district have formed "Wall Street Women United." Union women have organized in the Bay area, California, under the name, "Union W.A.G.E." (Union Women's Alliance to Gain Equality).

Another type of group marginal to this study are the feminist organizations recently formed by minority women. These include the equal rights oriented "National Conference on Black Women," of Pittsburgh, groups like the "Black Women's Employment Program," of Atlanta which concentrates upon getting jobs for black women, and the more politically oriented "National Black Women's Political Leadership Caucus." Blacks also have formed coalitions with other nonwhite women —for example "Women United for Justice and Equal Rights," of Maryland and the "Third World Women's Alliance" of New York City.

These groups exemplify how, on the local and on the national levels, women from particular interest groups—racial, occupational, etc.—have formed their own organizations. Some of the groups have thousands of members; others less than a hundred. They range from active to inactive, powerful to weak, a dedicated to an uninterested membership. While many of them function in ways similar to the Women's Rights groups discussed in this and the previous two chapters, and while many have made very important contributions to the feminist cause, they are too numerous and too varied to include in the present study.

WOMEN'S RIGHTS GROUPS

The Women's Equity Action League

After NOW, WEAL is one of the best-known of the Women's Rights groups.[1] Like NOW, WEAL was founded by a handful of persons. Led by Dr. Elizabeth Boyer, who had previously recruited actively for NOW in her home city of Cleveland, these founders believed that NOW was too unconventional. Further, some of them, including Dr. Boyer, disagreed with the 1967 NOW national meeting's decision to make abortion law repeal part of its official program.

In founding WEAL, Dr. Boyer limited the organization's objectives to the attainment of equality through the full enforcement of existing laws, the passage of antidiscriminatory legislation, and the encouragement of girls to prepare for more rewarding jobs than they have in the past. Since 1967 WEAL members' activities have been confined largely to working for legislative and legal changes that attack discrimination against women in education, industry, and other areas of life. For example, WEAL has brought charges of sex discrimination against almost 300 colleges and universities through the Department of Health, Education, and Welfare under Executive Order 11246 as amended. In Washington, D. C., the National Capital Chapter has investigated and reported on sex discrimination by the major foundations and fellowship programs, both federal and private. In 1971 Texas WEAL presented carefully documented charges of discrimination to the Dallas banks,[2] and in 1972 the national organization followed up by filing charges of sex discrimination against the city of Dallas under the new 1972 Equal Employment Opportunity Act.[3] Tampa, Florida, WEAL has requested the Internal Revenue Service to investigate the tax returns of more than two hundred employers who have run male/female segregated help-wanted advertisements in violation of the 1964 Civil Rights Act. The chapter argues advertising expenses are normally tax deductible but that, since the advertisements were segregated by sex, the deduction would be illegal.

The Dallas and the National Capital chapters are relatively recent additions to WEAL's organizational structure. At first WEAL, like NOW, was organized on a purely national level; unlike NOW, however, its original plan included the formation of chapters. With state chapters in over forty states, WEAL is roughly as broadly distributed as NOW. WEAL does not make public its membership figures but the requirement of a minimum of twenty-five members to form a chapter puts a lower bound of 1,000 on their 1973 membership. The actual total is probably considerably larger than this. During 1972 the organization's central office was moved from Cleveland to Washington so that WEAL could work more effectively with the government.

Smaller Women's Rights Groups

A number of Women's Rights groups, formed in the 1970s, have a very small membership (generally less than a hundred). A few other groups lie on the borderline of the present study by virtue of the fact that membership is in effect though not in principle limited to a few people. Many of these groups, together with many of the feminist interest groups mentioned above, were founded by NOW members who felt strongly about some particular problem and wanted to pursue their ideas independently.

In September 1971, the Women's Legal Defense Fund (not to be confused with NOW's Legal and Educational Defense Fund) was incorporated in Washington, D. C., with a membership of "Lawyers and other concerned persons . . . . Members will work for equal rights through litigation and other means in a wide range of areas, including employment, education, and public accommodations."[4] In 1973 it had about 200 members. The Fund, based in Washington, D. C., has taken on selected cases including a complaint to the Equal Employment Opportunity Commission charging that the food chain, Giant Foods, discriminates against women with regard to pay and promotions; and a suit on behalf of an Alexandria, Virginia, high school girl who was forced to drop out of school because she was pregnant. With a view to pressing other legal suits, the Fund has also undertaken a study of credit practices regarding mortgages granted by the Veteran's Administration, and loans and credit cards approved by FDIC banks.

The Women's Action Alliance, Inc., based in New York City, was formed early in 1972 to help women working on local action projects by providing technical assistance, a referral service, and an information clearinghouse. To provide this assistance the Alliance does not need a large membership: although it has a 34-person board of directors, including people like Congresswoman Patsy T. Mink, seven people do most of the work. They have developed a non-sexist curriculum for early childhood education, and an information kit on organizing a child care center; they observe and report on projects that provide continuing education for low-income adult women and that will inform women employed in local government about the problems of sex discrimination; and they cooperate with other feminist and non-feminist groups in an effort to stimulate people's awareness of discrimination suffered by people like female high school students and household employees.

Washington (D. C.) Opportunities for Women is one of the oldest Women's Rights groups. Since 1966 it has provided advice and information to women who wish to rejoin the labor force after being full-time housewives for a number of years. WOW encourages women to study or work part-time or full-time, and to plan ahead for a career when their children are grown.

In August 1972, Women United for Action, a New York City group of unknown size but probably at most fifty people, announced that it had been set up as a national organization "to fight the injustices that particularly affect women." Its first campaign designed to protest "skyrocketing" food prices involved demonstration protests at the offices of the Price Commission in Washington, D. C. and the National Association of Food Chains. The specific objectives, which were of particular concern to poor women, included demands that stores rollback food prices 25 percent, carry the same quality goods and adopt the same pricing policy in poor and middle-income neighborhoods, and stop marking up food prices on the days when welfare and social security checks were delivered.[5]

The International Institute for Women's Studies of Washington, D. C. has an academic orientation and a very small staff. It was formed in the latter half of 1971 to carry out, encourage, and sponsor "research on women's nature and behavior," to serve as a clearinghouse for scholarly information on women, and to publish an interdisciplinary journal concerned with empirical and theoretical works on women.[6]

Women Involved of Cambridge, Massachusetts, formed in 1972, gives guidance to women activists. In order to facilitate "greater participation of women in all sectors of American society," it provides women with the skills and training necessary to their involvement in such institutions as "government politics, universities, and service organizations," and plans to achieve this objective through holding conferences and training institutes, as well as conducting research to find out in what areas women are most in need of help.[7]

Human Rights for Women (HRW) is a group of six women, three

of them lawyers, who incorporated in 1968 to undertake legal action in support of women denied their legitimate rights. Its secondary objectives are to promote research and education into the area of women's rights. HRW has provided legal assistance to women (at the Colgate-Palmolive Company) who argued that their exclusion from jobs requiring the lifting of thirty-five pounds or more had the discriminating effect of excluding them from high-paying jobs. It has filed *amicus* briefs supporting, for example, William Baird when he was convicted of violating a Massachusetts statute prohibiting the sale or gift of contraceptives to single people; and it has helped finance research on the oppression of the black woman and on female sexuality.

Another small organization, the Women's Lobby, formed in 1972 has the express purpose of lobbying in the federal government for the passage of legislation felt by the group to be in the interests of women. It is concerned with such areas as child care and education, the reform of social security, welfare, and credit laws, increasing the wages paid to domestic workers, and health care for women.

In 1970 some ten to twenty women, mostly from the Washington, D. C., area who were working in high-level government and professional posts founded Women United. Many of the founders had worked unsuccessfully for passage of the Equal Rights Amendment in the 1970–1971 legislative session. Their aim in creating Women United was to secure passage of the amendment. During the succeeding session they worked to coordinate the activities of proamendment groups, ranging from Women's Rights to Women's Liberation and from the Business and Professional Women's Clubs to the American Civil Liberties Union. After the amendment was passed at the federal level, Women United continued to distribute information on and encourage people to work for ratification by the states.

Similar groups have sprung up at the local level. Examples include "Pennsylvanian's for Women's Rights," "Women in Leadership" (a Philadelphia group offering to help women in local communities "who are seeking to effect change"), the "St. Louis Organization for Women's Rights," the "Oregon Council for Women's Equality," "Equal Opportunities for Women in the Augusta [Maine] Area," and "Focus on Equal Employment for Women" in Ann Arbor, Michigan.

Several independent small groups collect, publish, or distribute new feminist literature, bibliographies, and films. They include the Feminist Book Mart and the New Feminist Bookstore, which sell feminist books at reduced prices; four small presses—KNOW, Inc., The Feminist Press, Daughters, Inc., and Lollipop Power (non-sexist children's books); distributors of films, tapes and slide-shows—Media Plus, Inc., New Feminist

THE RANGE OF WOMEN'S RIGHTS GROUPS

Talent Associates, and Women on Words and Images; and an independent library, the Women's History Research Center. Some of these groups are off-shoots from NOW. Most are non-profit organizations trying to make enough money to cover expenses and to provide subsistence income to the people principally involved.

POLITICALLY ORIENTED WOMEN'S RIGHTS GROUPS

At the same time that NOW began to move into party politics a new variety of Women's Rights group appeared—one devoted primarily to political action. The first of these, the National Women's Political Caucus (NWPC) was organized in Washington, D. C., by a group of NOW women along with Betty Friedan, Congresswoman Bella Abzug, Gloria Steinem, and Congresswoman Shirley Chisholm. The caucus was designed to achieve the maximum representation of women and sympathetic men in local, state, and federal elections. The first meeting attracted a wide range of groups, including religious organizations, the League of Women Voters, Welfare Rights, the Business and Professional Women's Clubs, unions, and the new feminist groups. Between 500 and 700 local units have been formed subsequently: each drew from between thirty to several hundred women—on occasion as many as a thousand—to their initial meetings. On the whole, the more successful units have been led by women who had previously been involved in party politics, but this organization, like NOW, shows considerable internal variation.

In cooperation with other feminist groups and sympathetic organizations, the NWPC facilitated passage of the Equal Rights Amendment in the House and Senate and has been instrumental in more than doubling the proportions of women representatives at the 1972, as compared with the 1968, Republican and Democratic conventions (Republican: 38 vs. 17 percent; Democrat: 40 vs. 13 percent). State and local caucuses have lobbied and testified for women's issues in local legislatures, worked for state ratification of the Equal Rights Amendment, encouraged and supported women candidates for political office, and pressured local government officials to select women for appointive posts. By 1973 the caucus was realizing its hopes of being an umbrella organization for politically involved women whatever their race, religion, or political persuasion. The NWPC was not technically a membership organization until early 1973. At that time the national office reported a mailing list of 30,000 to 35,000 and estimated that there were thousands of participants in local caucuses who were not on the national mailing list.

Another politically oriented group, the Feminist Party, was formed in New York City in November 1971 by Florynce Kennedy, Ti-Grace

Atkinson, Rosalyn Baxandall, Bill Baird, and others. Like the Political Caucus, it organized into chapters (having eighty-five in the summer of 1972)[8] and planned to pressure the major political parties to incorporate feminist views and to select sympathetic male and female candidates. In contrast to the Political Caucus, however, it has given relatively more attention to issues which are not directly related to party politics; for example, the repeal of all abortion laws, and protests over women's "brutal and unlawful arrests by police."[9]

The Feminist Party and the Women's Political Caucus represent a recent trend in many Women's Rights groups and an occasional Women's Liberation group: a demand for the reallocation of traditional political power in the society. Feminists want to share political office and policy making with the established political parties.

MEMBERSHIP IN WOMEN'S RIGHTS GROUPS

Early in 1973 about 70,000 or 80,000 people belonged to Women's Rights groups (including NOW but excluding the women's interest groups mentioned earlier in this chapter). The total number of participants in Women's Rights and Women's Liberation groups was probably between 80,000 and 100,000. This figure is arrived at by adding the best available membership estimates for the groups discussed: I have no way way of estimating the possible overlap in membership among the groups. Membership may seem small unless one realizes that it includes only participants in what I have called Women's Rights and Women's Liberation groups. Large numbers of people sympathize with the feminist cause without joining a feminist organization. Many other sympathizers join other types of feminist groups. The actual participants in any group advocating a social change typically are a very small proportion of all those sympathetic to the change in the population at large. In the following chapter I will give evidence that the Women's Rights and Women's Liberation participants similarly are leading a trend toward the acceptance of feminist ideas by the society as a whole.

ORGANIZATION

The Women's Rights groups range from conservative to radical. Examples of conservative groups are the Women's Equity Action League, the Women's Legal Defense Fund, Women United, and Human Rights for Women. Examples of relatively radical groups are Women United for Action, and the Feminist Party. No simple continuum exists, however, between more and less conservative Women's Rights groups. Like any of the several segments of NOW, a given group may be conservative in some respects and quite radical in others.

Cutting across these intragroup and intergroup differences are patterns of organizational development comparable to patterns I have already identified for NOW: these involve increasingly sophisticated forms of organizational management combined with an attempt to remain uniquely concerned with the welfare of the individual member. Not all groups have gone through such a development; those which were founded more recently usually started with a more traditional sort of operation.

Individual members are being urged to prepare carefully before plunging into social action. As a result, for example, members of a Political Caucus chapter have held practice debates on the pros and cons of the Equal Rights Amendment in preparation for the public debates that would precede state legislatures' discussions of ratification.

> Do you turn pale when someone says "Do you want your 18-year-old daughter to slough through the mud in Viet Nam. . . ." If you do, come to our next meeting to learn both one-line 'zinger' and 35-minute esoteric responses.[11]

Members and subgroups within an organization have grown increasingly careful to allocate scarce time and energy efficiently. For example, they have become more discriminating in the legal work they take on, selecting cases and issues that, for the same amount of work would create more total legal impact and bring them more publicity. Dr. Bernice Sandler, a psychologist, launched WEAL's wide-ranging attack on sex discrimination in the universities when she learned that, under the provisions of Executive Order 11246 as amended by Executive Order 11375, the Department of Health, Education and Welfare was required to investigate any complaint of sex discrimination in organizations receiving government contracts. Since essentially all universities have substantial government contracts, WEAL could avoid the time and expense of individual lawsuits by working through HEW. Since WEAL's complaints were accompanied by quantities of carefully compiled data, all parties concerned—colleges, universities, WEAL, and HEW—knew that the complaints had to be treated seriously. Similarly, WEAL recognized that expert testimony by its lawyers at government hearings on such issues as the reputation of gas and electric companies regarding sex discrimination was more economical of their own time and money and would have more total effect upon the position of women in general than would the successful completion of a few individual lawsuits.

In general, when Women's Rights groups have taken on individual lawsuits, they have selected cases that set legal precedents or that attack the practices of a large or a representative company. For example, NOW lawyers won Lorena Weeks's suit against Southern Bell Telephone and Telegraph Company, forcing Southern Bell to give Ms. Weeks a job as a switchman and over $30,000 in back pay. The case was significant because it was the first interpretation of the "bona fide occupational qualification" exception to Title VII of the Civil Rights Act of 1964. The Fifth U.S. Circuit Court interpreted the exception narrowly, giving Ms. Weeks her job and indirectly opening to women a wide range of jobs. Similarly the Women's Legal Defense Fund has attacked discrimination within the unions by representing a research assistant employed by the Communication Workers of America and filing complaints in her name with the EEOC and the Office of Contract Compliance.

Legislation is another area where these new organizations, like NOW, have rapidly learned to make effective use of their able but hard-worked personnel. By 1973 they were commonly reporting in newsletters and circulars the status of proposed legislation that was of potential interest to women. They described "desirable" and "undesirable" bills that were currently in local and national legislatures, evaluated their chances for passage, and explained which representatives members should contact if they wished to express support or opposition. In 1971 both Women United and WEAL began sending out reports on the status of pending federal legislation.[12] These reports not only provided information on what others were doing, but also on what readers could do for themselves. For example, they stated the positions of senators and congressmen regarding the Equal Rights Amendment, said which legislators were fence-sitting and were most likely to be influenced by constituents' mail, and gave the official wording of the amendment as supported by the women's groups. All these details greatly simplified the task of constituents who wished to write their legislators. (The same publications report statements made by major political figures regarding feminist questions. Thus they simultaneously inform the woman who is "on their side" and, by informing legislators that their views are being publicized, exert pressure on the politicians themselves.)

When bills have been passed Women's Rights groups have summarized in newsletters the bills' contents, their possible effects, and the actions women should take to benefit by the legislation. Thus in 1972 many groups passed on to members information concerning federal legislation permitting tax deductions for child care, changes in the social security laws which made them more equitable in their treatment of women and men, and the extension of the Federal Equal Pay Act (through the medium of the 1972 Higher Education Act) to apply to executive, administrative, and professional employees.

Such information was passed on also at the workshops that have become a major part of local and national conferences. By 1972 and 1973 workshops had shifted their emphasis from discussion (e.g. "The Problems of Working Women") to social action (e.g. "How to Organize Working Women"). Newsletters assumed a similar approach: the Indiana Women's Political Caucus newsletter explained "How to Organize a Local Caucus":

> After you have started . . . make sure that your organizing activities continue to reach a broad cross-section of women in your state or community. Build a good relationship with the media. . . . Let the caucus act as a catalyst.[13]

The North Carolina Caucus used its newsletter to explain in detail how local political units operate and how they can best be influenced:

> Political units, precincts or wards are made up of people on your block or your road who are registered to vote or who are not registered. A precinct which is the usual term is a geographical unit with boundaries and with a specific place to vote. Average precincts range from 500 to 2000 voters and about one-third will not be registered.
>
> The boundaries of your precinct and the names of those who are registered are available for use and inspection at the local registrar's office in your most local governmental unit, your town, county or city. They also have information you need on the legal requirements to register and when and where to register.[14]

A number of groups, like NOW, have started to distribute "kits," "packets" of information, or booklets dealing with specific issues. In 1973 the "Materials Division" of WEAL's national office was distributing to state divisions packets of practical information on such topics as the pros and cons of the Equal Rights Amendment and "how to prepare a job resume." In December 1972 the National Women's Political Caucus reported plans for publishing a booklet based upon the actual experience of women political candidates explaining, for example, what factors they had found most helpful and most detrimental in their campaigns, analyzing whether involvement in the women's movement helped or hindered women candidates, and explaining where they found money and volunteer help.[15]

Many groups have compiled and distributed feminist bibliographies, particularly of newly published books. More recently they have listed publications that have immediate practical application. For example, Human Rights for Women lists federal government publications on "Equal Pay in the United States," "Continuing Education Programs and Services for Women," "The Equal Rights Amendment and Alimony and

Support Laws," Senate and House Hearings on the Equal Rights Amendment, "Who Are the Working Women," and its own publication by Mary Eastwood, "Fighting Job Discrimination—Three Federal Approaches."[16] Similarly, the Women's Legal Defense Fund is selling a booklet that deals with questions commonly asked by women who want to change their names.[17]

Responding to the frequently heard complaint by employers that qualified women are not available, a number of groups have created some form of job roster. Their early efforts to place women in jobs were largely wasted because the enormous volume of clerical work never got done, because job information could rarely be distributed to potential applicants before deadlines expired, and because potential employers would not use the services. Recently, a few groups (such as the state Political Caucuses) have compiled lists of government jobs together with lists of employed and unemployed women qualified to fill these positions as a strategy to convince local officials that qualified women are, in fact, available for government posts.

Fund-raising is another area where the Women's Rights groups are growing more experienced. Almost all rely heavily upon members' contributions and (steadily increasing) dues. Their fund-raising efforts run the same gamut as those devised by NOW.

Several groups have established tax-exempt subdivisions comparable to NOW's Legal and Educational Defense Fund, or have achieved tax-exempt status for the organization as a whole. WEAL created its Education and Legal Defense Fund in 1972; the Women's Action Alliance and Human Rights for Women were founded as tax-exempt non-political groups, and the Women's Legal Defense Fund amended its by laws in late 1971 to meet the requirements for tax exemption.

COOPERATION AND COMMUNICATION

During the early 1970s the Women's Rights groups increasingly worked in cooperation with Women's Liberation groups, with all other feminist groups, and with nonfeminist groups. Such cooperation has been assisted greatly by an improvement in the communications based upon feminist publications and, to some extent, the mass media. The mass media spread general ideas about feminism and the feminist literature spreads specific information. The first new feminist publications began primarily as newsletters for individual Women's Liberation and Women's Rights groups; but during the early 1970s a number of these broadened their scope to report the activities of the full range of feminist groups, from radical to conservative. Thus radical women were informed about the activities of NOW and WEAL, while conservative women learned about Women's Liberation actions and ideology. Periodicals that were addressed to radical and moderately radical women included *Off Our Backs* (Washington, D. C.), *The Majority Report* (New York City), *Pandora* (Seattle), and *Her-self* (Chicago). Publications that appealed to more conservative women included *The Spokeswoman* (Chicago), *Women Today* (Washington, D. C.), and *The Woman Activist* (Arlington, Virginia).

While feminist periodicals have kept interested women informed about relevant developments inside and outside of the movement, cooperation among feminist groups depends, ultimately, upon personal contacts. At local and national levels, feminists meet each other at conferences (such as the organizing sessions of the Women's Political Caucuses), legislative hearings, public meetings, panel discussions, demonstrations, local school board meetings, and so forth.

Cooperative endeavors generally center around legislative and legal issues. The most notable of these has been work for passage of the Equal Rights Amendment. In Washington, Women's Liberation and Women's Rights groups joined with such old-established groups as the Business and Professional Women's Clubs, the American Association of University Women, and the American Civil Liberties Union to work for passage of the amendment. Similar coalitions, usually spearheaded by one organization, have worked for ratification in individual states.

The Women's Legal Defense Fund has worked with the Liberation-oriented Women's National Abortion Action Coalition challenging the legality of the District of Columbia abortion regulations, in particular the required twenty-four-hour waiting period. Also in Washington, local chapters of NOW and WEAL, the staff of *Off Our Backs*, and other groups have opposed the budget request for the Women's Detention Center because, they said, women prisoners were systematically neglected and received even worse treatment than male prisoners in the district system. Many NOW chapters regularly worked with Liberation groups on the abortion issue. Typically, NOW members would provide legal testimony, while Liberation group members would provide testimony of women's actual experiences. For a sit-in designed as a joint effort to "desexigrate" a restaurant's luncheon facilities in a west coast city, one Liberation member reported wearing a dress and stockings for the first time in months. Women's Rights groups commonly collaborate on legal cases with one group filing suit and others filing *amicus* briefs.

Cooperation of both Women's Liberation and Women's Rights groups with the traditional women's organizations or other reform groups as well as with each other has increased rapidly. Early in 1972, NOW members began to list their names with the Business and Professional

Women's Talent Bank. In Ohio, WEAL was instrumental in forming a state-level lobbying group, the Network for the Economic Rights of Women, consisting of representatives from NOW, the ACLU, the United Auto Workers, and the Amalgamated Meatcutters. NOW, WEAL, and several women's caucuses from professional societies and other organizations have sued the National Institutes of Health for sex discrimination in making appointments to NIH public advisory groups. A coalition of seven women's organizations, including five Women's Rights groups, the Center for Women's Policy Studies, and the Women's Project of the ACLU, has sought George Meany's support as president of the AFL-CIO in achieving an expanded role for women within the trade unions. Another coalition of groups from Maryland and the District of Columbia selected November 1972 as a month in which to pressure credit card companies to issue credit cards to women in their own names (e.g., Mary Jones, not Mrs. John Jones) and without regard to their marital status. The Women's Legal Defense Fund has represented a coalition of NOW chapters, Women's Political Caucus chapters, WEAL, and the District of Columbia chapter of FEW in a petition to the Federal Communications Commission to deny the D. C. area station, WRC-TV, renewal of its license on the grounds that the station discriminated against women at all levels of employment and that on the air its treatment of women and women's issues was biased. In New York City the WLDF joined NOW in presenting a similar petition to block the renewal of WABC-TV's license.

These, and many other cooperative ventures, have certainly increased the impact of feminist groups at local and national levels. They have not, however, been free of problems. The most serious difficulties arise when groups differ in style and ideology. At times these differences are simply annoying to participants; on other occasions they are disruptive. One such incident occurred at the organizing conference of the National Women's Political Caucus (Washington, D. C., 1971). While the details of the incident are disputed, it is clear that a violent debate arose over the question of whether Senator Eugene McCarthy and Dr. Benjamin Spock were to be allowed to address the meeting as arranged by some of the organizers. More conservative members of Women's Rights groups, union representatives, and representatives of the National Welfare Rights Organization were dismayed at the interruptions and heckling from a few of the more radical members of NOW. A black woman from the NWRO finally lost patience: dressed in a simple cotton frock with none of the middle-class chic of most of the black and white women present, she firmly expressed her anger at the rudeness. The interruptions stopped, to the visible relief of the majority of those present.

For their part, the radicals regarded it as a compromise of feminist principles to listen respectfully to a man who once supported woman's traditional role as enthusiastically as Spock did. Unsoothed by Spock's promises of a "revised edition," and dissatisfied with McCarthy's response to their challenge over one of his votes regarding the Equal Rights Amendment, they argued that Spock and McCarthy were exploiting the Caucus for their own political advantage. Moreover, they were disappointed to see a feminist group like the Caucus adopting the norms of the male establishment—following the private decision of an "elite" group rather than operating by consensus reached by open discussion, and showing hypocritical politeness in the name of parliamentary procedure. They feared that the changes they observed symbolized a decline of new feminist idealism.

A second criticism made by radical feminists of the conservative Women's Rights groups' cooperative endeavors is that they are oriented toward the interests of middle-class and professional women. The Women's Rights activists object strongly to such suggestions. They point out that most of the job discrimination cases they take on involve women in the lowest wage categories; that they are trying to work with the trade unions; that their work for improved child support laws will give most help to poor women because poor women are least likely to receive adequate payments under the existing system;[18] and that abortion law repeal helps poor more than middle-class women because, when abortions are illegal, only middle-class women can afford medically safe (if illegal) abortions. Liberation groups and radicals within Women's Rights groups, on the other hand, point out that other feminists are working to bring middle-class women into the higher echelons of business, government, religion, colleges and universities, politics, and the law.

As with all efforts at social change, it is very difficult to measure the impact of Women's Rights activities upon any one group of people. Whether (and in what respects) middle-class women are helped more than lower-class women will, at least for a while, remain uncertain.

PART FIVE

FEMINISM AND AMERICAN SOCIETY

CHAPTER ELEVEN

THE ORIGINS, SPREAD, AND FUTURE OF THE NEW FEMINIST MOVEMENT

The most satisfactory explanation of feminism's recent revival lies in an analysis of the long-term development of male and female roles within the context of the developing American society.[1] Since any such effort to set the present movement into the context of decades, even centuries, of social change requires a volume in itself, I shall here identify only the movement's proximate causes and relate them to the equivalent causes of the analogous nineteenth-century movement.[2]

THE ORIGINS

Social Climate and Social Reform

It has frequently been observed that both the nineteenth- and the twentieth-century feminist movements appeared at times of unusual enthusiasm for social reform. In addition, since both abolition in the nineteenth century and civil rights in the twentieth preceded a feminist movement, the suggestion frequently arises that the movement for black equality somehow "caused" the women's movements. Either women's rights ideologies are considered a logical and obvious outgrowth of the blacks' rights ideologies or women are seen as applying attitudes toward blacks to their own social position. This sort of explanation, while not inaccurate, is overly simplified.

Underlying the emergence of each feminist movement has been a reformist ideology which provided a rationale for the emergence of many reform movements. The nineteenth-century feminists, like their near-contemporary abolitionists, argued for the cause by referring to prevailing "radical" ideas about the "natural rights" of all persons, who shared a "common humanity," and "deserved justice." Yet, they also agreed with most of their contemporaries that although blacks and whites, and men and women were more nearly equal than had previously been assumed, important differences between the groups would always remain. In the women's case, all but a few reformers believed that the home would always be woman's primary concern.

Imbued with the optimism of its era, the early-to-mid-nineteenth-century reform ethic also stated that once downtrodden people were given freedom, or a job, or a new start in life they could, by their own efforts, make their lives personally rewarding. Very few reformers envisioned that drastic changes in American institutions were necessary if the pursuit of happiness was to be a reasonable goal for most people. The feminists, following the same reasoning, believed that women's position could be reformed within the existing societal context: once women achieved legal and educational equality, they would by their own efforts be able to transform their lives. Only the most radical feminists, such as Elizabeth Cady Stanton, disagreed.

A hundred years later a new set of feminist ideas grew out of the new radical ideologies of the 1960s. Two aspects of these ideologies were developed in particular by both the civil rights and the feminist movements. First, it was argued that socialization, not biological inheritance accounted for minority group members' differences in ability, temperament, and so forth. Out of this argument came the feminists' belief that female socialization was a debilitating experience of fundamental importance. Of equal significance was the notion that individuals and groups are oppressed not simply by other individuals and groups but also by a multitude of institutions ranging from industry through schools to politics. Thus, in addition to legal and attitudinal change, reform depended upon structural change. This idea encouraged the nascent feminists to question the organization of such institutions as the family and industry and the traditional division of labor between the sexes.

Although faith in the efficacy of social structural change constitutes the basis of the modern radicals' faith in progress, they have not described their ideal social forms but, instead, believe that these must be discovered through trial and error. "The commitment to action in the knowledge that the consequences of action can never be fully predicted in advance . . . remains the single most characteristic element of the thought-world of the New Left."[3] In the same way the feminist finds it unnecessary to describe the ideal society and ideal male and female roles: she believes that these can best be discovered through experiment.

Interestingly, the twentieth-century movement's founders report personally that they did not draw their inspiration from their nineteenth-century predecessors. They began to examine the earlier movement's ideas only after their own movement was established. The contemporary movement owes its existence far more directly to the radical ideologies of the 1960s than to the feminist ideology of the nineteenth century.

Thus, the nineteenth- and twentieth-century feminist movements drew upon the prevailing ideas of social reform in creating their respective ideologies. Yet, neither emerged with a completely synthesized analysis: rather, in the process of, first, forming and, later, working for feminist groups, participants elaborated the ideas in their own distinctive way.

Relative Deprivation

Neither the nineteenth- nor the twentieth-century feminist movements appeared as a simple response to the radical reform ideologies of its day. Each movement arose following a period during which women's discontent, or sense of relative deprivation, was gradually aggravated.

In the nineteenth century, just as in the twentieth, feminism's chief advocates came from the middle class. These relatively well-to-do women were, historically speaking, a step ahead of lower-class women in that they were less preoccupied with the material concerns of daily life and had more energy to devote to other matters. But they found few outlets for this energy. Intellectually and physically American men were exploring new frontiers from which women were excluded by the Victorian "cult of true womanhood." According to this conception of femininity, inside the home woman's spiritual and moral superiority enabled her to be guardian of the virtuous life while outside the home her physical and intellectual weakness compelled her to defer to men's natural superiority. In an era, then, of generally rising expectations, women, in contrast to men, were not only prevented from aspiring to new goals, they were also subject to a new set of psychological restraints in the form of an extreme conception of the traditional feminine role. As these restraints became progressively more institutionalized and thus less bearable, women became progressively more disposed to support a feminist movement.[4]

The contemporary middle-class woman is likely to experience a sense of deprivation comparable to that of her nineteenth-century predecessors but derived from quite different sources. She is educated to meet the challenges of life outside as well as inside the home; and she expects to meet those challenges. Yet, in actuality, discrimination and social disapproval of the employed woman have discouraged her efforts. In addition homemaking is no longer so demanding (and perhaps so satisfying) as it was before the introduction of labor-saving devices, the mass production of food, clothes, and home furnishings, and the advent of effective birth control technology. Outside the home the professionalization of much of the more stimulating and responsible volunteer work meant that women were excluded from activities which, traditionally, had been a legitimate outlet for their creative abilities. William Henry Chafe has documented the gradual buildup of women's sense of frustration during and after World War II.[5] Having first broken into the job market in significant numbers during the war, more and more women (in particular married women over the age of thirty-five) joined the work force in the years following 1945. An increasing proportion of middle-class women experienced the problems of discrimination, and of coping with their dual roles as homemakers and workers; at the same time, the expressed societal values praised full-time motherhood and implicitly or explicitly criticized the working woman, especially the woman who worked for personal satisfaction rather than because her family needed the money. The discrepancies between expectations and realized goals continued to grow throughout the 1950s and 1960s.

Eventually there appeared a counterbalance to the general emphasis upon the woman's traditional role. While the dominant view of woman's place remained unchanged, a growing number of popular writers and scholars began to question this role. Betty Friedan's book *The Feminine Mystique*[6] has been by far the most popular presentation of the nontraditional view. Other writers who before or shortly after Friedan elaborated the same or similar themes included Simone de Beauvoir, Doris Lessing, Ruth Hershberger, Edith de Rham, Eve Merriam, and Florida Scott-Maxwell.[7] Policy makers and scholars analyzed the "new" woman problem. President Kennedy appointed his Commission on the Status of Women in 1961; in 1963 the first legislation involving sex discrimination, the Equal Pay Act, was passed. Symposia on the new role of women in American society were held at the Massachusetts Institute of Technology, presented in an issue of *Daedalus*, and in a book by the Alliance of Unitarian Women.[8]

Despite the changes, the prevailing ethos in American society extolled the woman's traditional role. That some women's ideas were at odds with this ethos is illustrated in my interviews. About half of my respondents who were over the age of twenty-eight read *The Feminine Mystique* shortly after it was first published in 1963. About half of these said that they were seriously influenced by Friedan's ideas and greatly relieved to discover that someone shared their worries. The comments made by two of these women illustrate the nonconformist's isolation; "It hit me like a bomb. . . . For one thing, I knew then there were two kooks in the world"; and, "By the time I had . . . [read] Friedan . . . and Simone de Beauvoir . . . I had thought it all out but there was no response to my ideas and I had not time enough and was not pushy enough [to protest]." Most people, however, accepted the inconsistency: women of all social classes were in paid employment but the only place that they belonged was in the home. For the most part, people's attitudes had not caught up with the changed reality of women's participation in the work force and their desire for greater involvement in the society at large. Only when the new feminist movement crystallized a minority's discontent did the majority consider whether women were, or should be, satisfied in their traditional role.

Creation of a Feminist Ideology

From among the many women who personally experienced a growing sense of deprivation, a small minority founded the nineteenth- and twentieth-century feminist movements. During each period, nascent feminists came together in the course of their work for other reformist groups. They exchanged ideas about their social situation, shared experiences, and, inspired by the reformist ideology of their time, developed their own ideology.

During the nineteenth century many women who eventually became active feminists started out in the movement for abolition and in the course of the Civil War worked for service organizations on the northern side. Their experiences dramatically demonstrated the severe restrictions placed on women at that time. When they carried antislavery petitions from house to house men and women mocked them for unwomanly behavior: a husband or brother should be there to protect them. Furthermore, a woman had no right to urge people to sign petitions—such political work was for men.[9] Thus, women who were disposed to become feminists took what was, for the nineteenth century, the radical step of joining a reform movement. Their experiences working for reform then made some of these nascent feminists acutely conscious of their oppression as women.

Two women who were later to be key figures in the feminist movement shared a particularly dramatic experience of the restraints placed upon women when they attended the 1840 World Antislavery Convention held in London. Elizabeth Cady Stanton and Lucretia Mott, along with other women, were denied seats on account of their sex, despite the fact that, informally, they represented the many thousands of women who worked for the antislavery cause.

Working for another reform—temperance—Susan B. Anthony encountered great anti-female prejudice in her efforts to organize women in temperance societies. The men's opposition and the women's complete economic dependence on their husbands caused the demise of all the local groups she founded. Four years of such experiences between 1848 and 1852 helped to solidify her lifelong commitment to the feminist movement.

Other women were "radicalized" during the Civil War. Among them were women who worked for the Sanitary Commission, the organization which served as informal quartermaster and nursing agency to the Union soldiers, run primarily by women. Women in some 7,000 local societies organized bazaars and other events to raise funds. Others worked in the hospitals, distributing supplies and nursing the wounded. Yet men led the commission; for the time being most of the women accepted this secondary status, but some of them began to question their complete dependence upon the male world.

Thus, working together for reform in nonfeminist areas, these women realized how greatly they were disadvantaged by both law and custom. Given the social climate of the time, they believed their claim to greater equality clearly justified. It was these rights that the reformer-feminists began to advocate at the series of Women's Rights conventions held between 1848 and 1860 and to request in their petitions for government reform of women's legal status. They urged, for example, that married women retain title to property they brought into a marriage and that they have the right to keep any wages they earned after marriage. (At that time most feminists considered suffrage too radical a proposal to have a chance of acceptance even among their own ranks.)

Similar processes characterize the development of the contemporary feminist movement. The protest groups of the 1960s performed in less than ten years the same function as the reform movements of the forty years from 1830 to 1870—within them women became first radicalized then organized. Women participants in the civil rights, antiwar, and other movements personally experienced and objected to the socially imposed limits on their behavior. The movements were supposed to be democratic, but that democracy did not extend to them. Women performed the routine organizational chores; the men disregarded their efforts to get into the action, and the decision-making core of the movement was kept exclusively male. The feminists complained that influence was bought at the price of establishing sexual liaisons with male leaders. Some of these radical women eventually formed the Women's Liberation movement.[10]

The second group of modern feminists, those who founded NOW, were brought together mostly by their work for the federal and state Commissions on the Status of Women. Although they worked in a liberal climate that stressed equality of opportunity, they despaired of achieving change through established government channels, and they resolved to fight for the feminist cause as an independent group, the National Organization for Women.

Like their nineteenth-century predecessors, the founders of the twentieth-century feminist groups were bothered by the relative deprivation of the female as compared with the male role. Working together in what contemporary society regarded as radical or reformist activity, they exchanged ideas and came to realize the extent to which other women shared their sense of constraint; the prevailing philosophy of social reform served as a base from which to develop and then enlarge upon their own feminist ideology; and, finally, the movement's founders drew upon their experience with other reformist organizations in creating their own exclusively feminist organizations.

WHY FEMINISM IN THE UNITED STATES?

Many people ask: "Why should American women, who are the most liberated in the world, start a new feminist movement?" They argue that in the underdeveloped countries, such as India, women are far more "oppressed" than they are in America. Even in highly industrialized countries, such as England, the traditional role of woman-in-the-home is generally accepted and rarely protested.

The answer lies in the women's personal expectations and aspirations. Those in most of the underdeveloped countries learn from childhood that male and female roles are quite distinct. Whatever the authority relationships between husband and wife, women know that their assigned role brings them certain rights as well as responsibilities. Unlike American middle-class women, they have not also learned conflicting societal values relating to a general achievement ethic. Moreover, it can be argued that for them, the female role is more satisfying than is the equivalent American role since these women are necessary to the household in a way that American women are not. Thus, unlike American women, they have not learned to expect more from society than it can offer them, and they have a meaningful role to play in both family and community.[11] Finally, the social change which would benefit such women most is an improvement in the standard of living. Since men want the same change, the women do not need to form a separate movement to work for it.

Other industrial societies, generally comparable to the United States, differ from this country in two ways which are crucial to the development of the new feminist movement. First, women can still perform a significant, and satisfying, job even if they confine themselves entirely to life in the home because the job is more demanding than it is in the more highly mechanized American household. Second, the middle-class women who might spearhead a feminist movement have been *relatively* more successful in finding household help in the form of relatives or of working-class women. (In many industrial countries, however, this situation is changing rapidly and support for "women's rights" is growing.)

Other factors, too, contribute to the American woman's comparatively greater dissatisfaction. The work ethic, the belief (accurate or not) in the "land of opportunity," and the example of the "pioneer" woman, all encourage women to "do something" with their lives. In the United States such self-expression is often seen in terms of paid employment while in other countries leisure activities are more likely to be socially approved and practically available outlets for self-development. Thus men as well as women can gain personal satisfaction and social recognition by developing talents for gardening, sports, home maintenance, or just plain sociability. This is not to suggest a drastic contrast between the United States and other industrialized nations; it merely suggests that *on the whole* American society channels the opportunities for personal development into remunerative work, and correspondingly, it sets a high value upon this sort of achievement. Denied access to the more rewarding forms of paid employment, and denied socially applauded alternative activities inside and outside of the home, American women have initiated, out of their sense of frustration, the twentieth-century revival of feminism.

THE SPREAD OF NEW FEMINIST IDEAS

The Women's Liberation and Women's Rights groups are the small, highly visible core of a large-scale modern feminist movement. During the three years between 1970 and 1973 their new feminist ideology became a matter for serious concern. Much of what they said was accepted by men and women throughout the society. The women's movement galvanized these people into action.

Among the many traditional feminist organizations that have found new feminist ideas consistent with their past orientation is the YWCA. At its national convention in the spring of 1970, it adopted a series of resolutions to "strengthen women's freedom." In May of the same year a YWCA "Women's Resource Center" was established to act as a "catalyst for . . . change in the cultural concepts of women and their life styles and in the institutions that discriminate against them." The center provided opportunity for:

> dialogue in small group settings where women might clarify their feelings, think about new life styles, and mobilize to change the dehumanizing aspect of the society in which women and men live today, thus engaging themselves in the very process of liberation. . . . [We] are grateful to the many offshoots within the women's liberation movement who have lifted up in new ways many issues which we in the YWCA are *for*— and have been over the years. . . . In numbers few women are men haters unless the term is applied to those who confront males who discriminate, exploit or oppress women deliberately or unconsciously.
>
> Women can be their own worst enemy . . . when they raise children in a dwarfing atmosphere of stereotypes . . . when they perpetuate racist practices . . . when they live only through men.[12]

Later that year the Resource Center reported a survey of YWCA teenage leaders. It found, for example, that approximately 60 percent of the respondents were in favor of child-care facilities outside of the home, believed that men should help with household chores, and that a husband's identity should not be given priority at the wife's expense.[13]

Among the other traditionally feminist groups, the American Association of University Women stated in 1970: "We believe . . . woman is about to flex her muscles, stand tall, and seek nothing short of full equality of the sexes."[14] And, the same year the American Home Economics Association demanded an end to sex discrimination in education, business, industry, and government; it supported the Equal Rights Amendment; and it advocated repeal of laws restricting or prohibiting abortions.[15]

Women have also become progressively more active within a wide range of institutionalized groups. These include professional societies and even trade unions. Members of the American Newspaper Guild lobbied for, and achieved, a conference on sex discrimination within both the guild and the newspaper world at large. Later, the guild's house organ reiterated in a lead article the conference's conclusion that unequal treatment for women would "no longer be tolerated."[16] Women telephone operators were hesitant about participating in a July 1971 strike against the American Telephone and Telegraph Company but were willing once they found out that company retaliation against strikers was illegal. Referring to how the women had been ignorant of their rights, one operator commented, "Maybe it's about time for a little more women's lib in the Union."[17] Women white collar workers at a Chicago insurance brokerage firm affiliated themselves with the Communication Workers of America even though they believed the union to be antifeminist. They argued that women had to build themselves a strong base *within* the union movement.[18]

Women members of the professional organizations joined early to fight against subtle and overt forms of sex discrimination. Between 1969 and 1973 about twenty-five of the national societies in such fields as microbiology, political science, mathematics, library science, psychology, sociology, and physics set up women's caucuses or their equivalent. Caucus members have conducted surveys of discrimination, held panel discussions at their national society meetings, and successfully introduced to the business meetings motions in favor of equal opportunity, the Equal Rights Amendment, provisions for child-care facilities at national meetings, endorsement of the principle of parenthood leaves (for men as well as women), the creation of courses on women,[19] and the abolition of nepotism rules.

In a related professional group, the American Association of University Professors' "Committee W" (on the status of women in the professions) has been activated for the first time since 1928. Groups with similar goals have been formed within limited geographical areas. For example, in Ann Arbor, women created the organization PROBE to protect the rights of all women employed by the University of Michigan.

Women have also become progressively more active within a wide range of institutionalized religious groups. As early as 1970 Church Women United accused John Gardner's Common Cause organization of discrimination because its board contained only three women—and their names were left off the brochure advertising the group. (In subsequent years Common Cause has become a strong advocate of women's rights.) In September 1972 women's task forces from the United Church of Christ and the United Presbyterian Church in the U. S. A. joined NOW in filing a petition with the Securities and Exchange Commission seeking rules to require members of the national stock exchanges to take affirmative action to eliminate sex discrimination in employment. Within the Catholic Church activist nuns have created a new umbrella organization "Sisters Uniting" with the objective of helping member groups play a more active role in religious, political, and economic affairs.[20] The National Council of Churches has established a Corporate Information Center with the purpose of evaluating the policies of American corporations regarding the hiring and promotion of minority groups and women. The president of the National Women's Division of the American Jewish Congress urged an "intensified drive for women's equality in housing, employment, social rights and other areas where stubborn discrimination against women as women has not yet yielded to the times."[21] In the Protestant churches, women seminary students are demanding the opportunity not only to be ordained but also to fill jobs traditionally held only by ordained men.

Organizations with broadly liberal goals have recently adopted feminist positions often without direct pressure from feminist groups inside or outside the organization. The American Civil Liberties Union made "women's rights" its top priority program for 1972.[22] Common Cause, responding to pressure by the Women's Political Caucus, Church Women United, and other groups had, by the end of 1971, announced its commitment to women's rights including support for the Equal Rights Amendment, support for the Equal Employment Opportunity Commission's authority to enforce rulings concerning sex discrimination and, in its own internal organization, the election of seven women to its governing board. Ralph Nader's Public Citizen has demonstrated its expressed concern for discrimination against women by awarding a $10,000 grant to the newly formed Center for Women's Policy Studies; and Zero Population Growth has supported antidiscriminatory measures.

Even the political and government establishment show signs of responding to a general feminist climate of opinion. In the summer of 1972 the Republican and Democratic parties made serious attempts to increase the proportion of women delegates at the national conventions. Politicians from both parties expressed approval of the formation of the National Women's Political Caucus in July 1971. The federal administration specifically encouraged women to apply for the prestigious White House Fellowships. The U. S. Air Force, in a questionnaire survey, showed sensitivity to feminist issues by adopting a questionnaire which spoke of an officer's spouse rather than wife, and of the officer as he/she.[23] The navy reversed a long-standing tradition by assigning female personnel to duty on warships.

In the business world, some firms have begun to reevaluate their use of womanpower. Some, responding to newly established legal precedents, have modified their maternity leave requirements and a few have guaranteed women the right to return to their jobs after childbirth. Some have responded to pressures to establish child care facilities. Others are encouraging (or at least permitting) women to move into management posts.

Newspapers and periodicals are continually listing women's "first's"— a police captain in New York City, a Supreme Court justice in New Mexico, a jockey, the president of the National Council of Churches, a rabbi, and U. S. Army generals. Equally common are feature stories on women who hold such traditionally male jobs as field engineer, truck driver, executive, zoo keeper, minister, and air conditioning and refrigeration engineer.

By 1971 the press routinely discussed the reorientation of male and female roles. While it showed little enthusiasm for this aspect of the movement, it was beginning to comment favorably on the feminist groups working for legal, economic, and political equality. Articles documenting sex discrimination became common. When the National Women's Political Caucus was formed, many parts of the press reacted enthusiastically: the feminists had become more respectable. It seemed that they wanted to work within the existing political parties for such idealistic goals as the elimination of sexism, racism, violence, and poverty. *The New York Times* commented editorially on the "falling off of the noisier aspects of the women's liberation movement . . . leaving the emphasis where it belongs on the incontrovertible case that inequality between the sexes does exist."[24] *Time* magazine, while not without reservations, was generally in favor of the Caucus and, significantly, was critical of President Nixon's negative reaction. It quoted the secretary of state, William Rogers, as saying that a photograph of four caucus leaders looked " 'like a burlesque' " and President Nixon as replying, " 'What's wrong with that?' " *Time* deplored the remarks: "Faced with that kind of crude, belittling response, it is no wonder that women are often provoked to sharp recriminations, and sometimes to stretching a point beyond reason."[25] Toward the end of 1971 *Women's Wear Daily* claimed that it was the first national publication to adopt the use of Ms. in place of Miss or Mrs.[26] Soon after, the Minneapolis *Star* became the first newspaper to drop experimentally the use of Miss and Mrs.: its first reference to a woman would be as "Mary Doe"; second and later references would read simply "Doe." Ms. would not be used.[27]

Comparable sensitivity to the new movement has been shown by the publishers of *American Men of Science* in their decision, made in 1971, to change the reference work's name to *American Men and Women of Science*. Even *The Farmer's Almanac* has been rethinking (though not reversing) its attitudes toward women. In 1972 it announced that although the following edition would still contain such advice as "One of the best ways for a woman to catch a man is to keep her trap shut," it would have a two-page article "quite complimentary to the role of women in the world" because "The belief that 'It's a man's world,' quite evidently becomes less valid with every passing day and year."[28]

Advertisers, public relations men, manufacturers, and publishers have become sensitive to feminist issues and the possible adverse financial effects of slighting women. In December 1972 a travel goods store advertised in the *New Yorker* "Peace on Earth, Goodwill Toward Men and Women." Pharmaceutical manufacturers advertise about the valuable service the registered pharmacist performs: "That means he (or she, because 20% of today's pharmacy students are women). . . ." The U. S. government selling silver dollars, and manufacturers selling baby carriers, skis, or academic gowns are careful to refer to purchasers or recipients as "he or she." Some newspapers have relabeled "Women's Pages" as "Family

Living," "Living Styles," or "family, food, fashion, furnishings." Textbook publishers have asked authors to avoid "sexist" writing:

> Girls and women should not be shown as more fearful of danger, mice, snakes, and insects than boys and men are in similar situations. . . . Both men and women should be shown cooking, cleaning, making household repairs . . . taking care of children . . . making decisions; participating in sports; writing poetry; working in factories, stores, and offices.[29]

Many liberal outsiders to the feminist movement responded to the demands for women's equality with as much guilt-triggered alacrity as they had brought to demands for black equality. In this respect the feminist movement was carried along on the coattails of the civil rights movement: people who a few (or even many) years before had recognized the inconsistency between the American ideal of equality and social treatment of blacks now recognized a similar inconsistency in the treatment of women.

Since the first Women's Liberation and Women's Rights groups were founded in 1966, the new feminist ideas have been accepted in one form or another by a large number of people. Because, however, these ideas have spread through the society in a relatively conservative form, many people could espouse them while still rejecting their immediate source—the new feminist groups. Even antifeminists will assert that they believe in equal pay for equal work. Others support the divorced woman's right to receive some recompense for her years of housework and child care, oppose comic strips and television variety programs whose jokes are made at women's expense, or believe that women should be free to take any jobs for which they are qualified. Again and again, in private conversations and in printed interviews, a person makes a long series of statements squarely in line with new feminist ideology, ending with, "But of course I'm not one of those Women's Libbers." Such people rarely have any accurate perception of the goals of Women's Liberation or Women's Rights groups: "Women's Lib," like sin, is bad by definition.[30]

Despite the growing acceptance of feminist ideas if not of the Women's Liberation and Women's Rights segments of the movement themselves, these ideas still have many opponents. A columnist still advises teenage girls that the secret of success with boys is to learn about male interests: "You shutouts better start reading the sports pages. . . . Girls can still be feminine while talking about center forward and the Stanley Cup. And this makes conversation comfortable and easy for their male companions."[31] A female professor, speaking in opposition to a proposal that her university adopt a sex-blind admission policy, asked rhetorically, "Can you *conceive* of a sex-blind admission policy?" Television stations regularly air comedy programs whose jokes put down women in ways that the producers would not dare to put down blacks. Even women who, in fact, are leading relatively independent, "liberated" lives as professionals, local politicians, or writers will still assert firmly that a woman's primary place is in the home looking after her husband and family.

Very few of the avowed antifeminists have actually organized any opposition to the new movement. The few organized antifeminist groups which I have been able to locate include Stop E.R.A., whose principal objective is to prevent ratification of the Equal Rights Amendment. Headed by Mrs. Phyllis Schlafly, Stop E.R.A. has several thousand members and is strongest in the southern and central states. These same states, plus California, contribute most of the 10,000 members reported by the Happiness of Womanhood (HOW).[32] Founded by Mrs. Jaquie Davison, HOW's principal objective is to emphasize the joys of womanhood and the art of femininity. It sees the Equal Rights Amendment as jeopardizing these joys and this art. Another group, the Feminine Anti-Feminists, was formed in Cleveland in 1970 to urge their senators to oppose the Equal Rights Amendment then in the U. S. Senate. Some 3,000 women, chiefly from suburban and ethnic Cleveland, signed the petitions which were circulated by Feminine Anti-Feminists.[33] The organized antifeminists seem to be primarily middle- and lower middle-class housewives and mothers between the ages of thirty and forty.

Judging primarily from HOW's literature, from speeches made by members of HOW and of Stop E.R.A., and from one interview with a member of FAF, I would suggest that, unlike many nonfeminists, the antifeminists clearly recognize the new feminist movement's threat to the woman's traditional role and are determined that this role should not change. For example, the Feminine Anti-Feminists insisted that their members put their husbands and families ahead of the organization. "We told people, 'If your husband wants to go out that evening, you don't do the FAF work. You drop it and go out with your husband.' " They argue that the feminists want passage of the Equal Rights Amendment in order to take away men's jobs and their pay; and, they continue, women are not equal to men physically or emotionally. HOW elaborates on the traditional role theme. Housewives should treat their husbands like kings so that "they will in return treat us like queens." Women should "make the home a haven where our husbands can come . . . to regain their simple humanity."[34] Its members should "always have the soft, gentle, tender qualities of feminity." "Man's role is guide, protector, provider. Woman's role is wife, mother, homemaker."[35] As Ralph McMullen, senior editor of HOW's *Men's Auxillary Newsletter*, put it, "Capitalism set women free to find their own level and the result is what we have today."[36]

Underlying the antifeminists' attacks on the women's movement is a distinct ambivalence toward the traditional role—a need to protest too much. HOW asks its League of Housewives to promise "Never again to say, 'I am JUST a housewife,' and to do all I can, within my power, to dispel the idea that HOUSEWIVES are frumpy."[37] One individual antifeminist leader expresses this ambivalence in more detail: the ideal way of life for a woman is

> doing whatever is best for her; whatever makes her happiest. Whatever gets her fulfillment, and yet be aware of her responsibility. Doing what you get your best fulfillment out of, whether it is a career out of the home [or not]. . . . Not every woman needs to be a wife and mother. Only, if they do, they ought to fulfill their contract. . . . Believe me, raising kids doesn't raise your spirits. . . . If you are not on call [for the children] it sure hurts them. You mold their minds and dispositions. You've got to be there for that because . . . there's no way of replacing [you]. Because I'm sure if there were, I'd have found it. . . . Women go through what we call a mental depression. They think everyone hates them. Women used to be strong. Now they go through this depression and they look for more things to do. [This sends them to Women's Liberation] . . . and to psychologists and tranquillizers for excitement—to get away from everyday responsibilities. They are bored with remaining home. They want competition and excitement. They are on pills because they are not involved in the rest of the world. They should get out and relax once a week. Lift your spirits.

The organized antifeminists thus use a rationale very similar to that of the feminists as the ultimate justification for their position. They too believe in self-realization and the return to greater humanity in everyday life. The similarities go further: they object to societal imposition on their personal freedom and urge the cultivation of greater individual responsibility. The means whereby these goals are to be achieved— traditional womanhood or new feminism—are, however, very different.

Another interesting contrast between the feminists and their organized opponents lies in their general political philosophy. While the feminists' philosophy usually ranges from liberal Republican to various kinds of socialist, the antifeminists' ranges from conservative Republican (with a strong anticommunist or antisocialist element) to a philosophy primarily focused on opposing "government influence," whether that government be Republican or Democrat.[38]

These philosophies indicate that the feminists and the antifeminists are grappling with another shared problem: the loss of community in American society. The antifeminists believe that we can regain the old sense of real involvement in society if we return to the old values. The new feminists believe that we cannot turn back but must look to new means to achieve the same goal.

Despite the traditionalists' fears, and despite the general societal sensitivity to feminist issues, currently there is more talk about the problems than there is remedial action. So long as the response to the contemporary feminists remains at the level of words more than deeds, the primary cause of the movement's appearance—women's sense of relative deprivation—will remain. Indeed, the rising expectations stimulated by the lip service now paid to the idea of equality will in all likelihood result in an even greater sense of frustration. If, as seems likely, the gap between women's expectations and realizable goals increases, we can predict an increase in feminist protest. Insofar as the established institutions have committed themselves to the idea of women's equality, they are likely to remain committed: to state otherwise would be equivalent to telling blacks that, after all, they have no right to equal treatment. Established institutions, traditional feminist organizations, and women's interest groups within established institutions are all likely to respond to any feminist protest by acting primarily in the area of equal rights. The future actions of Women's Liberation and Women's Rights groups will depend in large part upon their resolutions of the ideological questions they have faced during the first years of the 1970s.

THE NEW FEMINIST MOVEMENT: A DILEMMA

The great majority of new feminist movement members advocate far greater flexibility in the interpretation of and a drastic but not complete redefinition of the female role. They favor greater opportunity for all forms of self-development while retaining a belief in personal consideration and rejecting selfish forms of individualism. They want to expand their horizons beyond the home without becoming slaves to the work ethic. They oppose such traditionally feminine traits as dependency, submission, and self-sacrifice but still adhere to the equally traditional traits of concern for others and personal expression of feelings. They firmly reject the accusation that they want to be men, claiming that in its own way the traditional male role is as demanding and as stultifying as the traditional female role. They believe that men should not have to suppress emotions or to deny themselves close personal friendships for the sake of maintaining the obviously impossible ideal of being in control of every situation. Men, they say, need not always be aggressive and assertive; nor need they maintain their present morbid concern with achievement.

Most new feminists recognize that the female role cannot be changed in isolation; change also must be introduced in the interdependent male role, in social institutions, and in the whole society. Yet even members of Women's Liberation have lost most of their early optimism and have reached the conclusion that such large-scale societal change is very hard to produce. Instead, movement members believe that, for the immediate future, the possible tangible improvements will be primarily in the area of women's rights, rather than in the social definition of the woman's role. Such concrete accomplishments enable women to join the "masculine world"—primarily the world of work. There, they risk seduction by the objectionable masculine values which the movement despises; it becomes all too easy to accept the normal ways and normal standards of behavior. They are caught, therefore, in a dilemma. By accepting available opportunities to broaden their roles (basically by joining the paid work force) they are trying to trade off despised parts of the traditional feminine role for admired parts of the traditional male role. Yet, at the same time, they fear that they may, in fact, also lose admirable parts of their traditional role and adopt what they consider to be unacceptable parts of the traditional male role.

Aware of these issues, members of Women's Liberation and Women's Rights groups are very sensitive to any suggestion that they wish, simply, to join the male world. Privately they have always supported any woman's right to be a nonachiever, including being a "happy housewife." The problem has been aired in public particularly since 1970: for example, a Women's Liberation periodical described the difficulties of combining a professional career or a factory job with the demands of the home. It pointed to the "cut-throat competition" of the job, the "need to fight off male predators," and the requirement to conform to regular work hours. The article did not pretend that at the present time the housewife's job is pleasant. However, it argued, a housewife who is paid for her work, who is not dominated by her husband, and who has had "a real choice about both work and [personal] relationships" can be happy. Thus, it concluded, "You don't have to have a career to be a 'Liberated Woman.'"[39]

Members of the Women's Rights groups have been equally sensitive about their ambivalence toward the housewife. Despite frequent avowals that this is a perfectly acceptable role so long as it is voluntarily chosen, many still despise it. For example, when five members of one eastern chapter were composing a questionnaire to be sent out to other NOW members, they considered using "housewife" as one item in a checklist for occupation; they were sure, however, that it would make others angry to say they were "merely housewives," and they commented that, if possible, they personally would check off "student" or "unemployed" rather than housewife. Two members of west coast chapters, discussing the matter, agreed that it was desirable to "be a housewife and do your own thing"; whereupon one suddenly added, "But in my heart, I don't believe it." Considering the sorts of conflicts that encouraged these women to join the movement, and the societal values which they brought with them, it is to be expected that many would be ambivalent about the housewife role.

Feminist activities have produced serious repercussions among non-members. As the NBC news commentator Barbara Walters put it, with some exaggeration, the new feminists have "given women who want to stay home a national inferiority complex."[40] It seems unlikely that the movement could change people's attitudes so effectively. More likely, the feminists have simply verbalized an idea many people already accepted implicitly. As Wilma Scott Heide, the president of NOW, said in 1972:

> Feminists are accused of putting down the suburban housewife or home-maker. The thing that most people are not aware of is that there is a difference between making an . . . observation . . . and having created . . . values. What we've observed is that *society* does not value the housewife, homemaker roles. If there is any doubt about this, one has only to look at how well the people are paid that substitute for these housekeeping and child care jobs. In the Dictionary of Occupational Titles, over 21,000 occu-pations are listed and categorized according to points. Homemaker is at the bottom with the *lowest* evaluation points of all the other 21,000 jobs.[41]

Feminists, therefore, want social approval for women (and men) who perform traditionally female tasks and for those who have long been involved in activities that, simply because they are outside of the home, have been considered unfeminine.

Behind the movement's ambivalence to the housewife lurks concern for the dilemma mentioned earlier—that involvement in the male world may cause them to deemphasize traits like humanity and personal concern and to emphasize traits like "calculating" and "inhuman" rationality. Grad-ually the more radical members of the Women's Rights groups have moved toward the Women's Liberation position: women's roles cannot be changed satisfactorily unless the whole society is also changed for the better. Two NOW members put the matter metaphorically: women not only "need a piece of the pie," they also need to explore how "to make the pie itself less repellent and indigestible."[42]

The new feminists' awareness that equality of opportunity would not, by itself, solve women's problems and might, in fact, create even worse problems came early. It was evident at the organization meeting of the National Women's Political Caucus in July 1971. Speakers at the first plenary session were not content simply to discuss the role women might play in party politics. Instead they repeatedly reassured their audience that a major part of this role would be to "humanize" society. Seven out of eight official speakers referred to this issue. For example, Dorothy Haener (International Division, UAW) urged women to participate in party politics in order to "build a better system where men and women will develop their full potential." Gloria Steinem expressed her belief that "we can humanize the machinery of politics to make a better society." Fanny Lou Hamer, of the Mississippi Freedom Democratic Party, argued that there would be less war if women had more power. Betty Walker Smith (state legislative-chairman, AAUW) urged, "Let's humanize America and save her." Paula Page, the director of the Women's Center of the National Student Center, wanted human liberation; she did not want "to play the political game by men's rules," and she stated clearly the view that attainment of women's rights would not bring a solution to women's problems. Three-quarters of the audience stood to applaud Congresswoman Bella Abzug when she said, "We have the capacity to build a humanistic society. I hope we will get down to decide how to do this. . . . What is good for women will turn out to be good for the country."

Betty Friedan's speech discussed the dilemma in more detail:

> Women do not seek power over men or to use power as men have used it. I believe that women's voice in political decisions will help change our whole politics away from war and toward the critical human problems of our society—not because women are purer or better than men, but because our lives have not permitted us to evade human reality as men have, or to encase ourselves in the dehumanizing prison of machismo, the masculine mystique. Shana Alexander suggested that our slogan should be "Women's Participation—Human Liberation."

(I must emphasize here that these new feminists are seriously concerned not only to redefine the feminine role selectively, but also to establish their position as quite different from that of their nineteenth-century predecessors. They reject the nineteenth-century notion that women's inherent nature befits them to improve the world; instead, they argue that confinement within the traditional role has given women a more objective view of society and of its failure to pursue humane objectives.)

These discussions about the need to legitimize the pursuit of human values echo the work of writers from Marx and Weber to Roszak and Reich when they ask how modern technological society can provide satisfactorily for human needs. Not only have the new feminists recognized this problem, they have actively sought solutions. The solutions which they choose will determine the movement's future. If the Women's Rights and Women's Liberation groups decide to work primarily for equal rights, then the groups themselves, not just their more conservative ideas, probably will be coopted by the society at large. The whole movement would then take the path of the conservative few among the Women's Rights groups, pursuing in a conventional fashion what have become relatively conventional goals.

Many members have argued that achievement of these objectives will itself stimulate desirable social change. They point out that if the values held by one element in a society shift away from the generally accepted values, then other elements will make corresponding, if lesser, shifts in the same direction. Thus, if some women try out a new role, other women will follow them at least part of the way. At the same time some men will be persuaded to reinterpret the masculine role. The argument appeals; however, it lacks any statement of the mechanics whereby this change will occur except insofar as it assumes that once some people find a more satisfying way of life, others will imitate them.

Other movement members have developed this argument to include the mechanics of change. Their position resembles that stated in the 1960s by participants in Women's Liberation: women's equality cannot be achieved within the present structure of American society; it was restated, for example, by a relatively radical NOW member in 1970: "NOW is getting something done" but it is "treating the symptoms more than the causes . . . [whereas] Women's Liberation is getting little done" but it is "going to the root causes." A more recent, conservative, and optimistic version of this position is that women can only achieve true equality if legal and legislative change is accompanied by social structural change. For example, a further increase of women in the work force would demand changes in the country's economy; if a variety of child-care facilities were created by private, government, and business groups, children would be socialized differently (although we do not know in what the difference would consist); if mothers on welfare develop a more powerful pressure group than they have at present, they may find new ways to attack problems of poverty; if many more husbands and wives were both employed, public and private housing projects might provide communal restaurants, just as today they provide common laundry facilities and swimming pools. Thus, it is argued, if women attain equal rights, structural changes will, necessarily, follow. Moreover, such structural change may in turn facilitate and even require a redefinition of male and female roles. For example, American children brought up in a more communal setting might be less competitive and more sensitive to interpersonal relations; men and women who worked together might gradually abandon their stereotyped definitions of each other; people who lived in more cohesive communities centered around child-care and other facilities might become more concerned with the rewards of friendship rather than the rewards of achievement. Of course, all such changes would be influenced simultaneously by a large number of other social factors including internal and external political developments, economic conditions, educational reforms, and urban growth.

In contrast to the pragmatic approach of those who narrow their goals to specifically feminist areas are the heady ideals of the humanist feminists who seek a general improvement in the quality of everyone's life. If their ideas predominate in the new feminist movement, its future will be far more venturesome and far less predictable. As members recognize, many Women's Rights and most Women's Liberation groups have the organizational and ideological flexibility to pursue the general humanist goal. But to do so involves enormous problems deciding on and pursuing specific objectives. The more radical feminist groups currently are committed to this path. Perhaps their hopes of causing a revolution in human values and so creating a better society for women and men are utopian; even so, many members prefer to seek such a utopia rather than to resign themselves to being watchdogs in the payroll office and the employment center.

APPENDIX I

METHODOLOGY

The material presented in this book is based primarily on interviews with movement members, participant observation in a full range of movement events, and analysis of the newsletters, periodicals, pamphlets, and books published by the movement members themselves.

Personal interviews were by far the most important source of information. I have visited seven major cities—Boston, Cleveland, New York, Pittsburgh, San Francisco, Los Angeles, and Washington, D. C.—where I interviewed women from as many as possible of the different sorts of Women's Rights and Women's Liberation groups.

In the summers of 1970 and 1969 respectively I interviewed a nonrandom sample of twenty-four members of Eastern Massachusetts NOW and twenty-three participants in Boston's Women's Liberation groups. The NOW sample was selected arbitrarily from a list of the first 125 people to join the chapter. The Boston Women's Liberation sample was selected from names suggested by participants I interviewed. I asked each respondent for the names of several "average" and "well known" members and, from these, selected a range of less active and more active participants.

When I was interviewing people in cities outside of the Boston area, I followed different strategy for selecting respondents. I arrived at a city with the names of several people to contact. When I telephoned them and described the research, they would suggest other people to call, and the number of names rapidly snowballed. Within the first two days of the visit and in the course of many telephone calls I had put together a superficial picture of what was happening in that area, and I was able to select specific people to interview.

The interviews conducted in the Boston area ranged in length from forty-five minutes to four hours, with a median length of one and three quarter hours. Between November 1970 and July 1971 I talked with fifty-seven women in the other major cities in interviews lasting from thirty minutes to six and a quarter hours, with a median length of one and a half hours. I also spoke informally with many women from these cities and throughout the country while attending meetings and conferences. In the course of the research I took extensive notes, wherever possible recording people's comments verbatim. I did not use a tape recorder even for the long interviews, because some women were suspicious of having their comments taped and, more important, because background noise, interruptions by children or the telephone, and a generally informal atmosphere made a tape recorder both impractical and, socially, out of place.

In order to find out how the groups operated, as well as how the members themselves felt, it was important to include in the respondents women who had expert knowledge of specific groups. For example, one could get a reasonably complete perspective on a NOW chapter by talking with the incumbent president, several rank-and-file members, and with someone who, whether or not she was now a member, had participated in earlier years. Secretaries and treasurers often provided the most reliable estimates of membership figures and financial conditions. Certain members who did not play particularly visible roles in the group nevertheless had an especially broad and objective view of its operation. It was, therefore, very important first to locate and then to interview such people.

As a general rule, the better a person was known outside of the movement, the less likely she was to provide me with useful information. Public figures are so accustomed to being interviewed that they tend to produce a series of set responses based upon the questions they repeatedly receive. Furthermore, many such women carefully avoided any comments that could be construed as harmful to the movement: their experience with the sensationalism of the press had, with reason, made them unwilling to risk misrepresentation. A third factor that made interviews with popular figures less useful than one might have expected was their own ignorance about the feminist groups' day-to-day operation: they were often so busily involved in proselytizing for the new feminism that they had lost close contact with the groups to which they officially belonged.

In addition to learning about the ways in which the various groups functioned, I wanted to know the reasons for individual members' original and continuing involvement. Beyond talking to someone about her particular group, therefore, I also, when time permitted, asked questions about her personal experiences.

I tried to select my sample to include a full range of members: active and inactive, rank-and-file as well as leaders, and those who were only marginally concerned as well as those who were deeply involved. Ideally, this would be done by a stratified random sample. This was impractical, if only because very few groups have complete or up-to-date membership lists. Many (particularly among the Women's Liberation groups) keep no formal records. And, even where complete records were available, the turnover in membership and the problems involved in tracking down individual respondents would have made it impractical to obtain a suitable sample.

At one time is seemed reasonable to compare the sample of participants with a matched sample of nonparticipants. Nonparticipants, however, are an enormously heterogeneous group, and it would have been impossible to select and interview a suitable sample in the time available for this project.

In order to compensate for possible bias in the selection of the sample and for its obvious bias toward large cities of the east and west coasts, I made every effort to gather data from movement members living in other parts of the country. I used opportunities while I was attending conferences or visiting in other states or while these people were passing through Boston and New Haven, the cities in which I have lived while working on this book. Often such women were able to describe not only their own characteristics but also those of the other movement members in their home communities. As usual, whenever possible, I cross-checked the information they gave.

The response to my telephone calls and to the interviews was almost always favorable, and often enthusiastic. I introduced myself as a sociology professor who was writing a history of the contemporary feminist movement. Most people were not interested in knowing more about the specific details of the project, but whenever they were, I went on to explain my plans in more detail. Only in the summer of 1969 did I get any seriously hostile responses. At that time three out of twenty-six Women's Liberation participants I contacted refused to be interviewed. Like some of the members of the New Left to which they were then still closely allied, they objected to my questions as a matter of principle: to cooperate with a professional social scientist was to cooperate with the disapproved "establishment." Furthermore, they were afraid that the government, or some agency of the government, would use the interviews of a social scientist like myself to help root out radical elements in the society.[1]

By 1970 or 1971 very few movement members retained any serious fear of such establishment spying, although several cases of "infiltration" were reported to me by members themselves and in the movement periodicals. A number of people discussed my work with other movement members but, as far as I know, only one person and a group with whom she was connected objected seriously to what I was doing.

The interviews consisted of open-ended questions designed, on the one hand, to get at the way a particular group worked and, on the other hand, to learn why the respondent participated. All interviews were to some extent tailored to suit the respondent. For example, when I asked the more radical members of Women's Liberation to describe their view of the ideal society and, later of how this society was to be achieved, their answers often included terms such as "socialism" and "revolution." I had, then, to ask them to interpret these widely used but ill-defined terms—and found a broad range of interpretations. In contrast, members of those Women's Liberation groups which were composed of suburban housewives had rarely thought about drastic changes in the political and social organization of society and I had little reason to examine their views of social change in any detail.

One of the contrasts between participants in Women's Liberation and members of Women's Rights groups emerged in the interview process itself. Members of the Women's Rights groups generally accepted the idea of research without question; they were satisfied to know simply that I was a sociology professor and that I was writing a book about the movement. In contrast, members of Women's Liberation, particularly the more radical people, were far less inclined to accept my formal academic credentials as a justification for my interest. They often asked who was funding my research and why the funding agency was interested in the project; a few asked how much money I had been given; more often they wanted to know where I was planning to publish the book, whether I intended to keep any profits for myself or to donate them to the women's movement, and how exactly I intended to write up the material.

In the interview itself, some looked over my shoulder and openly read my notes. Others criticized my research methodology. A few chastised me for asking what they considered to be deceitful questions; for example, when I asked one person to tell me what she believed to be the differences between NOW's objectives and those of Women's Liberation, she objected on the grounds that I already knew the answer. As a result, I subsequently modified that question, saying to someone that, while I had my ideas about NOW's objectives, I would be interested in learning hers.

Members of Women's Liberation were also much more likely than members of Women's Rights groups to believe that they deserved some recompense for the interviews they gave. Occasionally they asked for a copy of the book I was writing; sometimes they discussed the respondent's right to be paid for interviews, although no one actually asked me for such payment. Most frequently I was left with the feeling that I had been granted a favor I could not return. In contrast, someone in one of the Women's Rights groups more commonly would act as if my research justified itself and viewed her cooperation as part of her general social responsibility.

On four occasions two or more Women's Liberation respondents asked to be interviewed together;[2] they argued that no one person could adequately represent their group's views. On some of these occasions it was not possible to complete all the individual questions for each person present (thus twelve of the forty-three Women's Liberation personal interviews were incomplete). At these group interviews, however, members were able to give a composite picture of the Women's Liberation activities going on in their group and/or their area.

There was one respect in which most of the interviews contrasted with my previous research experience. In the past I have, for example, interviewed people involved in antifluoridation campaigns, I have talked to managers of small businesses about their work, I have asked middle- and upper middle-class people about their lives in a small residential community, and I have asked church members about their religious beliefs. In all these cases the respondents rarely asked me any personal questions. Those who did so brought up such topics as my work as a professor, where I lived, or whether I had had difficulty finding their house. The feminists with whom I talked, on the other hand, asked me many questions. They treated me as someone whom they wanted to know and like, not as an impersonal "interviewer." They wanted me to talk freely about my feelings on feminist issues and about my experiences as a woman. They were also anxious to know what I had learned about the movement in the rest of the country. I was very willing to talk about this after the main interview, with the one reservation that I kept confidential the names of groups and persons I used to illustrate my comments, as I have done in this book. I felt comfortable discussing my experiences and feelings on feminist issues, because I am a confirmed feminist. Of course, I could not agree with all the factions within the movement: but most people did not expect me to do so. Occasionally I felt uncomfortable because someone mistakenly believed that I agreed with all of her ideas. In these cases I let the misunderstanding go by unless the differences in our attitudes were large or unless I believed the misunderstanding could lead to serious consequences.

In my manner, dress, and general behavior I tried to fit into my surroundings without violating my own integrity. For example, I wore informal sweaters and skirts for Women's Liberation meetings but did not wear the near-universal jeans or slacks because I feel uncomfortable in them. When interviewing several people on one day I would often wear the same knitted dress to meet someone from WEAL and someone from Women's Liberation. For the WEAL interview, I would add a gold pin and slightly dressy shoes—the sort of outfit in which I might lecture; for the Women's Liberation interview, I would add a sweater and change to plain shoes—the sort of outfit I might wear to go to a movie. I give the details to show that I tried to present myself as honestly as possible and with the personal integrity that women in the feminist movement rightly regard so highly.

The interviewer can never tell whether respondents are for their part being completely honest. Considering the ease with which people discussed their ideas and actions, the time they devoted to interviews, and the large number of personal confidences they offered, I believe that they did answer openly.

While interviews and discussions with individual movement members form the basis of the present research, participation in feminist activities broadened my perspective on the movement. I attended local Women's Liberation and Women's Rights groups' meetings in most of the citiees I visited, three Women's Liberation regional conferences, and five Women's Rights regional and national conferences. I participated in a consciousness-raising group for nine months. (The members of this group are not included in my interview sample and no personal details about them are recorded in this book.) I visited five Women's Centers (representing the Women's Liberation movement) and one NOW office in a total of four cities. I also took part in one demonstration. In this way I was able to observe the groups in operation and to talk informally to many more people from a much larger geographical area than I was able to reach in the formal interview. In this way I learned, for example, about movement activities in many other parts of the country. Except for the more superficial contacts, I always explained to people that I was present as a sociologist as well as a feminist.

As the final part of my research strategy, I followed the extensive literature put out by the movement members and by groups within the movement. This includes seventy-eight active and defunct Women's Liberation periodicals (newsletters, newspapers, and magazines), forty Women's Rights periodicals and five periodicals which appeal equally to Women's Liberation and Women's Rights readers.

Ten major and three minor Women's Rights periodicals have been put out by groups devoted exclusively to publishing. These range from *The Spokeswoman* (a biweekly survey of women's progress in their work for equality in all areas of life) to *The New Woman* (a slick popular magazine that has attempted to attract the so-called "liberated woman" who is dissatisfied with *Homes and Gardens* but is not actively involved in the Liberation or Women's Rights groups).

Such published materials have to be used with caution. Most of the women who put out movement magazines and newspapers and, less commonly, newsletters, belong to one of the radical wings of the new feminism and are by no means representative of either Women's Liberation or Women's Rights. Usually such periodicals are written and produced by a small collective of from six to twelve people whose views, as they themselves declare, do not necessarily correspond to those of other local movement members. Newsletters give a more accurate picture; since, however, the people who compile them generally gather information by word of mouth, the activities they hear about and report are usually the kind in which the newsletter staffs themselves are interested.

In the text I have not documented statements which are general knowledge in the movement or which have been corroborated by several movement members; and, to preserve their anonymity, I have not identified the respondents whose comments I quote. On the other hand, I have documented quotations which have already appeared in print or statements for which I have relied primarily upon a single published source. Unattributed material within quotation marks can be assumed to be a verbatim quote from a movement member.

This methodology, which involves careful piecing together of information from many sources of varying quality, has, like all methodologies, its weaknesses. The data may be incomplete, the sampling may be insufficiently representative, the interview responses may be biased. But though the resulting book cannot be the definitive work on the contemporary women's movement, two very important features distinguish this methodology. First, it is appropriate to the phenomenon under scrutiny. Active social movements in general cannot be studied by conventional social-scientific methods. The women's movement in particular is too fluid and its members too hostile to the impersonal approaches of highly quantitative sociology, which they feel loses sight of the total picture.

Second, not only is my approach to the study of the new feminist movement the only one practical at the present time, it also records data that, some years from now, will be lost to both the sociologist and the historian. Documentary materials on the movement will in the future consist of periodicals, leaflets, newsletters, minutes of meetings, and reports by the mass media. Except for the newsletters and minutes, these documents are biased toward the ideological statements and biographical accounts of a very small, unrepresentative sample of movement members. Newsletters, and minutes of meetings, while less distorted in this direction, concentrate primarily on decisions made and actions taken. Very little of this material will tell the future student about the internal processes whereby the groups arrived at these decisions and how members felt about their actions. Since much of this information is exchanged at meetings or over the telephone, and is never recorded, it will be lost to the future scholar. Of course, some letters will remain,[3] but ours is not a letter-writing age; nor is it a diary-keeping age. If, for the future, we wish to know what today's feminists are thinking, we must ask them. Unlike the student of the nineteenth-century women's movement, the scholar concerned with today's movement will have far more promotional literature to evaluate and many fewer personal records to illuminate the individual and group thinking that produced such literature. We must, therefore, record this part of history while it is being made if we are not to lose it forever. By doing a small part of this work I hope to repay to future feminists the debt I owe to the contemporary feminists who have helped in this research.

APPENDIX II
LIST OF
ORGANIZATIONS

This list is limited to the resource centers and Women's Rights organizations referred to in the text.

Daughters, Inc., Publishers of Books by Women, Plainville, Vermont 05667.

Equal Opportunities for Women of the Augusta Area, 190 Alden Road, Augusta, Maine 04330.

Feminist Book Mart, 162-11 Ninth Avenue, Whitestone, New York 11357.

The Feminist Party, 311 West 24th Street, New York, New York 10011.

The Feminist Press, c/o State University of New York at Westbury, Box 334, Old Westbury, New York, 11568.

Human Rights for Women, 1128 National Press Building, Washington, D. C. 20004.

International Institute for Women's Studies, 1615 Myrtle Street, N.W., Washington, D. C. 20012.

KNOW, Inc., P. O. Box 86031, Pittsburgh, Pennsylvania 15221.

Lollipop Power (non-sexist children's books), P. O. Box 1171, Chapel Hill, North Carolina 27514.

Media Plus, 60 Riverside Drive, New York, New York 10024.

National Organization for Women, 1957 East 73rd Street, Chicago, Illinois 60649.

National Women's Political Caucus, 1302 18th Street, N.W. (#603), Washington, D.C. 20036.

The New England Free Press (also publishes nonfeminist "underground" literature), 791 Tremont Street, Boston, Massachusetts 02118.

New Feminist Bookstore, 1525 East 53rd Street (Room 503), Chicago, Illinois 60615.

New Feminist Talent Associates, 250 West 57th Street, New York, New York 10019.

Oregon Council for Women's Equality, P. O. Box 8168, Portland, Oregon 97207.

Pennsylvanians for Women's Rights, 23 West Chestnut Street, Lancaster, Pennsylvania 17603.

St. Louis Organization for Women's Rights, Box 3025, St. Louis, Missouri 63130.

Washington Opportunities for Women, 1111 20th Street, N.W., Washington, D.C. 20036.

Women in Leadership, 730 Witherspoon Building, Philadelphia, Pennsylvania 19107.

Women Involved, 1572 Massachusetts Avenue, Cambridge, Massachusetts 02138.

Women on Words and Images, P. O. Box 2163, Princeton, New Jersey 08540.

Women's Action Alliance, 370 Lexington Avenue (Room 313), New York, New York 10017.

Women's Equity Action League, 538 National Press Building, Washington, D.C. 20004.

Women's Legal Defense Fund, 1736 R Street, N.W., Washington, D. C. 20009.

Women's Lobby, 1345 G Street, S.E., Washington, D. C. 20003.

Women United, Crystal Plaza 1, Suite 805, 2001 Jefferson Davis Highway, Arlington, Virginia 22004.

Women United for Action, 58 West 25th Street, New York, New York 10010.

Women's History Research Center (also known as the International Women's History Archive), 2325 Oak Street, Berkeley, California 94708. Publications on file at the Center are available on microfilm from Bell and Howell, Drawer "E," Wooster, Ohio 44691.

NOTES

Introduction

1. Each of these terms gives a somewhat erroneous impression about the groups to which it refers. However, the usage I have chosen is the one emerging within both the women's movement and the social-scientific literature; e.g., Judith Hole and Ellen Levine, *Rebirth of Feminism* (New York: Quadrangle Books, 1971) pp. 17–166; and Alice S. Rossi and Ann Calderwood, eds., *Academic Women on the Move* (New York: Russell Sage Foundation, 1973).

Chapter One: Ideas and Issues

1. As used by students of social reform movements, the term "ideology" carries none of the negative connotations associated with its use by Mannheim and other students of the sociology of knowledge. It denotes, instead, the set of ideas, arguments, and principles which together make up the rationale for the movement's existence. See Karl Mannheim, *Ideology and Utopia* (New York: International Library of Psychology, Philosophy and Scientific Method, 1936), and Joseph R. Gusfield, ed., *Protest, Reform, and Revolt: A Reader in Social Movements* (New York: Wiley, 1970), pp. 395–398.

2. In accordance with a promise made to my informants during the field research, I have not identified any of the people whose unpublished remarks are quoted in this book.

3. *Women: A Journal of Liberation*, vol. I, no. 1 (Fall 1969), p. 27.

4. *The Feminine Mystique* (New York: Norton, 1963).

5. From the time that vaginal sprays were first advertised on a large scale in 1969, members of Women's Liberation scorned them. They asked themselves whether women had really been walking around for years smelling unpleasant? Wasn't washing enough? Toward the end of 1971 the American Medical Association's, the Federal Drug Administration's, and the Federal Trade Commission's investigations of the products corroborated the feminists'

beliefs: the sprays were little, if any, more effective than soap and water, and they could have potentially harmful side effects.

6. Erik H. Erikson, "Inner and Outerspace: Reflections on Womanhood," in *The Woman in America*, ed. Robert Jay Lifton (Boston: Beacon, 1965), pp. 1–26. Bruno Bettelheim, "The Commitment Required of a Woman," in *Women and the Scientific Professions: The M.I.T. Symposium on American Women in Science and Engineering*, eds. Jacquelyn A. Mattfeld and Carol G. Van Aken (Cambridge, Mass.: The M.I.T. Press, 1965), p. 15.

7. Psychologically disposed critics of the movement point out that a lack of self-confidence is symptomatic of personality disturbances in the women being described. The new feminists counter with the argument (familiar in the works of people such as Erich Fromm and Abraham H. Maslow) that some societies are so constructed that, to get along in them, the average member (in this case, the average woman) has to develop personal characteristics which by the psychologists' own definitions of that elusive concept "mental health" would indeed, be called unhealthy. For one of the supporting pieces of research, see Inge K. Broverman et al., "Sex Role Stereotypes and Clinical Judgments of Mental Health," *Journal of Consulting and Clinical Psychology*, vol. XXXIV, no. 7 (1970), pp. 1–7.

Chapter Two: Social and Personal Characteristics of the New Feminist

1. Chapter members in Women's Rights organizations usually estimated their average member's age to be the late twenties or early thirties, although they often emphasized that there was a broad age range. Median figures for age in my interviews are as follows:

Age of Women's Rights Respondents

	Median Age (years)	Range (years)
NOW (Boston area)	32	25–44
NOW (other cities)	38	26–55
WEAL	47	29–67
($N = 61$)		

Median ages for NOW members outside the Boston area interviewed were higher because those respondents were more frequently leaders (e.g. chapter presidents); and in general, leaders are older than rank-and-file members.

Members of Women's Liberation groups throughout the country estimated that most participants were between twenty-five and thirty years old.

Age of Women's Liberation Respondents

	Median Age (years)	Range (years)
Boston	26	21–59
Other cities	27	21–37
($N = 43$)		

2. *Marital Status of Respondents: Women's Rights*

	NOW (Boston)	NOW (other cities)	WEAL	Total	Percent
Married	20	11	4	35	57%
Divorced or separated	3	7	1	11	18%
Single	1	9	5	15	25%
Total	24	27	10	61	100%

Percentages for my sample are different from those reported by individual chapters and those cited in the text because outside of Boston I interviewed a disproportionate number of unmarried leaders.

3. *Marital Status of Respondents: Women's Liberation*

	Boston	Other cities	Total	Percent
Married	9	3	12	28%
Divorced or separated	4	7	11	26%
Single	10	10	20	46%
Total	23	20	43	100%

These figures, and those for the Women's Rights groups, can be compared with data for the United States female population: in 1969 about two-thirds of the white women in their early twenties and almost 90 percent of those in their late twenties were married; and between 2 and 3.4 percent were divorced. Source: Albert L. Ferris, *Indicators of Trends in the Status of American Women* (New York: Russell Sage Foundation, 1971), pp. 327–328.

4. For a range of interpretations of movement members' "personalities" and attempts to define characteristic features of these personalities see: J. Allen Broyles, *The John Birch Society: Anatomy of Protest* (Boston: Beacon, 1964),

pp. 149–151; Hadley Cantril, *The Politics of Despair* (New York: Basic Books, 1958); H. T. Dohrman, *California Cult: The Story of "Mankind United"* (Boston: Beacon, 1958), p. 119; Kenneth Keniston, *Young Radicals: Notes on Committed Youth* (New York: Harcourt, Brace & World, 1968), pp. 44–105; Thelma Herman McCormack, "The Motivation of Radicals," *American Journal of Sociology,* vol. LVI (1950), pp. 17–54; Ralph H. Turner and Lewis M. Killian, *Collective Behavior* (Englewood Cliffs, N. J.: Prentice-Hall, 1957), p. 441; William W. Wood, *Culture and Personality: Aspects of the Pentecostal Holiness Religions* (The Hague: Mouton, 1965), pp. 68–110.

5. For further discussion of this issue see Reinhard Bendix, "Complaint Behavior and Individual Personality," *American Journal of Sociology,* vol. LVIII (1952), pp. 292–303; and George Devereux, "Two Types of Personality Models," in *Studying Personality Cross Culturally,* ed. Bert Kaplan (New York: Harper & Row, 1961), pp. 227–241.

6. E.g., sociologists Mirra Komarovsky, "Cultural Contradictions and Sex Roles," *American Journal of Sociology,* vol. LII (1946), pp. 184–189 and *Women in the Modern World* (Boston: Little, Brown, 1953); Helen Hacker, "Women as a Minority Group," *Social Forces,* vol. XXX (1951), pp. 60–69; Florence Rockwood Kluckhohn, "Dominant and Variant Value Orientations," in *Personality in Nature, Society, and Culture,* eds. Clyde Kluckhohn, Henry Miller, and David M. Schneider (New York: Knopf, 1955), chap. 21, especially pp. 356–357; Cynthia Epstein, *Woman's Place: Options and Limits in Professional Careers* (Berkeley: University of California Press, 1970); and popular writers, Ruth Herschberger, *Adam's Rib* (New York: Farrar, Straus & Giroux, 1948); Betty Friedan, *The Feminine Mystique* (New York: Norton, 1963).

7. Documentation of the specific traits stereotypically attributed to males and females is found in Inge K. Broverman et al., "Sex-Role Stereotypes and Clinical Judgments of Mental Health," *Journal of Consulting and Clinical Psychology,* vol. XXXIV (1970), pp. 1–7.

8. This observation reached through my interviews is supported indirectly by a piece of research on the characteristics of the movement supporter. The "one compelling characteristic that sets her off from the . . . [nonsupporters and opponents] is her very strong desire for autonomy. In comparison to both the opposed [college] women and to college girls in general, she wants to be independent, self-sufficient and free from external control." Judith Worell and Leonard Worell, "Supporters and Opposers of Women's Liberation: Some Personality Correlates" (Paper presented at the American Psychological Association meetings, Washington, D. C., September 1, 1971), p. 4.

9. Phoebe A. Williams reaches a similar conclusion in a long-range study of women who have had successful careers in medicine. "A relationship with an encouraging adult was mentioned many times as having had an important influence on the final career decision." "Women in Medicine: Some Themes and Variations," *Journal of Medical Education,* vol. XLVI (1971), p. 590.

10. *Off Our Backs,* vol. II, no. 2 (October 1971), p. 9.

11. Ann Rosenberg, "They All Want to Come," *Women: A Journal of Liberation* (Fall 1970), p. 52. Reprinted by permission.

12. Jody Aliesan, "Bridal Suite," Part I, *Pandora*, vol. II, no. 6 (December 28, 1971), p. 4. Reprinted by permission.

13. *Everywoman*, vol. II, no. 17 (issue no. 28, December 1971), p. 14.

14. E.g., Mirra Komarovsky, *Blue-Collar Marriage* (New York: Random House, 1962); Lee Rainwater, Richard P. Coleman, and Gerald Handel, *Workingman's Wife* (New York: Oceana, 1959).

15. Louis Harris and Associates, Inc. "The 1972 Virginia Slims American Women's Opinion Poll: A Survey of Attitudes of Women on their Roles in Politics and the Economy," p. 4 is an example.

16. Unlike certain feminist theorists, black women do not see racial discrimination and, particularly, economic privation as part of the feminist issue.

17. Representative of the range of colleges and universities which have had active Women's Liberation groups are San Diego State, the University of Texas, Yale, Berkeley, the University of Minnesota, Slippery Rock (Pennsylvania) State College, and San Francisco State College.

18. Some members of Women's Liberation and Women's Rights groups believe that the movement is beginning to move down into the high schools They point out that since the spring of 1970 high schools have increasingly requested their groups to send speakers. However, students' interest in such an obvious social phenomenon as women's liberation should not necessarily be interpreted as belief in the cause.

Chapter Three: Becoming a New Feminist

1. The first Women's Liberation groups were founded in Chicago, Toronto, Detroit, Seattle, and Gainesville, Florida.

2. It is sometimes hypothesized that social movement members are persistent "joiners" who move from one protest group to another in search of some unattainable, personal goal. My respondents do not fit this model. The first participants in Women's Liberation were the only ones who frequently had belonged to several such groups, and even their migrations from civil rights to antiwar to politically radical groups represent a concern for social issues rather than for personal problems. The hypothesis about persistent "joiners" may apply more accurately to members of communes, religious sects, and cults. For documentary examples see H. T. Dohrman, *California Cult: The Story of "Mankind United"* (Boston: Beacon, 1958), especially pp. 110–117; and Benjamin Zablocki, *The Joyful Community: An Account of the Bruderhof, a Communal Movement Now in Its Third Generation* (Baltimore, Md.: Penguin, 1971), especially chap. 6, pp. 239–285.

3. The National Organization for Women, the National Women's Political Caucus, and probably other groups experienced a second surge in membership during 1972. Details on NOW's membership are given in Chapter Eight, note 3.

4. The following analysis of conversion to the new feminist perspective draws upon the work of other students of social movements, in particular Luther P. Gerlach and Virginia H. Hine, *People, Power, Change: Move-*

ments of Social Transformation (Indianapolis, Ind.: Bobbs-Merrill, 1970), pp. 99–158; Hadley Cantril, *The Politics of Despair* (New York: Basic Books, 1958), pp. 79–116; and Ted Robert Gur, *Why Men Rebel* (Princeton, N. J.: Princeton University Press, 1970), pp. 59–154.

5. Peggy White and Starr Goode, "The Small Group in Women's Liberation," *Women: A Journal of Liberation*, vol. I no. 1 (Fall, 1969), p. 57.

More recently the guidelines suggested by *Ms.* magazine in July 1972 have been adopted by newer groups whose members are not part of the informal Women's Liberation communication network. *Ms.*, vol. I, no. 1 (July 1972), p. 18ff.

6. It has been suggested that the consciousness-raising groups perform amateur psychiatry. In some respects they do resemble therapy groups: their members encourage mutual trust, the expression of emotions, and the discussion of personal problems; they suggest ways to tackle individual problems and encourage each others' efforts to modify behavior. In these respects they do, in practice, serve certain therapeutic ends. The consciousness-raising groups strenuously reject any psychotherapeutic purpose, however. They argue that they are dealing with role-related problems, not "personal hangups."

A few groups go further and take the position that any problems their members have are role-related—that is, are caused when society forces them into predetermined molds. Pushing this position to its logical conclusion, these groups forbid their members to participate in therapy at all. It should be noted that many activist members of Women's Liberation are opposed to analytic psychology in general: they believe that most psychoanalysts encourage their patients to adjust to the existing situation rather than to change either the situation or themselves, and that the analysts support the idea that women are inferior. Very few groups, however, carry this objection to psychoanalytic theories to the extent of excluding women who are in therapy.

7. Interestingly, a number of authors of popular magazine articles on new feminism have, in the course of their research, undergone a consciousness-raising experience through which they have achieved a new sense of perspective on women. Examples include Father Jeremy Harrington, editor of *St. Anthony Messenger*, published by the Franciscans; Special issue on women, vol. LXXVIII, no. 10 (March 1971); H. Dunbar, "Women's Lib: The War on Sexism," *Newsweek*, March 23, 1970; Richard Gilman, "The FemLib Case Against Sigmund Freud," *New York Times Magazine*, January 31, 1971.

8. William H. Masters and Virginia Johnson, *Human Sexual Response* (Boston: Little, Brown, 1966).

9. Throughout the women's movement any feminist is warmly received by members of all the individual groups. In a strange city she immediately finds people she can trust and who will trust her with offers of accommodations, advice, and a genuine friendliness. This friendliness is based in part upon the participants' emphasis upon sisterhood. In addition feminists, like ministers or members of the armed forces, create among themselves a sort of gemeinschaft based upon members' overlapping interests, shared activities, and common understanding.

10. *Women: A Journal of Liberation*, vol. II, no. 2 (Winter 1971), p. 14.

Chapter Four: The Radical Feminist

1. "Caste and Class (excerpts)," *No More Fun and Games,* no. 3 (November 1969), pp. 6–9. Complete version circulated as a leaflet by author Roxanne Dunbar.

2. E.g.: the April 1971 Conference on Indo-China held in Toronto. About fifty American and Canadian feminists met for three days of discussions with each other and with six Indo-Chinese women (two from South Vietnam, two from North Vietnam, and two from Laos).

3. These feminists draw their inspiration from Engels who in turn drew upon the research of the nineteenth-century anthropologist Lewis H. Morgan. Frederick Engels, *The Origin of the Family, Private Property and the State, in the Light of the Researches of Lewis H. Morgan* (New York: International, 1942).

4. Probably karate rather than judo was chosen for two reasons. First, karate is less of a sport and more directly a means of self-defense and second, effective results depend less on physical size.

5. The Feminists' prediction that, eventually, babies would be produced in test tubes received even more attention in the media.

6. In October 1971, *Everywoman,* a Women's Liberation newspaper published in Venice, California, suggested that a medical technique developed as a means to extract menses from the uterus could be used as a method of birth control or abortion. When, at the time of a normal monthly period, a Karman cannula was inserted into the uterus and a vacuum syringe used to remove the menses, any fertilized eggs would also be removed. *Everywoman* advised women that the practice of menstrual extraction required skill and great care. Shortly afterward, many other movement publications warned readers that the practice was very dangerous and advised them not to attempt it. Peggy Grau, "Menstrual Extraction," *Everywoman,* vol. II, no. 15 (October 26, 1971), pp. 2–3. Menstrual extraction is also discussed in the context of women's control of their bodies in Ellen Frankfurt, *Vaginal Politics* (New York: Quadrangle, 1972).

7. Report of a ten-person lesbian rap session. "Coming Out," San Francisco *Women's Liberation Newsletter* (June 1972), unnumbered p. 8.

Other women in the lesbian rap session quoted reported that they "came to women . . . from a growing sexual awareness." (Ibid.) There is no evidence, however, that the movement, broadly defined, creates lesbians. A survey conducted by *Psychology Today* (March 1972) shows that very few women have become lesbians as a *result* of participation, although a small percentage of previously practicing lesbians has been attracted to the movement.

8. *Ain't I a Woman,* vol. I, no. 15 (April 31, 1971), p. 3.

9. Three of my 104 respondents obviously were not wearing bras. Only one woman looked bizarre: she had a penis appliqued on the front of her jeans.

10. We would expect that the conflict between the traditional feminine role and the larger American values is more acute for these women than for women who lack either beauty or intellectual ability.

11. *Everywoman,* vol. I, no. 13 (January 12, 1971), p. 14; Dana Densmore, "Speech Is the Form of Thought: With a New Glossary," *No More*

Fun and Games, no. 4 (April 1970), pp. 9–15; Cheryl Flemming Libbey, "Hey, What Are *You* Doing After the Revolution?" *Women: A Journal of Liberation* (Winter 1971), pp. 36–40; and Kate Miller and Casey Swift, "De-sexing the English Language," *Ms.*, preview issue (Spring 1972), p. 7.

12. Since 1972 the commune Twin Oaks in Louisa, Virginia, has been atempting to use "co" when the pronoun refers to both male and female members. They report, however, that members have trouble making this linguistic change.

Chapter Five: The Emergence and Growth of Women's Liberation

1. Robin Morgan, ed., *Sisterhood Is Powerful: An Anthology of Writings from the Women's Liberation Movement* (New York: Random House Vintage, 1970), "Introduction: The Women's Revolution," p. xxi; Joan Robins, *Handbook of Women's Liberation* (North Hollywood, Calif.: Now Library Press, 1970), p. 104. The first paper to be circulated, "A Kind of Memo" by Casey Hayden and Mary King, reached New Left women in the fall of 1965. See Jo Freeman, "Origins of the Women's Liberation Movement," *American Journal of Sociology*, vol. LXXVIII (1973), p. 800.

2. Some years later many people still believed that Carmichael was still of the same opinion. In fact he, like other nationally known opponents such as Dr. Benjamin Spock, has since voiced his support for much of the movement's basic analysis.

3. Heather Booth, Evi Goldfield, Sue Munaker, "Toward a Radical Movement," April 1968, reprinted by New England Free Press; Judith Hole and Ellen Levine, *Rebirth of Feminism* (New York: Quadrangle Books, 1971), p. 112; Robins, *Handbook*, p. 104.

4. Morgan, *Sisterhood*, p. xxi.

5. Hole and Levine, *Rebirth of Feminism*, p. 113.

6. At that time Kathie Amatniek had not yet taken the feminist surname "Sarachild."

7. "Notes from the First Year," June 1968, p. 25.

8. *Voice of the Women's Liberation Movement*, no. 6 (February 1969).

9. WITCH, the name of one of the first New York City Women's Liberation groups, was an acronym for its complete title—"Women's International Terrorist Conspiracy from Hell."

10. A consequent misunderstanding reported by one woman present was that, when Webb spoke about the men trying to castrate the women, many men heard this as a threat by the women to castrate the men.

11. One of these women published *Voice of the Women's Liberation Movement* which, a few months later, had a circulation of 2,000. At that time (January 1969) only three other Women's Liberation periodicals were being published: *S.P.A.Z.M.* (Berkeley), *No More Fun and Games* (Boston), and *Lilith* (Seattle).

12. "The Siege of Columbia," *Ramparts*, June 15, 1969, p. 6.

13. Robins, *Handbook*, p. xxii.

14. In "Notes from the Second Year: Women's Liberation—Major Writ-

ings of the Radical Feminists," April 1970. In the cases of women who have been known in the movement under their birth names as well as new names of their own choice, I have inserted their birth names in parentheses following the first use of their chosen names.

15. The figure 40 and the reference to New Orleans and Durham are taken from Lyn Wells, "American Women: Their Use and Abuse," "Introduction" (Pamphlet reprinted by the New England Free Press, 1969).

16. Robins, *Handbook*, p. 214.

17. Women's Liberation periodicals are here classified as newsletters when they are primarily concerned with reporting the activities of a particular group or of a number of groups. Other periodicals include newspapers and magazines which contain primarily national news, ideological discussions, or literary pieces intended for a wider readership. Generally newspapers and magazines also include some information on group activities in the locality where they are published. A list of titles and dates of publication appears in the Bibliography, pp. 211–216.

Six periodicals which are directed primarily toward lesbians are included in the 1973 figures. Others exist, but I have not kept such a careful check on them as on the periodicals which focus upon the liberation of all women, including lesbians. A partial list of lesbian periodicals is given in the Bibliography.

18. *Female Liberation*, December 6, 1971, p. 29 (on occasion, *Female Liberation* has been published weekly); *The Second Coming*, vol. I, no. 2 (October 25, 1971), unnumbered p. 2; *Awake and Move*, vol. I, no. 5 (October 1971), p. 3; *Pandora*, vol. II, no. 13 (April 4, 1972), unnumbered p. 9; *Sister*, vol. II, no. 1 (April 1972), n.p.; *L[os] A[ngeles] Women's Liberation Newsletter*, vol. II, no. 6 (January 1972), p. 3.

19. This sort of decentralized, informal, independent, and inconspicuous structure is characteristic of contemporary (and perhaps past) social movements. Examples include the commune movement, draft resistance, the Black Power movement, and the Pentecostal movement. See: Luther P. Gerlach and Virginia H. Hine, *People, Power, Change: Movements of Social Transformation* (Indianapolis, Ind.: Bobbs-Merrill, 1970), especially pp. 33–78; and Barrie Thorne, "Resisting the Draft: An Ethnography of the Draft Resistance Movement" (Ph.D. dissertation, Brandeis University, 1971).

20. *Coalition* (Women's Liberation Coalition of Michigan Newsletter), vol. II, no. 2 (February 1971).

21. Although the actual responsibility for financial obligations is shared, the legal responsibility usually is assumed by one or two people.

22. *Voice of the Women's Liberation Movement*, no. 6 (February 1969).

23. "Marriage, From a Gay Perspective," *Kansas City Women's Liberation Union, Newsletter*, vol. II, no. 2 (January 1972), p. 15.

24. First published in the *Monthly Review*, September 1969.

25. All of these articles were first presented or published in 1968 or 1969.

26. *Essecondsex*, vol. II, no. 12 (October 1972).

27. This model of communication—the two-step flow— was first described by Elihu Katz and Paul F. Lazarsfeld in *Personal Influence* (New York: Macmillan, 1955).

Chapter Six: Women's Liberation: Actions

1. Many groups' interest in "children's liberation" illustrates their genuine concern for their children's welfare. For example, a group from New Haven commented: "Although most of us are rejecting the Freudian notion that the only fulfillment of a woman's life is her children, many of us see children as a beautiful and important part of our lives. We want to be able to provide settings which will allow our children to grow and develop happily." *Sister*, New Haven (Connecticut) Women's Liberation Newsletter, vol. II, no. 1 (1972), unnumbered p. 9.

2. By the Boston Women's Health Collective (Boston: New England Free Press, 1971).

3. E.g., "Little Miss Muffet Fights Back" compiled by Feminists on Children's Media (New York, 1971).

4. E.g., books published by Lollipop Power, Inc., North Carolina.

5. Barbara—— and Carrie——, "Birth—Two Women Speak," *Womankind* (Louisville, Kentucky), vol. I, no. 7 (July 1971), p. 20.

6. Such clinics vary greatly in their size, quality, the extent of their facilities, and the training of their staff. Most are small and run by Women's Liberation members with the help of paraprofessionals and consultant physicians. By the end of 1973 cities in which clinics had been founded included San Diego, Sacramento, Santa Cruz, Berkeley, San Francisco, Boston, and Seattle. The Los Angeles area had four clinics, and twelve are reported in New York State.

7. The participants' real need for such information is illustrated by the large proportion of the total space in Women's Liberation periodicals that is devoted to nonemotional, factual articles on pregnancy and childbirth.

8. "People's Law," *Off Our Backs*, vol. II, no. 2 (October 1971), p. 7; *Philadelphia Women's Center, Newsletter* (January 1972), p. 4.

9. *Second Coming*, vol. I, no. 2 (October 25, 1971), p. 2.

10. Rosalyn Baxandall, "City Money for Nursery Schools Now Available," *Women's World*, vol. I, no. 1 (April 15, 1971), pp. 6–7.

11. "Sexist Advertising," *Everywoman*, vol. II, no. 11 (July 30, 1971), p. 2.

12. "Ma Bell," *Everywoman*, vol. II, no. 11 (July 30, 1971), p. 5.

13. The minority of the feminists who oppose the Equal Rights Amendment believe that it would harm working women because it would require repeal of protective legislation. Proponents of the amendment argue that protective legislation has been used to keep women out of high-paying jobs. (The requirements for being a store manager, for example, might include lifting weights of over 25 pounds.) They also point out that, in any case, such legislation should be extended to apply equally to any woman or man who would be harmed by performing a particular job.

14. *Female Liberation Newsletter*, Boston, (November 16, 1971), p. 6.

15. Three of the bills were actually passed. *Goodbye to All That*, no. 26 (February 25–March 16, 1972), p. 2.

16. *Womankind* (Chicago Women's Liberation Union), vol. I, no. 6 (June 1972), p. 6.

17. *The Hand that Rocks the Rock*, vol. III, no. 3 (February 1972), p. 3.

18. *Female Liberation* (July 26, 1971), p. 4.

Chapter Seven: Women's Liberation: Organization

1. For a statement of this generally accepted ideological position see Kathy Sarachild, "Consciousness Raising and Intuition," reprinted in *The Radical Therapist*, vol. I, no. 3 (August–September 1970), p. 6.

2. During 1972 women from the YSA began to drop out of the Women's Liberation groups and to devote relatively more attention to the antiabortion law coalition, the Women's National Abortion Action Coalition (WONAAC).

3. A number of the observations in the remainder of this section are also made by Gail Stickler in an untitled paper on New York feminist groups submitted to the Department of Sociology, Columbia University, by a movement member, Jo Freeman, "The Tyranny of Structurelessness," *Berkeley Journal of Sociology: A Critical Review*, vol. XVII (1972–73), pp. 151–164 (also published in several Women's Liberation periodicals), and by other movement members.

4. Manuscript by anonymous conference participant.

5. It is likely that a number of women including Roxanne Dunbar, Ti-Grace Atkinson, and Marlene Dixon, dropped out of the movement at least temporarily because they were unable to tolerate such personal attacks.

6. By 1973 the practice had become less common, partly because speakers have grown in confidence and partly because many groups were more willing to allocate responsibilities among their members.

7. Report of the Grass Roots Organizing Workshop, National Women's Political Caucus Conference, July 10–11, 1971.

8. After a year or more in Women's Liberation, most members accept the fact that group decision-making is frequently a lengthy process and a small but noticeable proportion take knitting, sewing, macramé and other forms of handwork to occupy themselves during the long meetings.

9. *Female Liberation Newsletter*, Minneapolis-St. Paul, no. 24 (March 1971), unnumbered p. 14.

10. Ibid., unnumbered pp. 16–20.

11. *Ain't I a Woman*, vol. II, no. 8 (May 19, 1972), p. 3.

12. *The Feminist Voice*, vol. I, no. 9 (June 1972), pp. 3–4. Article reprinted in the *Berkeley Journal of Sociology*; see note 3 above.

13. *Women: A Journal of Revolution*, vol. II, no. 4 (Spring 1972), p. 4.

14. Leaflet accompanying vol. II, no. 13 (April 4, 1972), and *Pandora*, vol. II, no. 14 (April 18, 1972), p. 4.

15. Groups with centers or offices usually find that rent of $100–$150 a month is the largest item and that total expenses amount to about $200 a month exclusive of members' contributions of time. Newsletters and periodicals involve greater expenses, generally ranging from $50 to $500 a month, again excluding overhead.

16. *Women's Liberation Newsletter*, San Francisco (November 1971), p. 3.

17. *The Spokeswoman*, vol. II, no. 1 (July 1, 1971), p. 7.

18. The Women's History Research Library in Berkeley is a special case. From early 1969 to mid-1971 Laura X, the library's founder, used her own funds to make a large but relatively unorganized collection of new feminist literature, most of which she stored in two rooms of her own house. In 1972 the library obtained outside financial support from Bell and Howell (Wooster, Ohio) which published a microfilm edition of the Library's holdings at $550 a set. By mid-1972 most new feminist magazines and many newsletters and periodicals were cooperating in the Bell and Howell scheme by sending copies of all issues to Bell and Howell to be microfilmed as well as to the Women's History Research Library.

19. *Kansas City Women's Liberation Union, Newsletter*, vol. II, no. 3 (March 1972), p. 4.

20. Newsletter (September 11, 1971), p. 1.

21. *Sister*, New Haven, Connecticut, Women's Liberation newsletter, vol. II, no. 1 (1972), unnumbered p. 6.

22. *Off Our Backs*, vol. II, no. 5 (January 1972), p. 21.

23. (April 1972), p. 2.

Chapter Eight: National Organization for Women: Emergence and Growth

1. National Organization for Women (NOW), Statement of Purpose, October 29, 1966.

2. NOW, first press release [1966].

3. Voluntary organizations like NOW typically have difficulty keeping accurate figures on membership in part because record keeping is not felt to be as important as social action and so is not as thorough as it might be; but also because officials have considerable difficulty keeping check of membership renewals, lapsed memberships, and new memberships.

NOW: Membership Figures
December 31

	1967	1968	1969	1970	1971	1972
Total membership	1,122	1,313 (est.)	3,033 (est.)	4,289	5,801	14,924
Percentage increase over previous year	—	17%	131%	41%	35%	157%

Source: Financial Statement of the National Organization for Women, December 31, 1972.

The figure of 20,000 for the spring 1973 membership is based on the estimate of a national NOW official.

4. "North Suburban," *Act NOW* (Chicago NOW newsletter), vol. III, no. 10 (October 1971), unnumbered p. 2.

5. Marilyn Freifeld, "NOW Gets into Consciousness Raising," *NOW: Eastern Massachusetts, Newsletter*, vol. III, no. 3 (March 14, 1972), pp. 4–5.

6. [Roberta Benjamin], "Text of President's Farewell Address," Decem-

ber 13, 1971, *NOW: Eastern Massachusetts, Newsletter*, vol. III, no. 1 (January 14, 1972), p. 5.

7. *L[os] A[ngeles] Women's Liberation Newsletter*, vol. I, no. 13 (May 1971), p. 3.

8. *NOW: Berkeley Newsletter*, vol. II, no 7 (July 1971), p. 4.

9. "Resolutions of the 1971 Conference," "Revolution: From the Doll's House to the White House!," Report of the Fifth Annual Conference of the National Organization for Women (NOW), Los Angeles, California, September 3–6, 1971, p. 16. We should note, however, that unlike Women's Liberation groups, NOW chapters have not divided informally into lesbian and straight groups, nor have heterosexual NOW members felt under any pressure to try engaging in lesbian relationships. The great majority of NOW lesbians have no desire to be publicly identified as lesbians; they work for NOW in the capacity of feminists, not lesbian feminists.

10. E.g.: female college students were asked to state on a six-point scale how willing they would be to apply for each of thirty-two jobs (originally advertised in segregated newspaper columns) assuming that they were qualified to fill any of the posts. Compared with women for whom the advertisements were integrated, women for whom they were segregated were significantly less likely to rate highly jobs that had originally been designated "male interest" by the newspaper in which they appeared. See Sandra L. Bem and Daryl J. Bem, "Sex-Segregated Ads: Do They Discourage Female Job Applicants?" Pittsburgh: KNOW, Inc., 1970.

11. New York NOW, "NOW Equal Rights Divorce Reform Bill," [1971].

12. The women involved in this experiment were not told that some were given real birth control pills while others took placebos. All were also given and told to use contraceptive foam. Either ten or eleven women became pregnant (none of the half-dozen women's movement periodicals reporting the experiment indicates the total sample size).

13. Aileen Hernandez, Keynote address to the opening session of the Fifth Annual Conference, NOW, Los Angeles, September 4, 1971. Published in "Revolution: From the Doll's House to the White House!" p. 2.

"Humanist" is a term adopted by NOW to indicate positive values that are sex-neutral—"human" rather than "masculine" or "feminine."

14. "Resolutions of the 1971 Conference," in "Revolution: From the Doll's House to the White House!" p. 13.

15. Letitia Sommers, and Kerstin Joslyn, "Volunteer Beware!" Berkeley NOW [1971], p. 2.

Chapter Nine: National Organization for Women: Internal Organization

1. "Interim Report to Members of NOW," July 21, 1967.

2. NOW Financial Statement, December 31, 1972.

3. Bert [Roberta] Benjamin, Memo to Board Members, Eastern Massachusetts NOW, July, 1971.

4. All voluntary protest and social service groups depend greatly upon

members' contribution of time and their payment of personal expenses. Unlike more institutionalized reform groups, however, NOW works on a national scale without the financial support of a broad membership. For example, NOW's 1972 gross income of $160,000 for a 1972 membership of 15,000, compares with a gross budget of $4 million for the NAACP (approximately 400,000 members). NOW's income per member is roughly the same as the NAACP's but the gross is far smaller. See "NAACP Annual Meeting," *The Crisis,* vol. LXXIX, no. 3 (March 1972), p. 95ff.

5. *Act NOW,* Chicago NOW Newsletter, vol. IV, no. 2 (February 1972).

6. *NOW Acts,* vol. V, no. 1 [1972], p. 7.

7. NOW Financial Statement, December 31, 1972.

8. Ibid.

9. The student of voluntary organizations will be familiar with arguments suggesting that democratic organizations become oligarchies. See the classic work of Robert Michels, *Political Parties* (New York: Dover, 1959), First English edition, 1915.

10. See: Carole Pateman, *Participation and Democratic Theory* (London: Cambridge University Press, 1970); and Dennis F. Thompson, *The Democratic Citizen: Social Science and Democratic Theory in the Twentieth Century* (London: Cambridge University Press, 1970).

11. It would be very interesting (and very difficult) to discover exactly how much interpersonal conflict exists in NOW compared with other nonfeminist groups. Conceivably, if overt conflict is permitted, as in NOW, the total amount of covert and overt conflict is actually reduced.

12. *Do It NOW* (June 1972), unnumbered p. 4.

Chapter Ten: The Range of Women's Rights Groups

1. See Appendix II for the addresses of WEAL and of the other Women's Rights groups referred to in this and other chapters.

2. *WEAL, National Newsletter,* vol. IV, no. 2 (May 1972), p. 3.

3. *WEAL, National Newsletter,* vol IV, no. 3 (August 1972), p. 4.

4. Women's Legal Defense Fund, circularized letter from Temporary Steering Committee, July 9, 1971.

5. From letter, Women United for Action [October 1972].

6. From letter, International Institute of Women's Studies, September 7, 1971.

7. Announcement, Women Involved [1972].

8. *Feminist Party News* (Summer 1972), unnumbered p. 2.

9. *Feminist Party News* (October 1972), unnumbered p. 1.

10. *Women Today,* vol. II, no. 26 (December 25, 1972), p. 1.

11. *Women's Political Caucus, Greater Indianapolis, Newsletter,* vol. I, no. 6 (August 1, 1972), p. 1.

12. *Women United, News Releases;* and *WEAL Washington Report,* National Capital Chapter of WEAL.

13. "How to Organize a Local Caucus: Part II," *Women's Political Caucus, Indiana, Newsletter*, vol. I, no. 2 (August 1, 1972), p. 3.

14. "Political Action in Your Own Political Unit," *Women's Political Caucus, North Carolina, Newsletter*, vol. I, no. 5 (October [1972]), p. 4.

15. "Where Do We Go from Here?" *National Women's Political Caucus, Newsletter*, no. 6 (December 1972), p. 3.

16. *Human Rights for Women, Newsletter*, no. 6 (September 1971), pp. 5–6; no. 7 (February 1972), pp. 3–4, 8.

17. "Manuals on Name Change Available," *Women's Legal Defense Fund, Newsletter*, no. 6 (September 4, 1972), p. 5. The booklet is written by Virginia Carson.

18. See: Citizens Advisory Council on the Status of Women, "The Equal Rights Amendment and Alimony and Child Support Laws" (Washington, D. C.: Department of Labor [1972]).

Chapter Eleven: The Origins, Spread, and Future of the New Feminist Movement

1. For example, Janet Zollinger Giele, "Centuries of Womanhood: An Evolutionary Perspective on the Feminine Role," *Woman's Studies*, vol. I, (1972), pp. 97–110.

2. The analysis of movement origins which follows in particular draws upon the work of William Henry Chafe, *The American Woman: Her Changing Social, Economic, and Political Roles, 1920–1970* (New York: Oxford, 1972); Eleanor Flexner, *Century of Struggle: The Woman's Rights Movement in the United States* (Cambridge, Mass.: Belknap Press of Harvard University Press, 1966; Janet Zollinger Giele, "Social Change and the Feminine Role: A Comparison of Women's Suffrage and Women's Temperance, 1870–1920," Ph.D. dissertation, Harvard University, 1961; William L. O'Neill, *Everyone Was Brave: The Rise and Fall of Feminism in America* (Chicago: Quadrangle Books, 1969); Andrew Sinclair, *The Emancipation of the American Woman* (New York: Harper & Row, 1965).

3. Staughton Lynd, "Towards a History of the New Left," in *The New Left: A Collection of Essays*, ed. Priscilla Long (Boston: Extending Horizon Books, Porter Sargent, 1969), p. 5.

4. O'Neill, *Everyone Was Brave*, pp. 3–9.

5. *The American Woman*, pp. 135–244.

6. (New York: Norton, 1963).

7. Simone de Beauvoir, *The Second Sex*, translated by H. M. Parshley (New York: Knopf, 1953); Doris Lessing, *The Golden Notebook* (New York: Simon & Schuster, 1962); Ruth Hershberger, *Adam's Rib* (New York: Farrar, Straus & Giroux, 1948); Edith de Rham, *The Love Fraud: A Direct Attack on the Staggering Waste of Education and Talent among American Women* (New York: Pegasus, 1965); Eve Merriam, *After Nora Slammed the Door* (Cleveland, Ohio: World, 1962); Florida Scott-Maxwell, *Women and Sometimes Men* (New York: Knopf, 1957).

8. Seymour M. Farber and Roger H. L. Wilson, eds., *The Potential of Women: A Symposium* (New York: McGraw-Hill, 1963); Robert J. Lifton ed., "The Woman in America," *Daedalus* (Spring 1964); Beverly Benner Cassara, *American Women: The Changing Image* (Boston: Beacon, 1962).

9. Flexner, *Century of Struggle*, p. 51.

10. Several writers have suggested that the existence of an unusually large proportion of young single women in the late 1960s contributed to the pool of potential Liberation movement members. Unhampered by marital responsibilities, these women were free to work, first, for radical causes and, later, to participate in the feminist movement. This phenomenon, which Paul C. Glick has called the "marriage squeeze," is a delayed consequence of the baby boom that followed immediately after World War II. Girls born between 1946 and 1948 reached their early twenties in the latter half of the 1960s. Since women ordinarily marry men who are on the average two years older than themselves, their potential mates were born during the pre-baby boom years of 1944 and 1945. Thus, statistically speaking, there were simply not enough marriageable men. See Census Bureau reports and Robert R. Parke, Jr., and Paul C. Glick, "Prospective Changes in Marriage and the Family" (paper presented at the American Sociological Association Meetings, August 31, 1966).

11. There is an apparent inconsistency between the low status of women in India and Ceylon and those countries' acceptance of women prime ministers. I would hypothesize that in societies which have a strong caste or class system the majority of people see such a person in terms of her caste or class rather than her sexual status. Similarly, such women as Catherine the Great of Russia and Elizabeth I of England were seen by the country at large as monarchs first and women second.

12. Helen F. Southard, "National YWCA Resource Center on Women," *The YWCA Magazine* (January 1971), p. 4.

13. *The Spokeswoman*, vol. I, no. 6 (October 1970).

14. Betsy Williams, "Women in Transition," *AAUW Journal*, vol. LXIV, no. 2 (November 1970), p. 1.

15. *Women Today*, vol. I, no. 14 (August 14, 1971).

16. *The Guild Reporter*, vol. XXXVII, no. 22 (December 11, 1970).

17. *The New York Times*, July 15, 1971.

18. *The Spokeswoman*, vol. III, no. 8 (March 15, 1973), p. 7.

19. In the academic year 1971–72, over 1,000 college-level women's studies courses were offered. (*Moving Out*, vol. III, no. 1 ([March] 1973), p. 42. By 1972–73, at least seventy colleges and universities had established formal programs in Women's studies including five for work at the M.A. level. (Florence Howe, lecture June 15, 1973, Women's Studies Evaluation Conference, Wesleyan University.)

20. The autonomous organizations 'hus federated include the National Coalition of American Nuns, the Conference of Mother Superiors of Women, the National Assembly of Women Religious, the National Sisters Formation Conference, and the National Sisters Vocation Conference. *The Spokeswoman*, vol. I, no. 11 (April 1, 1971), p. 5.

21. *Women Today*, vol. I, no. 17 (Steptember 20, 1971), unnumbered p. 2.

22. *Civil Liberties*, no. 284 (February 1972), p. 2.

23. United States Air Force, "Officer Sample Survey," Data Services Center, HQ USAF Washington, D. C., March 20, 1971, p. 17.

24. *The New York Times*, August 28, 1971.

25. Ruth Brine, "Women's Lib: Beyond Sexual Politics," *Time* magazine, July 26, 1971.

26. *Women Today*, vol. I, no. 22 (November 29, 1971), unnumbered p. 4.

27. *Women in Struggle* (January–February 1972), p. 3.

28. *The New York Times*, August 21, 1972.

29. Scott, Foresman and Company, "Guidelines for Improving the Image of Women in Textbooks" [1972], pp. 3–4.

30. The report of a Harris Poll reaches a similar conclusion, "While support for efforts to change women's status in society seems to be growing, the phrase 'women's liberation' remains an emotionally charged expression with negative implications for many women." Louis Harris and Associates, Inc., "The 1972 Virginia Slims American Women's Opinion Poll," p. 5.

31. "Ask Beth," *Boston Sunday Globe*, September 5, 1971.

32. *The New York Times*, January 15, 1973.

33. Another group, the Pussycat League, was formed in September 1969 to combat Women's Liberation's supposed man hating. The Pussycats wanted to promote fascinating, sexual, happy femininity even among women who supported such liberal aims as abortion law reform and equal pay. Lucianne Goldberg and Jeanne Sakol in *Purr, Baby, Purr* (New York: Pinnacle Books, 1972), claim that the Pussycats have chapters "from Portland, Maine, to Portland, Oregon" (p. xii); but I have not been able to find any traces of such an organization, and it seems more likely that the Pussycats started and ended as a publicity stunt.

34. "Welcome to H.O.W." [1971].

35. Ibid.

36. Ralph McMullen, *H.O.W., Men's Auxiliary, Newsletter*, (December 1971).

37. *Happiness of Womanhood, Newsletter*, League of Housewives section, p. 2 [March 1972].

38. "Creeping socialism," or "government interference" is identified in the busing of children to schools outside their neighborhoods, sex education in schools, the Supreme Court decisions against prayers in school, and against abortion statutes. All such changes are seen as undermining American patriotism, morality, the family (the "backbone of America"), free enterprise, all our "precious freedoms" (including free enterprise), "God and the red, white and blue."

39. "Do You Have to Have a Career to Be a Liberated Woman?" *Real Women* (Spring 1971), pp. 1, 3.

40. Barbara Walters, Commencement address at Ohio State University. Quoted in *Women Today*, vol. I, no. 6 (April 16, 1971).

41. From speech at John Carroll University, September 13, 1972. Quoted

in *Women Unite NOW*, newsletter of the Cleveland chapter of NOW, October 1972, p. 6.

42. Babette Chamberlain and B. J. Miller, Statement by candidates for joint office of cochairwomen. *NOW: Berkeley, Newsletter*, vol. II, no. 7 (July 1971), p. 3.

Appendix I: Methodology.

1. This problem was discussed at length at one of the earliest Women's Liberation conferences—the one held outside of Chicago in November 1968. From these and other discussions an informal but general policy of dealing cautiously with representatives of the media emerged.

Although only three women directly refused to be interviewed, of course some potential respondents in both Women's Liberation and Women's Rights groups proved to be unavailable for reasons apparently unrelated to my research.

2. At nine other interviews involving both Women's Liberation and Women's Rights group participants, a second and even a third person was present for part of the interview. Usually this was some movement friend of the respondent who happened to be there at the time. In two cases husbands listened to part of the interview. With the exception of one case when a husband was present, I do not believe the presence of other people significantly affected the respondents' answers.

3. E.g., Betty Friedan's correspondence and her personal collection of material relating to the first years of NOW. These are preserved in the Arthur and Elizabeth Schlesinger Library, Radcliffe College, Cambridge, Massachusetts, but unfortunately were not cataloged at the time of the research.

BIBLIOGRAPHY

BOOKS; ARTICLES IN AND WHOLE ISSUES OF
PROFESSIONAL JOURNALS

Hundreds of books and articles have been published on feminism and on the new feminist movement. The following list is limited to works cited in the text, and to important or characteristic feminist and antifeminist works published in book form or in professional journals.

Abbott, Sidney and Barbara Love. *Sappho Was a Right-on Woman: A Liberated View of Lesbianism.* New York: Stein & Day, 1972.

Altbach, Edith Hosino, ed. *From Feminism to Liberation.* Cambridge, Mass.: Schenkman, 1971.

Amundsen, Kirsten. *The Silenced Majority: Women and American Democracy.* Englewood Cliffs, N.J.: Prentice-Hall, 1971.

Bardwick, Judith M. *Psychology of Women: A Study of Bio-Cultural Conflicts.* New York: Harper & Row, 1971.

Bardwick, Judith M., Elizabeth Douvan, Matina S. Horner and David Gutmann. *Feminine Personality and Conflict.* Belmont, California: Brooks/Cole, 1970.

Beard, Mary R. *Woman as Force in History: A Study in Traditions and Realities.* New York: Macmillan, 1946.

de Beauvoir, Simone. *The Second Sex.* New York: Knopf, 1953.

Bem, Daryl J., ed. *Beliefs, Attitudes, and Human Affairs.* Belmont, Calif.: Brooks/Cole, 1970.

Bem, Sandra L. and Daryl J. Bem. "Sex-Segregated Ads: Do They Discourage Female Job Applicants?" Pittsburgh: KNOW, Inc., 1970 [?]. Also in Daryl J. Bem, ed. *Beliefs, Attitudes, and Human Affairs.* Belmont, Calif.: Brooks/Cole, 1970.

Bendix, Reinhard. "Compliant Behavior and Individual Personality." *American Journal of Sociology*, vol. LVIII (1952), pp. 292–303.

Bernard, Jessie. *Women and the Public Interest: An Essay on Policy and Protest.* Chicago: Aldine Atherton, 1971.

Bird, Caroline. *Born Female: The High Cost of Keeping Women Down.* New York: McKay, 1968. Revised 1970.

Blumen, Jean. "Selected Dimensions of Self-Concept and Educational Aspirations of Married Women College Graduates." Ph.D. dissertation, Harvard University, 1970.

Broverman, Inge K., *et al.* "Sex Role Stereotypes and Clinical Judgments of Mental Health." *Journal of Consulting and Clinical Psychology*, vol. XXXIV, no. 7 (1970), pp. 1–7.

Broyles, J. Allen. *The John Birch Society: Anatomy of Protest.* Boston: Beacon, 1965.

Burton, Gabrielle. *I'm Running Away from Home But I'm Not Allowed to Cross the Street: A Primer on Women's Liberation.* Pittsburgh: KNOW, Inc., 1972.

Cade, Toni, ed. *The Black Woman: An Anthology.* New York: New American Library, 1970. A Signet book.

Cantril, Hadley. *The Politics of Despair.* New York: Basic Books, 1958.

Cassara, Beverly Benner. *American Women: The Changing Image.* Boston: Beacon, 1962.

Chafe, William Henry. *The American Woman: Her Changing Social, Economic, and Political Roles, 1920–1970.* New York: Oxford, 1972.

Chesler, Phyllis. *Women and Madness.* Garden City, N.Y.: Doubleday, 1972.

Cooke, Joanne, Charlotte Bunch-Weeks and Robin Morgan, eds. *The New Women: A MOTIVE Anthology on Women's Liberation.* Indianapolis: Bobbs-Merrill, 1970.

Crook, Margaret Brackenbury. *Women and Religion.* Boston: Beacon Press, 1964.

Daly, Mary. *The Church and the Second Sex.* New York: Harper & Row, 1968.

Davison, Jaquie. *I am a Housewife! The Housewife is the Most Important Person in the World.* New York: Guild Books, 1972.

Deutsch, Helene. *The Psychology of Women.* New York: Grune and Stratton, 1944.

Devereux, George. "Two Types of Personality Models." In Bert Kaplan, ed. *Studying Personality Cross Culturally.* Elmsford, N.Y.: Row, Peterson, 1961, pp. 227–241.

Dohrman, H. T. *California Cult: The Story of "Mankind United."* Boston: Beacon, 1958.

Edwards, Lee R., Mary Heath, and Lisa Baskin, eds. *Woman: An Issue.* Boston: Little, Brown, 1972. (Also published as vol. XIII, nos. 1 and 2 (1972) of *The Massachusetts Review.*)

Ellis, Julie. *Revolt of the Second Sex.* New York: Lancer Books, 1970.

Engels, Frederick. *The Origin of the Family, Private Property, and the State, in the Light of the Researches of Lewis H. Morgan* (1884). New York: International Publishers, 1942.

Epstein, Cynthia Fuchs. *Woman's Place: Options and Limits in Professional Careers.* Berkeley: University of California, 1970.

"Equal Rights for Women: A Symposium on the Proposed Constitutional Amendment." *Harvard Civil Rights-Civil Liberties Law Review,* vol. VI, no. 2 (March 1971).

Farber, Seymour M. and Roger H. L. Wilson, eds. *The Potential of Women: A Symposium.* New York: McGraw-Hill, 1963.

Ferriss, Abbott L. *Indicators of Trends in the Status of American Women.* New York: Russell Sage, 1971.

Figes, Eva. *Patriarchal Attitudes.* New York: Stein and Day, 1970.

Firestone, Shulamith. *The Dialectic of Sex: The Case for Feminist Revolution.* New York: Morrow, 1970.

Flexner, Eleanor. *Century of Struggle: The Woman's Rights Movement in the United States.* Cambridge, Mass.: Belknap Press of Harvard University Press, 1959.

Forfreedom, Ann, ed. *Women Out of History: A Herstory Anthology.* The Editor, P. O. Box 2551A, Los Angeles, California, 90025.

Frankfurt, Ellen. *Vaginal Politics.* New York: Quadrangle, 1972.

Freeman, Jo. "The Origins of the Women's Liberation Movement." *American Journal of Sociology,* vol. LXXVIII (1973), pp. 792–811.

Freeman, Jo. "The Tyranny of Structurelessness." *Berkeley Journal of Sociology: A Critical Review,* vol. XVII (1972–73), pp. 151–164. Reprinted in *Ms.* (July 1973), pp. 76–78ff.

Friedan, Betty. *The Feminine Mystique.* New York: Norton, 1963.

Fromm, Erich. *The Sane Society.* New York: Rinehart, 1955.

Gerlach, Luther P. and Virginia H. Hine. *People, Power, Change: Movements of Social Transformation.* Indianapolis: Bobbs-Merrill, 1970.

Giele, Janet Zollinger. "Centuries of Womanhood: An Evolutionary Perspective on the Feminine Role." *Women's Studies,* vol. I (1972), pp. 97–110.

Giele, Janet Zollinger. "Social Change and the Feminine Role: A Comparison of Women's Suffrage and Women's Temperance, 1870–1920." Ph.D. dissertation, Harvard University, 1961.

Gilman, Charlotte Perkins. *Women and Economics: The Economic Factor Between Men and Women as a Factor in Social Evolution.* Edited by Carl N. Degler. New York: Harper & Row, 1966.

Goldberg, Lucianne and Jeannie Sakol. *Purr, Baby, Purr.* New York: Pinnacle Books, 1972.

Gornick, Vivian, and Barbara K. Moran, eds. *Women in Sexist Society: Studies in Power and Powerlessness.* New York: Basic Books, 1971.

Gurr, Ted Robert. *Why Men Rebel.* Princeton, N.J.: Princeton University Press, 1970.

Gusfield, Joseph R., ed. *Protest, Reform, and Revolt: A Reader in Social Movements.* New York: Wiley, 1970.

Hacker, Helen. "Women as a Minority Group." *Social Forces*, vol. XXX (1951), pp. 60–69.

Hennessey, Caroline. *I, B.I.T.C.H.* New York: Lancer, 1970.

Herschberger, Ruth. *Adam's Rib.* New York: Farrar, Straus & Giroux, 1948. New York: Harper & Row, 1970.

Hole, Judith and Ellen Levine. *Rebirth of Feminism.* New York: Quadrangle Books, 1971.

Horney, Karen. *Feminine Psychology.* New York: Norton, 1967.

Huber, Joan, ed. "Changing Women in a Changing Society." *American Journal of Sociology*, vol. LXXVIII (1973): whole issue.

Janeway, Elizabeth. *Man's World; Woman's Place: A Study in Social Mythology.* New York: Morrow, 1971.

Jenness, Linda, ed. *Feminism and Socialism: An Anthology.* New York: Pathfinder, 1972.

Johnston, Jill. *Lesbian Nation: The Feminist Solution.* New York: Simon and Schuster, 1973.

Kanowitz, Leo. *Women and the Law: The Unfinished Revolution.* Albuquerque: University of New Mexico, 1969.

Katz, Elihu, and Paul F. Lazarsfeld. *Personal Influence* (New York: Macmillan, 1955.

Keniston, Kenneth. *Young Radicals: Notes on Committed Youth.* New York: Harcourt, Brace & World, 1968.

Kennedy, Florynce, and Diane B. Schulder. *Abortion Rap.* New York: McGraw-Hill, 1971.

Klein, Viola. *The Feminine Character: History of an Ideology.* New York: International Universities, 1946, 1948.

Kluckhohn, Florence Rockwood. "Dominant and Variant Value Orientations." In Clyde Kluckhohn, Henry Miller, and David Schneider, eds. *Personality in Nature, Society, and Culture.* New York: Knopf, 1955, Chapter 21.

Komarovsky, Mirra. *Blue Collar Marriage.* New York: Random House, 1964.

Komarovsky, Mirra. *Women in the Modern World: Their Dilemmas.* Boston: Little, Brown, 1953.

Komarovsky, Mirra. "Cultural Contradictions and Sex Roles." *American Journal of Sociology*, vol. LII (1946), pp. 184–189.

Komisar, Lucy. *The New Feminism.* New York: Franklin Watts, 1971.

Kraditor, Aileen S. *Ideas of the Woman Suffrage Movement, 1890–1920.* New York: Columbia University, 1965.

Lerner, Gerda, ed. *Black Women in White America: A Documentary History.* New York: Pantheon, 1972.

Lessing, Doris. *The Golden Notebook.* New York: Simon & Schuster, 1962.

Lifton, Robert Jay, ed. *The Woman in America.* Boston: Beacon, 1965. First published as "The Woman in America." *Daedalus* (Spring 1964).

Long, Priscilla, ed. *The New Left: A Collection of Essays.* Boston: Extending Horizon Books, Porter Sargent, 1969.

Lopata, Helena Znaniecki. *Occupation: Housewife.* New York: Oxford, 1971.

Louis Harris and Associates, Inc. "The [1971] Virginia Slims American

Women's Opinion Poll: A Survey of the Attitudes of Women on their Role in American Society."

Louis Harris and Associates, Inc. "The 1972 Virginia Slims American Women's Opinion Poll."

Lundberg, Ferdinand, and Marynia F. Farnham. *Modern Woman: The Lost Sex*. New York: Harper, 1947.

Maccoby, Eleanor, ed. *The Development of Sex Differences*. Stanford: Stanford University, 1966.

McCormack, Thelma Herman. "The Motivation of Radicals." *American Journal of Sociology*, vol. LVI (1950), pp. 17–54.

McCracken, Robert D. *Fallacies of Women's Liberation*. Boulder, Colo.: Shields, 1972.

Mannheim, Karl. *Ideology and Utopia*. New York: International Library of Psychology, Philosophy and Scientific Method, 1936.

Martin, Del and Phyllis Lyon. *Lesbian/Woman*. New York: Bantam, 1972.

Maslow, Abraham H. "Self-Actualizing People: A Study of Psychological Health." In Clark E. Moustakas, ed. *Self: Exploration in Personal Growth*. New York: Harper, 1956.

Masters, William H., and Virginia Johnson. *Human Sexual Response*. Boston: Little, Brown, 1966.

Mattfeld, Jacquelyn A., and Carol G. Van Aken, eds. *Women and the Scientific Professions: The M.I.T. Symposium on American Women in Science and Engineering*. Cambridge: M.I.T., 1965.

Mead, Margaret. *Male and Female*. New York: Morrow, 1949.

Mead, Margaret, and Frances Balgley Kaplan, eds. *American Women: Report of the President's Commission on the Status of Women and Other Publications of the Commission*. New York: Scribner's, 1965.

Merriam, Eve. *After Nora Slammed the Door: American Women in the 1960's—The Unfinished Revolution*. Cleveland, Ohio: World, 1962.

Michels, Robert. *Political Parties*. New York: Dover, 1959. First English edition, 1915.

Millet, Kate. *Sexual Politics*. Garden City: Doubleday, 1970.

Mitchell, Juliet. *Woman's Estate*. New York: Pantheon, 1971.

Morgan, Robin, ed. *Sisterhood is Powerful*. New York: Random House, 1970.

Myrdal, Alva, and Viola Klein. *Women's Two Roles: Home and Work*. London: Routledge and Kegan Paul, 1956.

Myrdal, Gunnar. *An American Dilemma*. New York: Harper, 1941, 1944. Two Volumes. Appendix 5, "A Parallel to the Negro Problem."

Nye, F. Ivan, and Lois Wladis Hoffman, eds. *The Employed Mother in America*. New York: Rand McNally, 1963.

O'Neill, William. *Everyone Was Brave: The Rise and Fall of Feminism in America*. Chicago: Quadrangle Books, 1969.

Oppenheimer, Valerie Kincade. *The Female Labor Force in the United States: Demographic and Economic Factors Governing its Growth and Changing Composition*. California: University of California, Institute of International Studies, 1970.

Parke, Robert R., Jr. and Paul C. Glick. "Prospective Changes in Marriage and the Family." Paper presented at the American Sociological Association meetings, August 31, 1966.

Pateman, Carole. *Participation and Democratic Theory*. London: Cambridge University Press, 1970.

Rainwater, Lee, Richard P. Coleman, and Gerald Handel. *Workingman's Wife: Her Personality, World, and Lifestyle*. New York: Oceana, 1959.

de Rham, Edith. *The Love Fraud: A Direct Attack on the Staggering Waste of Education and Talent among American Women*. New York: Clarkson N. Potter, 1965.

Robins, Joan. *Handbook of Women's Liberation*. North Hollywood, Calif.: Now Library Press, 1970.

Rossi, Alice and Ann Calderwood, eds. *Academic Women on the Move*. New York: Russell Sage Foundation, 1973.

Salper, Roberta, ed. *Female Liberation: History and Current Writings*. New York: Knopf, 1972.

Scott, Ann Firor, ed. *What is Happening to American Women?* Atlanta: Southern Newspaper Publishers Association Foundation.

Scott-Maxwell, Florida. *Women and Sometimes Men*. New York: Knopf, 1957.

Sherfey, Mary Jane. *The Nature and Evolution of Female Sexuality*. New York: Random House, 1972.

Sherman, Julia A. *On the Psychology of Women: A Survey of Empirical Studies*. Springfield, Ill.: Thomas, 1971.

Sinclair, Andrew. *The Emancipation of the American Woman*. New York: Harper & Row, 1965.

Stambler, Sookie, ed. *Women's Liberation: Blueprint for the Future*. New York: Ace, 1970.

Suelzle, Marijean. *The Female Sex Role*. Urbana, Ill.: Univ. of Illinois Press, in press.

Tanner, Leslie B., ed. *Voices from Women's Liberation*. New York: New American Library, 1971.

Thompson, Dennis F. *The Democratic Citizen: Social Science and Democratic Theory in the Twentieth Century*. London: Cambridge University Press, 1970.

Thompson, Mary Lou, ed. *Voices of the New Feminism*. Boston: Beacon, 1970.

Thorne, Barrie. "Resisting the Draft: An Ethnography of the Draft Resistance Movement." Ph.D. dissertation, Brandeis University, 1971.

Turner, Ralph H., and Lewis M. Killian. *Collective Behavior*. Englewood Cliffs, N.J.: Prentice-Hall, 1957.

U.S. Department of Labor, Women's Bureau. *Background Facts on Women Workers in the United States*. Washington, D. C.: Government Printing Office, 1970.

U.S. Department of Labor, Women's Bureau. *1969 Handbook on Women Workers*. Bulletin 294, Washington, D. C.: Government Printing Office, 1969.

Ware, Cellestine. *Woman Power: The Movement for Women's Liberation.* New York: Tower, 1970.

Welter, Barbara. "The Cult of True Womanhood: 1820–1860." *American Quarterly,* vol. XVIII (1966), pp. 151–174.

Williams, Phoebe A. "Women in Medicine: Some Themes and Variations." *Journal of Medical Education,* vol. XLVI (1971), pp. 584–591.

Wollstonecraft, Mary. *A Vindication of the Rights of Woman with Strictures on Political and Moral Subjects.* New York: Norton, 1967.

"The Woman in America." *Daedalus* (Spring 1964). Published in book form; Boston: Beacon, 1965; Robert Jay Lifton, ed.

The Woman Question: Selections from the Writings of Karl Marx, Frederick Engels, V. I. Lenin, Joseph Stalin. New York: International, 1951.

"Women and the Law." *Valparaiso Law Review: Symposium Issue,* vol. V (1971).

Women's Studies: An Interdisciplinary Journal, vol. I (1972).

Wonderwoman. Introduction by Gloria Steinem. An Interpretive Essay by Phyllis Chesler. New York: A Ms. Book, 1973.

Wood, William W. *Culture and Personality: Aspects of the Pentecostal Holiness Religions.* The Hague: Mouton, 1965.

Worell, Judith and Leonard Worell, "Supporters and Opposers of Women's Liberation: Some Personality Correlates." Paper presented at the American Psychological Association meetings, Washington, D. C., September 1, 1971.

Zablocki, Benjamin. *The Joyful Community: An Account of the Bruderhof, A Communal Movement Now in Its Third Generation.* Baltimore, Md.: Penguin, 1971.

BIBLIOGRAPHIES

Astin, Helen, Nancy Suniewick and Susan Dweck. *Women: A Bibliography on their Education and Careers.* Sponsored by University Research Corporation and the Institute of Life Insurance. Washington, D. C.: Human Services Press, 1971.

Business and Professional Women's Foundation. "Woman Executives: A Selected Annotated Bibliography." Washington, D. C.: Business and Professional Women's Foundation, 1970.

Cisler, Lucinda. "Women: A Bibliography." New York: Cisler, 1968, 1969, 1970. Sixth edition (1970): Lucinda Cisler, 102 West 80 St., New York. New York 10024.

Cole, Johnneta B. "Black Women in America: An Annotated Bibliography." *Black Scholar,* vol. III (1971), pp. 42–53.

Drake, Kirsten, Dorothy Marks and Mary Wexford, "Women's Work and Women's Studies, 1971." Pittsburgh: KNOW, Inc., 1972.

Farians, Elizabeth J. "Selected Bibliography on Women and Religion." Revised. 6125 Webbland Place, Cincinnati, Ohio 45213.

Feminists on Children's Media. "Little Miss Muffet Fights Back: Recommended

Non-Sexist Books About Girls for Young Readers." New York: Feminists on Children's Media, 1971.

Frithioff, Patricia. *A Selected Annotated Bibliography of Materials Related to Women in Science*. Lund: Research Policy Program, 1967.

Hughes, Marija Matich. "The Sexual Barrier: Legal and Economic Aspects of Employment, 1970." Supplements I and II, 1971 and 1972. From the Compiler, 2116 F Street, N.W., Apt. 702, Washington, D. C. 20007.

Keiffer, Miriam and Patricia Warren. *Population Limitation and Women's Status: A Bibliography*. Princeton, N. J.: Educational Testing Service, 1970.

Radcliffe Institute. "Womanpower: Selected Bibliography on Educated Women in the Labor Force." Cambridge, Mass.: Radcliffe Institute, 1970.

Spiegel, Jeanne. "Continuing Education for Women: A Selected Annotated Bibliography." Washington, D. C.: Business and Professional Women's Foundation, 1967.

Spiegel, Jeanne. "Sex Role Concepts: How Women and Men See Themselves and Each Other. A Selected Annotated Bibliography." Washington, D. C.: Business and Professional Women's Foundation, 1969.

Spiegel, Jeanne. "Working Mothers: A Selected Annotated Bibliography." Washington, D. C.: Business and Professional Women's Foundation, 1968.

Steinmann, Ann. *Bibliography on Male-Female Role Research*. New York: Maferr Foundation, 1971.

U. S. Department of Labor. "Publications of the Women's Bureau." Washington, D. C.: Government Printing Office, current issue.

Westervelt, Esther Manning and Deborah A. Fixter. *Women's Higher and Continuing Education: An Annotated Bibliography with Selected References on Related Aspects of Women's Lives*. New York: College Entrance Examination Board, 1971.

Whaley, Sara Stauffer, ed. *Women Studies Abstracts*. Issued Quarterly. Vol. I (1972). P. O. Box 1, Rush, New York, 14543.

Women's History Research Center. Bibliographic materials available.

NEW FEMINIST MOVEMENT PAMPHLETS, ARTICLES, AND SPECIAL ISSUES OF PERIODICALS

The following is a selection from the numerous articles and pamphlets written and distributed by movement members. Most of them have been published in several places and reprinted, dittoed, or xeroxed many times. I have cited the year in which the piece was first presented, and the most accessible place or places where it has been reprinted.

Allen, Pam. "Free Space: A Perspective on the Small Group in Women's Liberation." 50 pages. New York: Times Change, 1970. Reprinted in "Notes from the Third Year."

Amatniek, Kathie. See Kathie Sarachild.

Beal, Frances M. "Double Jeopardy: To Be Black and Female." 6 pages. Reprinted in Cade, ed., *The Black Woman* and Cooke, *et al., The New Women.*

Benston, Margaret. "The Political Economy of Women's Liberation." *Monthly Review,* vol. XXI, no. 4 (September 1969). Reprinted in Tanner, ed. *Voices from Women's Liberation,* and Altbach, ed. *From Feminism to Liberation.*

Booth, Heather, Evi Goldfield, and Sue Manaker. "Toward a Radical Movement." 4 pages. April 1968. Reprinted by New England Free Press, 791 Tremont Street, Boston, Massachusetts, 02118.

Boston Women's Collective, Inc. "Women's Yellow Pages." 62 pages. The Sanctuary, Inc., 1151 Massachusetts Ave., Cambridge, Mass., 02138.

Boston Women's Health Collective. "Our Bodies and Ourselves." Boston: New England Free Press, 1971. Revised edition New York: Simon and Schuster, 1973.

Cisler, Lucinda. "Abortion Law Repeal (Sort of): A Warning to Women." 1970. Reprinted in "Notes From the Second Year," pp. 89–93 and Altbach, *From Feminism to Liberation.*

Cisler, Lucinda. "Unfinished Business: Birth Control and Women's Liberation." 44 pages. 1969. Reprinted in Morgan, ed. *Sisterhood is Powerful.*

Dixon, Marlene. "On Women's Liberation: Where Are We Going?" *Radical America,* vol. IV, no. 2 (February 1970), pp. 26–35. Reprinted in Altbach, ed., *From Feminism to Liberation.*

Dunbar, Roxanne. "Female Liberation as a Basis for Social Revolution." 5 pages. 1970. Reprinted in "Notes From the Second Year" and Morgan, *Sisterhood is Powerful.*

Freeman, Jo. "The Building of the Gilded Cage." 17 pages. 1970. Reprinted in "Notes From the Third Year."

Jones, Beverly. "Toward a Strong and Effective Woman's Movement." (The "Chambersburg Paper") 19 pages. 1972. Pittsburgh, KNOW, Inc., 1973.

Jones, Beverly, and Judith Brown. "Toward a Female Liberation Movement." 1968. Known as "The Florida Paper." Reprinted in Tanner, ed., *Voices From Women's Liberation.*

Jordan, Joan. "The Place of American Women: Economic Exploitation of Women." 22 pages. *Revolutionary Age,* vol. I, no. 3 (1968).

Koedt, Anne. "The Myth of the Vaginal Orgasm." 5 pages. Reprinted in "Notes From the First Year" and Tanner, ed., *Voices From Women's Liberation.*

Mainardi, Pat. "The Politics of Housework." 4 pages. 1968 and 1970. Reprinted in "Notes From the Second Year" and Tanner, ed. *Voices From Women's Liberation.*

Miller, Ruthann, Mary-Alice Waters, and Evelyn Reed. "In Defense of the Women's Movement." 15 pages. New York: Pathfinder Press, Merit Pamphlet, 1970. First published in *The Militant,* February 13, 1970; December 12, 1969; and February 6, 1970.

Mitchell, Juliet. "Women: The Longest Revolution." 27 pages. 1970. *New*

Left Review, no. 40 (November/December 1966), pp. 11–23. Reprinted in Altbach, *From Feminism to Liberation.*

"Mushroom Effect: A Directory of Women's Liberation." 1970. P. O. Box 6024, Albany, California, 94706.

"Notes From the First Year." 33 pages. June, 1968. Redstockings, P. O. Box 748, Stuyvesant Station, New York, New York, 10009.

"Notes From the Second Year: Women's Liberation—Major Writings of the Radical Feminists." 126 pages. April, 1970. Notes, Box AA, Old Chelsea Station, New York, New York, 10011.

"Notes From the Third Year: Women's Liberation." 142 pages. 1971. Notes, Box AA, Old Chelsea Station, New York, New York, 10011.

"Notes on Women's Liberation: We Speak in Many Voices." January and October, 1970. 75 and 86 pages. News & Letters, 1900 E. Jefferson, Detroit, Michigan.

Novack, George. "Revolutionary Dynamics of Women's Liberation." 22 pages. New York: Pathfinder Press, Merit Pamphlet, 1969. First published in *The Militant*, October 17, 1969.

Radical America. Issue on Women, vol. IV (1970).

Radicalesbians. "The Woman Identified Woman." 4 pages. Reprinted in "Notes From the Third Year."

Reed, Evelyn. "Problems of Women's Liberation: A Marxist Approach." 63 pages. New York: Pathfinder, 1969; revised and enlarged, 1970.

"Red Papers 3: Women's Fight for Liberation." 62 pages. Bay Area Revolutionary Union, Box 291, 1230 Grant Avenue, San Francisco, California, 94133.

"Revolution: From the Doll's House to the White House!" Report on the Fifth Annual Conference of the National Organization for Women (NOW), Los Angeles, California, September 3–6, 1971.

Sarachild, Kathie (Amatniek). "Consciousness Raising and Intuition." *The Radical Therapist*, vol. I, no. 3 (August–September 1970), p. 6.

Sarachild, Kathie. "A Program For Feminist 'Consciousness Raising'." 1968. In "Notes From the Second Year." Outline reprinted in Tanner, ed. *Voices From Women's Liberation.*

Sommers, Letitia and Kerstin Joslyn. "Volunteer Beware! Guidelines for Discussion." 14 pages. NOW Task Force: Women and Volunteerism, P. O. Box 7024, Berkeley, California, 94707.

"The Struggle for Women's Liberation: A Strategy for a Mass Movement." 13 pages. Young Socialist Discussion Bulletin, vol. XIV, no. 1 (November 9, 1970). Published by the Young Socialist Alliance, P. O. Box 471, Cooper Station, New York, New York, 10003.

Syfers, Judy. "Why I Want a Wife." 2 pages. 1971. Reprinted in "Notes From the Third Year."

Weisstein, Naomi. " 'Kinde, Kuche, Kirche' as Scientific Law: Psychology Constructs the Female." 10 pages. 1968. Reprinted in Cooke, *et al., The New Women;* Morgan, *Sisterhood is Powerful;* and Gornick and Moran, *Woman in Sexist Society.*

Weisstein, Naomi. "Woman as Nigger." *Psychology Today*, October 1969, pp. 20ff. Reprinted in Tanner, ed. *Voices From Women's Liberation;* and Gornick and Moran, *Woman in Sexist Society.*

Wells, Lyn. "American Women: Their Use and Abuse." 17 pages. 1969. Reprinted by New England Free Press, 791 Tremont Street, Boston, Massachusetts, 02118.

"Whole Woman Catalog." 1971. Portsmouth, New Hampshire.

Willis, Ellen. "Women and the Left." *Guardian* (New York), February, 1969. Reprinted in "Notes From the Second Year."

Women on Words and Images. "Dick and Jane as Victims: Sex Stereotyping in Children's Readers." 78 pages. 1972. Women on Words and Images, A Task Force of New Jersey NOW, Princeton, New Jersey.

NEW FEMINIST MOVEMENT PERIODICALS

This list of United States periodicals is not exhaustive: it indicates, however, the range of periodicals which have been produced. The place of publication is given. Newsletters, magazines and newspapers are distinguished from each other. "Newsletters" usually provide factual information of interest to a particular group (usually local, occasionally national). "Magazines" have a magazine format, a local or national circulation, and devote the majority of their space to ideological, biographical and other factual articles, short stories and poetry. "Newspapers" (which adopt a newspaper format) are usually part-newsletter and part-magazine. Their editors often seek a wider circulation than do editors of newsletters; they print news items of interest to groups in the area where they publish; and they include poetry, nonfiction articles and occasional short stories. Where a periodical is specifically lesbian/feminist or socialist/feminist, this fact is noted.

Publication dates are provided. For example: a periodical first published in March 1972 and last published in December 1972 is recorded "(March 1972–December 1972)"; a periodical first published in November 1971 and still being published in the first months of 1973 is recorded "(November 1971—)." When the exact date of publication is not known, a question mark in brackets follows the estimated date of publication.

At the end of the alphabetical list, a subsidiary listing of major Women's Rights groups' periodicals and major independent periodicals is provided.

It should be re-emphasized that periodicals, while important to the study of the new feminist movement, are not representative of the movement. Women's Liberation periodicals, in particular, are published by highly select groups of movement participants.

(a) Alphabetical List of Periodicals

Act NOW. Chicago, Illinois. Newsletter; Chicago NOW (1969—).

Action NOW. Detroit, Michigan. Newsletter; Metropolitan Detroit Chapter of NOW (Spring 1970—).

Ain't I a Woman. Iowa City, Iowa. Newspaper (Spring [?] 1970—).

ALAS's. South Bend, Indiana. Newsletter; South Bend Women's Liberation Coalition (Summer 1971–Spring 1972).

Amazon Quarterly: A Lesbian-Feminist Arts Journal. Oakland, California. Magazine (Fall 1972—).

Aphra. New York, New York. Magazine (Fall 1969—).

Aurora: Prism of Feminism. Suffern, New York, Magazine (Winter 1971—[?]).

Awake and Move. Philadelphia, Pennsylvania. Newspaper (January/February 1971–October 1971).

Battle Acts. New York, New York. Magazine published by socialist feminists (Fall 1970—).

Black Maria. River Forest, Illinois. Magazine (December 1971—).

Change: A Working Woman's Newspaper (formerly *A Change is Gonna Come*). San Francisco, California. Newspaper (December [?] 1970—).

Coalition. See *Women's Liberation of Michigan Monthly.*

Do It NOW. Chicago, Illinois. Monthly action newsletter of National NOW (March [?] 1971—).

Earth's Daughters. Buffalo, New York. Collection of loose-leaf notes, plans, etc. (February 1971–Summer [?] 1972).

Essecondsex. Rockport, Massachusetts. Newsletter; North Shore [Massachusetts] Feminists (Spring [?] 1971—).

Everywoman. Los Angeles, California. Newspaper (April 1970–April [?] 1972).

Feelings from Women's Liberation. Brooklyn, New York. Magazine (Spring 1970—[?]).

Female Liberation Newsletter. Boston, Massachusetts. Newsletter; Female Liberation (1970—).

Female Liberation Newsletter. Minneapolis-St. Paul. Newsletter, Twin Cities Female Liberation (1969 [?]–November 1971).

The Feminist Bulletin. Hartsdale, New York. Newsletter; Westchester [County] Women's Liberation Coalition (Spring 1972—).

Feminist Party News. New York, New York. Newsletter; Feminist Party (April [?] 1972—).

Feminist Studies. New York, New York. Journal (Summer 1972—).

The Feminist Voice. Chicago, Illinois. Newspaper (September 1971—).

FEW's Views and News. New Port Richey, Florida. Newsletter; Federally Employed Women (Fall [?] 1968—).

The Furies. Washington, D. C. Newspaper for lesbian feminists (January 1972—).

Goodbye to All That. San Diego, California. Newspaper (Summer 1970—).

The Hand (formerly *Lysistrata*, and *The Hand that Rocks the Rock*). Slippery Rock, Pennsylvania. Newsletter; Slippery Rock Women's Liberation (Spring [?] 1970—).

Happening. Menomonie, Wisconsin. Newsletter; The Center for Women's Alternatives, Inc. (March [?] 1972—).

Happiness of Womanhood, Newsletter. San Diego, California. Antifeminist (Spring [?] 1971—).

Happiness of Womanhood, Men's Auxiliary Newsletter. San Diego, California. Antifeminist (1971—).

Her-self: Community Woman's Newspaper. Ann Arbor, Michigan. Newspaper (Spring 1972—).

Human Rights for Women, Newsletter. Washington, D. C. (Summer 1970—).

It is Not My Baby (formerly *It Ain't Me Babe*). Berkeley, California. Newspaper (January 1970–1971).

Just Like A Woman. Atlanta, Georgia. Newsletter; Atlanta Women's Liberation (1970—[?]).

Kansas City Women's Liberation Union, Newsletter. Kansas City, Missouri. (1971 [?] —).

KNOW News Service. Pittsburgh, Pennsylvania. News bulletins (August 1970—).

The Ladder. Reno, Nevada. Magazine for lesbian women (1956–August/September 1972).

Lancaster Women's Liberation, Newsletter. Lancaster, Pennsylvania. (September 1971—).

Lavender Woman. Chicago, Illinois. Newspaper for lesbian women (November 1971—).

Libera. Berkeley, California. Magazine (Spring 1972—).

Lilith. Seattle, Washington. Magazine (January [?] 1969–September 1970).

The Link (formerly *The Alliance Link*). Chicago, Illinois. Newsletter; The Sisterhood (1971 [?] —).

Los Angeles Chapter NOW, Newsletter. Los Angeles, California. (Spring [?] 1969—).

L[os] A[ngeles] Women's Liberation Newsletter. See *Sister*.

Maine Women's Newsletter. Bangor, Maine. Newsletter; for Maine Women (February [?] 1972—).

Majority Report: A Feminist Newspaper Serving the Women of New York. Jamaica, New York. Newspaper (Spring [?] 1971—).

Matrix: For She of the New Aeon. Los Angeles, California. Anthology (Spring 1971–Fall 1971 [?]).

Momma: The Newspaper/Magazine for Single Mothers. Venice, California (December 1972—).

The Monthly Extract: An Irregular Periodical. Stamford, Connecticut. Newsletter (Summer [?] 1972—[?]).

Mother Lode. San Francisco, California. Newspaper (January 1971—).

Moving Out. Detroit, Michigan. Magazine (Spring [?] 1971—).

Ms. New York, New York. Magazine with national circulation (Spring 1972—).

Muthah. Sacramento, California. Magazine (Summer 1970–Fall 1970 [?]).

National Women's Political Caucus, Newsletter. Washington, D. C. (December 1971—).

The New Broadside: The Feminist Review of the News. New York, New York. Newspaper (October 1970–January 1971).

New Broom: A Legislative Newsletter for Massachusetts Women. Boston, Massachusetts (October 1970–November [?] 1971).

New Carolina Woman. Knightdale, North Carolina. Newspaper (January [?] 1971–Summer [?] 1971).

New Directions for Women. Dover, New Jersey. Newspaper (Summer [?] 1972—).

New Woman. Fort Lauderdale, Florida. Magazine with national circulation (June 1971—).

New York Radical Feminists, Newsletter. New York, New York (January [?] 1971—).

No More Fun and Games: A Journal of Female Liberation. Cambridge, Massachusetts. Magazine (September 1968–July 1971).

North Dakota Women's Liberation. Minot, North Dakota. Newsletter (Spring 1971–1972).

NOW Acts. Chicago, Illinois. Newsletter; National NOW (1968 [?]—).

NOW: Berkeley, Newsletter. Berkeley, California. (January [?] 1970—).

NOW: Eastern Massachusetts, Newsletter. Boston, Massachusetts. (January [?] 1970—).

Off Our Backs. Washington, D. C. Newspaper (January 1970—).

The Opening. Pittsburgh, Pennsylvania. Magazine (August 1971—[?]).

Oregon Council for Women's Equality. Portland, Oregon. Newsletter (1972 [?] —).

Pandora. Seattle, Washington. Newspaper (October [?] 1970—).

Philadelphia Women's Center, Newsletter. Philadelphia, Pennsylvania (1971 [?] —).

Prime Time: For the Liberation of Women in the Prime of Life. . . . Brooklyn, New York. Newsletter (Fall [?] 1971—).

Pro Se. Boston, Massachusetts. Newsletter; National Law Women (Summer 1971—).

RAT. New York, New York. Newspaper (1969 [?] taken over by women staff members–April 1972).

Real Women. St. Louis, Missouri. Newsletter; St. Louis Women's Liberation (1971).

San Francisco Women's Newsletter (formerly *Women's Liberation Newsletter*). San Francisco, California (1971 [?] —).

Scarlet Letter. Madison, Wisconsin. Magazine (April 1971–Summer 1972).

Second Coming. Austin, Texas. Newsletter; Austin Women's Liberation (November [?] 1970–November 1971).

The Second Page. San Francisco, California. Newspaper (Fall [?] 1970–April/May 1972).

The Second Wave. Boston, Massachusetts. Magazine (Spring 1971—).

Sister (formerly *L[os] A[ngeles] Women's Liberation Newsletter and Women's Center Newsletter,* Los Angeles (Spring [?] 1969—).

Sister. New Haven, Connecticut. Newsletter, New Haven Women's Liberation (1971—).

Sisters in Poverty. Albuquerque, New Mexico. Newsletter; NOW Task Force on Women in Poverty (January [?]1971 —[?]).

Skirting the Capitol: A Newsletter about Legislation and Women. Sacramento, California. Newsletter; California legislation (Winter 1967-8 [?] —).

S.P.A.Z.M. (formerly *Murra's Maxims*) Berkeley, California. Newsletter (April 1969–December 1969).

Spectre. Ann Arbor, Michigan. Newspaper for lesbian women (March/April 1971–January/February 1972).

The Spokeswoman. Chicago, Illinois. Newsletter (June 1970—).

Tell-a-Woman. Philadelphia, Pennsylvania. Newsletter; Media Workshop of Women's Liberation Center (March 1972—).

Tooth and Nail. Berkeley, California. Newsletter; San Francisco Bay Area Women's Liberation (September 1969–January 1970).

Triple Jeopardy: Racism, Imperialism, Sexism. New York, New York. Newspaper (Fall 1972—).

The Turn of the Screwed. Dallas, Texas. Newsletter; Dallas Area Women's Liberation (1970–Fall [?] 1971).

Union W.A.G.E. (Union Women's Alliance to Gain Equality). Berkeley, California. Newspaper (1971 [?] —).

Up From Under: by, for and about Women. New York, New York. Magazine (May/June 1970–Winter 71–72 [?]).

Velvet Glove. Livermore, California. Magazine (Spring 1971–Summer 1972).

The Vocal Majority: NOW National Capital Area Newsletter. Washington, D. C. (January [?] 1970—).

Voice of the Women's Liberation Movement. Chicago, Illinois. Newsletter (Spring [?] 1968–Spring 1969).

WEAL, National Newsletter (formerly *WEAL's Word Watcher* and, *WEAL's Action*). State College, Pennsylvania. Newsletter; Women's Equity Action League (January [?] 1970—).

WEAL Washington Report. Washington, D. C. Newsletter; National Capitol Chapter (September [?] 1971—).

Whole Woman. Madison, Wisconsin. Newspaper (October 1972—).

Wildflowers. Santa Barbara, California. Magazine (1971— [?]).

The Woman Activist: An Action Bulletin for Women's Rights. Falls Church, Virginia. Newsletter (Winter 1970–71—).

Woman Becoming. Pittsburgh, Pennsylvania. Magazine (December 1972—).

Womankind. Chicago, Illinois. Newspaper; Chicago Women's Liberation Union (Summer [?] 1971—).

Womankind. Louisville, Kentucky. Newspaper (December 1970–November 1971).

Womanpower. Brookline, Massachusetts. Monthly Report on employment practices (Fall 1971—).

The Woman's Journal. Northampton, Massachusetts. Magazine (March 1971—).

Woman's World. New York, New York. Newspaper (April 1971—).

Women. Philadelphia, Pennsylvania. Newsletter; Philadelphia Women's Liberation (Spring [?] 1970–Fall 1970 [?]).

Women & Art. New York, New York. Newspaper (Winter [?] 1971—).

Women Involved, Newsletter. Cambridge, Massachusetts. (Fall 1972—).

Women: A Journal of Liberation. Baltimore, Maryland. Magazine (Fall 1969—).

Women in Struggle. Winneconne, Wisconsin. Newsletter (1971 [?]—).

Women Studies Abstracts. Rush, New York. Journal (Winter 1972—).

Women Today (formerly *Washington Newsletter for Women*). Washington, D. C. Newsletter (May 1970—).

Women Unite NOW. Cleveland, Ohio. Newsletter; Cleveland NOW (January 1971—).

Women United, News Releases. Washington, D. C. (April 1971—).

Women West. Studio City, California. Newspaper (Fall 1970–June [?] 1971).

Women's Center Newsletter, Los Angeles. See *Sister.*

Women's Legal Defense Fund, Newsletter. Washington, D. C. Newsletter (October 1971—).

Women's Liberation of Michigan Monthly (formerly, *Coalition*). Detroit, Michigan. Newsletter (Winter 1970–71–August 1971).

The Women's Page. San Francisco, California. Newspaper (October 1970–April/May 1971).

Women's Political Caucus, Connecticut, Newsletter. New Haven, Connecticut (Spring 1972—).

Women's Political Caucus, Greater Indianapolis, Newsletter. Indianapolis, Indiana (Spring [?] 1972—).

Women's Political Caucus, Indiana, Newsletter. Indiana (Spring [?] 1972—).

Women's Political Caucus, North Carolina, Newsletter. Durham, North Carolina (Spring [?] 1972—).

Women's Political Caucus, South Bend-Mishawaka, Newsletter. South Bend, Indiana (June 1972—).

Women's Press: A Women's News Journal. Eugene, Oregon. Newspaper (Winter 1970–71—).

Women's Rights Law Reporter. Newark, New Jersey. Journal (July/August 1971—).

Women's Studies Newsletter. Old Westbury, New York: The Feminist Press (Fall 1972—).

(b) Women's Rights Groups' Periodicals

NOW; national and local publications

Act NOW: Chicago NOW Newsletter.

Action NOW: Detroit NOW Newsletter.

Do It NOW. National NOW.

Los Angeles Chapter NOW, Newsletter.

NOW Acts. National NOW.

NOW: Berkeley, Newsletter.

NOW: Eastern Massachusetts, Newsletter.

Sisters in Poverty. Newsletter, NOW Task Force on Women in Poverty.

The Vocal Majority. NOW National Capitol Area Newsletter.

Women Unite NOW: Cleveland NOW Newsletter.

Other Women's Rights Groups' Periodicals

Feminist Party News.
Human Rights for Women, Newsletter.
WEAL National Newsletter.
WEAL Washington Report.
Women Involved, Newsletter.
Women United, News Releases.
Women's Legal Defense Fund, Newsletter.
Women's Political Caucus (National), Newsletter.
Women's Political Caucus, Connecticut, Newsletter.
Women's Political Caucus, Greater Indianapolis, Newsletter.
Women's Political Caucus, Indiana, Newsletter.
Women's Political Caucus, North Carolina, Newsletter.
Women's Political Caucus, South Bend-Mishawaka, Newsletter.

(c) Major Independent National Periodicals

Feminist Studies, Journal.
KNOW News Service.
Ms., Magazine.
New Woman, Magazine.
Skirting the Capitol, Newsletter.
The Spokeswoman, Newsletter.
The Woman Activist, Newsletter.
Womanpower, Newsletter.
Women Today, Newsletter.
Women's Studies, Newsletter.

INDEX

National Sisters Vocation Conference, 198 *n20*

National Student Center, Women's Center, 169

National Welfare Rights Organization, 29, 30, 139, 146

National Women's Political Caucus: address of, 180; actions of, 92, 133, 139, 143, 145–146, 161; attitudes toward, 146, 161, 162; described, 139, 140; foundation of, 16, 139, 168–169; size of, 139

Nepotism, rules, 160

Network for the Economic Rights of Women, Ohio, 143

New England Congress to Unite Women, 88

New England Free Press, The, 69, 180

New Feminist Bookstore, 138, 181

New feminist movement: emergence of, 1, 2; future of, 169–171; origins of, 125, 140, 151–152, 163; proportion of active members, 110, 123, 196 *n9*

New feminists: and antifeminists, 165–166; attitudes of, toward YSA/SWP women, 88–89; effects on, of participation in feminist groups, 32, 93, 108, 109, 110; and middle class image, 24, 29, 106, 117, 124; and nineteenth-century feminists, 10–11, 151–153, 155–157, 169; numbers of, 32, 37, 64–65, 67, 105, 127, 139, 140, 187 *n3*, 194 *n3*, 195–196 *n4*; proportion of members active, 72, 110, 128, 196 *n9*; reading habits of, 70; speculations concerning, 1, 2, 21. *See also* under specific headings

New Feminist Talent Associates, 138–139, 181

New Haven Women's Liberation, 97

New Left: attitudes of new feminists toward, 26, 62, 66; and emergence of Women's Liberation, 1, 37, 60, 61–63; "feminists" in, 61; ideology

of, 48, 49, 132; "politicos" in, 61; responses of male members to new feminism, 59–61, 62–63, 156

New Left Review, 69

Newsletters. *See* Periodicals

Newsweek, 134

New Woman, 178

New York chapter, NOW, 195 *n11*

New York City Women's Liberation Center, 97

New Yorker, The, 162

New York Radical Feminists, 87, 88, 108

New York Radical Women, 87

New York Times, The, 162

Nineteenth-century feminism, 10, 151–153, 155–157, 169

Nixon, Richard M., 80, 162

No More Fun and Games, 65, 190 *n11*

Nonparticipants, and the new feminist groups, 24, 175

Norms, of new feminist groups, 93, 125, 128–130, 131–132

Normlessness, 40–44. *See also* Community

North Carolina Women's Political Caucus, 143

Objectives, of new feminist groups, 16, 78–79, 104, 114–118, 131. *See also* under specific groups

Obscene language, 51, 62

Occupational status, of new feminists, 19–20, 123

Office of Federal Contract Compliance, 115, 142

Off Our Backs, 97, 145

Older Women's Liberation, 77

Oligarchy, 193 *n9*. *See also* Elitism

One, Varda, 55

Opposition to new feminism, 33, 60–61, 62–63, 163–166, 188 *n7*, 190 *n2*

"Oppression" of women: explained, 13–14, 51, 152; extreme interpretations of, 50; and lesbians, 69; and nine-